# Outrun the Wolf

*self-care in times of trouble*

**David Walton Earle, LPC**

**David Walton Earle**

*Souls do not grow in sunlight.*

**Fred Dent**

**David Walton Earle**

Other publications by David Walton Earle:

- *What to Do While You Count to 10*
- *Simple Communication for Complicated People*
- *Iron Mask*
- *Red Roses 'n Pinstripes*
- *Professor of Pain*
- *Love Is Not Enough*
- *Recovery Stories*
- *Joy of Dysfunctional Families* – Joke Book
- *Contents of a Small Boy's Pocket*
- *Purposeful Dreaming* – Not in My Lifetime
- *Purposeful Dreaming* –Happily Ever After
- *Purposeful Dreaming* –Meaning
- *The Wisdom of the Twelve Steps:*
    - *1st Step Workbook*
    - *2nd Step Workbook*
    - *3rd Step Workbook*
    - *4th Step Workbook*
    - *5th Step Workbook*
    - *6th Step Workbook*
    - *1st – 3rd Step Workbook*
    - *4th – 6th Step Workbook*

## Co-authored

- *Leadership – Helping Others to Succeed*
  by Senator George Mitchell et al.
- *Extreme Excellence*
  by Michael Higson, Arlene R. Taylor, et al.
- *You Might Need a Therapist If...*
  by John Carfi, Cliff Carle, et al

Most of these books can be found on Amazon.com under
David W. Earle or David Walton Earle.

**David Walton Earle**

**Trouble is**: pandemic, murders, suicide, wars, floods, earthquakes, robberies, insurrection, divorce, death, kidnapping, sabotage, rejection, separation, bankruptcy, tornadoes, snowstorms, hurricanes, typhoons, shots fired, arrested, sued, arbitration, move, hostile work environment, disinherited, mediation, financial crisis, rape, robbery, fraud, embezzlement, disowned, espionage, rockslides, avalanche, sexual harassment, arrested, volcanic eruption, shipwreck, conviction, imprisonment, sinking, torpedoed, revolt, riot, lightning strike, rock slide, forest fire, operation, broken bones, dislocation, fight, DUI, auto accident, death, disease, or stubbed toe.

When experiencing

any type of trouble,

crisis, or stress,

***Outrun the Wolf***

is a valuable resource.

***You are not alone.***


IDSN: 978-0-578-30104-4

## My Experience

In the early eighties, the Gulf Coast Region went through the oil depression. Since the petrochemical industry is the main economic driver in this region, its decline caused tremendous upheaval in Texas and Louisiana. I was the Executive Vice President of Sline Industrial Painters and had 1000 people working for me. Sline had just been bought out but was now under siege by our new owners, Hatel and Telling (H.A.T. as listed on the UK stock exchange). HAT's board of directors and president, David Telling put considerable pressure on our president, Charles Fox, and my boss, Dick Lack for good returns on their investment. They passed that pressure to me, and I quickly discovered my resiliency was severely lacking. The purchase agreement required us to make a certain profit or suffer financial punishment. Our fingers were about to be slapped.

The petrochemical industry, until then had enjoyed a booming economy even when the rest of the country suffered recessions. Previously profits were much easier, but now I felt woefully inadequate to lead the team in the fight for survival. Compounding this pressure, my marriage was falling apart, and we had two teenagers who were acting out. Back then I defined myself by my position, by my big over-priced house, and my exalted title. I was somebody!

The nagging worry about the future haunted my every moment and intensified the onset of depression. When I started writing this book, I asked myself: What did I need *but did not have* that would have provided relief from this dismal quagmire?

The insights included in *Outrun the Wolf* are valuable for **anyone** experiencing a crisis. Imagine yourself the CEO of a company under tremendous financial stress. This may be the trouble that prompted you to read this book. You don't have to be a carbon copy of our hero for these lessons to be effective. I created a narrative of a stressed-out executive who experienced financial pressures on his company. It is this story around which these suggestions, insights, and coping skills are built. To get in the frame of this executive, picture yourself as a CEO desperately trying to save your struggling organization. In this role, assume your corporate trajectory has an uncertain and frightening future. As the executive in this storyline, you are the hero, but your sense of security and comfort has long since run over the horizon deserting you. As you travel down this lonely road of worry and isolation, the reality is sucking you deeper into the swamp of despair.

*Outrun the Wolf* is about taking care of yourself and ***thriving*** despite the various pressures that are being thrust upon you. It is not about understanding balance sheets, negotiating with your bankers, or drawing Fish-Bone diagrams. You and your team are the driving force of your company but now may be consumed by the dark forces of despair that will make effective decisions difficult and hamper the results. The *breathing side of crisis* unfortunately is you. *Outrun the Wolf* provides tools to care for yourself during this crisis.

You already have many important decisions on your ever-growing to-do list, so the thought of adding something else like self-care seems burdensome, even counterproductive. Here is my suggestion: Read a little each day. Think about the insights, lessons, and new tools that are included. The concepts found in *Outrun the Wolf* can be your welcomed friend before bedtime or your eager companioned while having your morning coffee, before you address the burdens of the day. Allow this book to be your security blanket – something that is not part of the big bad wolf threatening to blow your house down.

On one side of this scale is *Status quo,* your present reality, and the other side is *Fear,* the fear of stepping out into the unknown and encountering the stark necessity of change. Reality is knocking loudly on your door and the noise has become intolerable. Change is now an absolute necessity for survival. Even when this relentless demand is in our face, humans tend to retreat into past comfort zones, especially *when we experience stress*.

***Fear and change are conflicting forces competing for your attention and dominance.***

Patrick Rettig with Rettig Corporation declares that your job, Mr./Ms. CEO, your difficult assignment is to "…renew trust, faith and, confidence in the employees, customers vendors, and stakeholders." You are the living, breathing side of this crisis, the soft side of hard facts. *Outrun the Wolf* will help you garner the strength necessary to accomplish this seemingly impossible task.

## Caution - Dangerous Curves Ahead

There is a well-worn joke in the corporate turnaround profession. The successful components of corporate crisis are 50% operational, 50% financial, and 50% debtor psychology! *Outrun the Wolf* covers half of the problem – debtor psychology. Most turnaround professionals focus on legal aspects, debt restructuring, factoring, investment banking, acquisitions, bankruptcies, and general corporate malaise. All of these are resources you may need for survival. However, fixing the corporate balance sheet is never the entire problem. Left-brain solutions are necessary, but they often mask the more profound problem, the *people*.

To successfully navigate this crisis, you need three things:

**Head** – ***flexible thinking***
**Means** – ***adequate resources***
**Heart** – ***determination to overcome***

**Head** – How a person thinks dictates how they react to external experiences. Some of your thinking has been excellent, some has been questionable, and some might need to be changed. You are, right now, the sum of the decisions you already have made.

**Means** – Your ability to turn this crisis into success may require more resources than you currently have. *Outrun the Wolf* has a useful reference in the Appendix section to Turnaround Management

Association. This group has many fine organizations dedicated to resources you may need.

**Heart** – Do you have enough heart, enough gas in your tank left to fight on? ***You have much more strength than you think.*** Learning to use the principles in this book will help rekindle the passion you've temporarily misplaced. Do you worry? Of course, you do, look at all your problems. Included in Part One is a wonderful coping skill to manage worry – any worry.

As the hero in this story (that's you), your business is in dire straits - maybe in free-fall, it may be threatening not only your livelihood but your very meaning. Understandingly you may ask the unanswered question. ***Who am I without this business? What will I do if my business fails?***

This traumatic thought can strike fear in the most hard-crusted leaders. Your challenge is not only to bring your company back from the brink but also to find balance in your personal life. Consider this a survival attitude. It does you little good if your company survives but you do not. *Outrun the Wolf*'s mission is holistic. Not only can it help you survive, but it will demonstrate how you can learn from this experience. Someday you will look back on this time and success will be yours when you can say, "This was a very difficult time, but I am glad to have had this experience. *I am a better person today.* ***Thank you, I am grateful for this trouble!"***

Mike Manes with Square One Consulting thinks all organizations (even profitable ones) need to be periodically dismantled and then rebuilt. This crisis provides a wonderful opportunity to re-examine your current existence, both for your company and for you personally. When the dust settles and this crisis is resolved, you will know a great deal more about yourself and your business than before.

NOTE: Even if you are not a CEO but your family is in crisis, the principals included are tools to help change your part of the family painful dysfunction.

## Along the Road

Robert Browning

I walked a mile with Pleasure
she chattered all the way
but left me none the wiser
for all she had to say.
I walked a mile with Sorrow
and ne'er a word said she
but oh, the things
I learned from her
when Sorrow
walked with me!

**Let's Begin**

There is a certain powerful force in life, a different way of living not widely known. When using certain coping skills (many included in these pages), you become much more powerful. As said in Star Wars, "*the force be with you.*" The pain of this upheaval could be a golden opportunity to learn how to live in ***The Force, a much more peaceful place to be.*** Once there, your life is much different and more enjoyable.

Half of what you need to live in ***The Force*** is found in Chapter I. You need these skills to regain control of your ship heading for the rocks. When learned, you will be happier, more successful, have considerably less stress, with much better relationships. No matter the roadblocks, the sooner you accept this challenge the more options are available. If you are prepared to go on this voyage, then let's begin.

This is a "... *required course. Only the time you take it is voluntary. Free will does not mean that you can establish the curriculum. It means only that you can elect what you want to take at a given time."*
A Course in Miracles

**Editor's note:** The author has used many examples and quotes from Alcoholics Anonymous, the 12 Steps, and other recovery programs. Please do not take them personally but allow them to provide powerful examples to help understand some of the insights found in this book.

*The Journey in life has many lessons transferable to business success.*
Clarity Management

# Four parts of *Outrun the Wolf*

Is it time to quit hitting the snooze button?

## Part I – Surviving

Staring down the wolf.

## Part II – Thriving

Change becomes an ally.

## Part III – Soaring

Wings for you to fly.

## Part IV– Community with Others

Together, we can turn the wolf into pot roast.

# Table of Contents

*I've missed more than 9000 shots in my career. I've lost almost 300 games. 26 times, I've been trusted to take the game winning shot and missed.*

*I've failed over and over and*
*over again in my life.*
*And that is why I succeed."*

Michael Jordan

# Surviving

## Staring down the wolf

# Chapter 1

## Inventory

Most businesses must account for their stock in the form of an inventory. Before you begin, I suggest you turn to the Appendix and take the Depression Inventory. With the pressures on you, I would not be surprised if you had some melancholy symptoms. Do not let your score disturb you. It's hard to get as far as you've come without a few dents and scratches.

This profile provides an understanding of the price you are currently paying. Included in your reading are many suggestions on how to handle shortages in your happiness quotient. The Inventory will also serve as a monitoring tool as you journey through this experience.

## Rallying Cry

Instead of your recent tidal wave of bad luck, a windfall of good news might be a welcome relief. Good luck is often the result of dedication, perseverance, and leadership. For a successful transformation, there must be first a reason, a rallying cry leading the flag of change.

Community Coffee Company in Baton Rouge, Louisiana has such a rallying cry, "We Are as good as Our Coffee." Many times, when a decision needs to be made, they ask themselves, "Is this as good as our coffee?" When it's not, they go back to the drawing board.

Dr. M. L. King invited us in his "I have a dream" speech to join us together. Many were shocked and angered with the acquittal of O.J. Simpson, but what the jurors heard as they went to consider was Johnny Cochran's rallying cry, "If it doesn't fit, you have to acquit." President Reagan's profound demand still echoes today, "Mr. Gorbachev, tear down this wall!".

*Where there is no vision people perish.*
Proverbs

I helped change the culture at Renewal Energy Group (REG) at their Geismar, Louisiana plant. I knew to be successful, we would need a rallying cry, a burning platform with enough heat to encourage for all employees and management to change. In a conversation with the plant manager, Peter Guay commented that his dream was to have "a first-class plant." Within six months, REG had experienced two terrible fires with injuries. These fires so damaged his dream that it seemed to be a far-off vision seemingly unattainable. I jumped into his dream and suggested a rallying cry for our changing the culture. "We're going to be a first-class plant!"

REG declared this as our mission. At first, the employees just rolled their eyes at management's seeming naivety. In the back of everyone's minds, they wanted to be part of a first-class plant but sincerely doubted we could. REG kept repeating this declaration in many ways many times. Then I started hearing comments, "This is not first-class," or "If they wanted to be a first-class plant, they would…" Eventually, a few became many, and the rallying cry changed to, "To become a first-class plant we need to …."

***When the employees start to own the change, results are greatly magnified.***

## Swampy

Swampy is a magical, malevolent elf with a gnarled nose, beady blood-red eyes, and heavy led boots. He has long arms to wrap around you and pull you deep into the dark, foreboding Swamp of Despair. He rides on your shoulder and challenges anything positive. You know who I am talking about, you just never had a name for him, or pretended he was not there.

A woman ran through the Atlanta airport hurrying to catch her plane. Swampy jumped on her shoulder and said, "You know you are late." She walked a little faster. He then said, "You are going to miss your plane." She increased her frantic pace. "You are going to get fired. You'll never get another job. You are just no good." In the middle of the Atlantic airport this highly skilled, polished executive stopped, put her briefcase down, then her purse. With a quick swipe of her hand, she knocked Swampy to the floor and for good measure, stomped on him. She then picked up her belongings and made her plane – without Mr. Swampy. No Swamp of Despair for this woman!

Listen closely when Swampy talks. Hear what he whispers in your ear. When you challenge his negative messages, your thinking will change. Once aware, just knock him to the floor. Swampy will leave you and slink off looking for someone weaker to peddle his doom and despair.

*"Whatever the mind can conceive and believe,*
*the mind can achieve."*
Napoleon Hill

## Worry

Feeling stress? Depressed? Worried? "Woe is me." Of course, you are! All humans occasionally feel these heavy emotions, especially when under stress. Although those are understandable, they come with an expensive price tag on your physical stamina, health, peace, faith in the future, and tremendous doubt about yourself and your company. You are going to be much more effective once you put these emotions in their proper place, pull your shoulders back, take a deep breath, and tackle the next task.

***Stress** is the gap between the demands you*
*perceive are being made*
*on you and your perceived resources*
*to meet those demands.*
Unknown author.

## Signs of Unmanaged Stress and Burn Out Symptoms

Decrease in self-esteem
Pessimistic outlook
Anxiety
Insomnia
Physical health decline
Depression
Hostility
Suicidal thoughts
Headaches
Stomach aches
Decrease in selfcare
Exhaustion, tiredness
Physically run down
Increased anger
Uncontrolled emotions
Weight gain/loss
Feeling helpless
Suspiciousness
Decreased in connection
Not enjoying pleasant things
Difficult concentration
Avoiding difficulties
Marital discord
Missing work
Running away/ hiding
Problems with the law
Making threats
Bitterness
Focus on Lack
Loss of faith
Feeling of failure
Child/spouse/employee abuse
Blame – a sacrificial lamb
Isolation from social network
Alcohol/drugs usage
Pessimistic mindset
Decrease in fun
Defensiveness
Irritation
Seeing little meaning
Worrying
Sense of being besieged
Feeling useless
Shortness of breath
Exploding easily
Anxiety attacks
Increased degree of risk taking
Acting out behavior
Argumentative
Decrease interest in sex
Procrastination
Decrease in communication
Foreboding / gloom
Missing deadlines
Resisting authority
Divorce
Wanting revenge
Disillusion
Decrease gratitude
Acting out kids

One of the greatest tools humans have - not found elsewhere in the animal kingdom - is humor. During any crisis, humor is available. Comic relief is wonderful stress relief. To celebrate that reality, aphorisms are scattered throughout this book. An aphorism is a statement of truth or opinion expressed in a concise and witty manner. Many were written by internet authors long forgotten by frequent forwarding. **When was the last time you laughed?**

People under stress often have some of these burnout symptoms. The next Exercise will demonstrate how the **Wisdom Chart** becomes a *powerful* method of managing the worry that may be robbing you of peace, calmness, and serenity. *Do not hurry through this exercise for it will pay you great dividends*.

**Exercise**

> Stress is the basic confusion created when one's mind overrides the body's desire to choke the living daylights out of some jerk who desperately deserves it!

What worries you about your current situation in life? Although you may be worried and concerned about many things, narrow down to one worry for this exercise. Briefly write your immediate worry in My Worry on the next page. Is the banker, whom, you once thought was a friend when you made the loan, now breathing down your neck with demands. How about the key employee who left your company for a greener paycheck. Maybe it could be a legal situation causing you heartburn or a Key Vendor who cannot supply what you desperately needed yesterday! Choose just one example causing you to fret and worry. If you worry about a loved one, that too will prove an even better worry to use in this exercise.

**My Worry**:

After defining your worry, answer this question: what about this problem ***can't*** you control? What is out of your control? See sample below. Spend some time listing everything about this problem that is out of your control.

An idiot will drag you down to his level and beat you with experience.

Below are a few sample questions that may belong on the ***Can't Control*** side:

- Can you control someone else's situation?
- Can you control if the other person changes?
- Can you control other people's behavior?
- Can you control other people's thoughts?
- Can you control other people's emotions?
- Can you control what others think about you?
- Can you control how they treat you?
- Can you control the economy?
- Can you control how your banker views your financials?

On page 10, write on the Wisdom Chart a bullet point list of what you can't control about your expressed worry. In addition, here are a few other thoughts about the ***Can't*** side. Can you control how other people treat you, or how they view the situation? Can you control others' perceptions? Can you control if they like you or not, or even respect you, or believe you? Record each one that pertains to you as a bullet point on the ***Can't*** side.

After you have made your list, take a moment, and study it. Looking at this list, ask yourself this critical question: Based on this list on the ***Can't* side,** can you control the ultimate ***outcome*** of this situation? **Yes/No?** Granted, you may influence the outcome, perhaps even more than you think, but considering all that is out of your control, is the outcome something you ***Can*** control? I think not.

Knowing what you cannot control is a powerful realization. Now go back to the sample worry you identified. When thinking about this identified worry, now answer this question: What about this problem ***Can*** you control? Add those bullet point items to the Wisdom Chart under the ***Can Control*** side. If you have difficulty getting started on what you ***Can*** control, review the sample below, using it for a starting point for your study.

What is your worry you wrote on page 7

Example *insufficient cash-flow*

| ***Can't Control*** | ***Can Control*** |
|---|---|
| Current economy | My behavior |
| Banker's requirements | My thoughts |
| Employee's commitment | My emotions |
| Employee commitment | My determination |
| Customers paying bills | My willingness to invest |
| If employees stay or go | Continue to fight or not. |
| Employee attitude | My attitude |

## Wisdom Chart

| **Part of the Problem**<br>***I CAN'T Control*** | **Part of the Problem**<br>***I CAN Control*** |
| --- | --- |
| | |

The Line between ***Can't*** control and ***Can*** control is your Wisdom line. This thin line is your ticket on the Stress Reduction Train. *All Aboard!*

| ***What do I experience?*** | ***What do I experience?*** |
| --- | --- |
| | |

By completing this Wisdom Chart, you are taking the first step towards reducing your stress.

## Warning:

The publisher ***cannot*** be held legally liable for any amount of smile restoration, calmness, and/or increased sense of wellbeing you experience.

Some people have difficulty with putting their *thoughts* and/or *emotions* on the ***Can*** Control side.

**Thoughts –**

You can choose to change your thinking. Suppose you did not like broccoli but for whatever reason you wanted to develop a taste for this vegetable. If you make a conscious effort to develop a taste for broccoli, could you? If you made the choice, could you decide to think good thoughts about a person who did you wrong? If you are forced to put your thoughts in one of the two columns, one labeled ***Can't,*** and other side labeled ***Can,*** where do your thoughts logically belong? *Not, easy, uh?*

**Emotions –**

People often have difficulty accepting that they can have control over their emotions. Until a person knows how to manage feelings, emotions tend to be in control. Here is a key (by the way, this question will be on Friday's quiz) where do your emotions/feelings come from?

**David Walton Earle**

Many say their heart, others think experience, but they are mistaken. ***Your feelings come from your thoughts!*** If you want to feel differently – the key to success is to change your thinking.

If you still say ***Can't*** for either the feelings or thoughts - humor me and put them in the ***Can*** column anyway, and then high-light them with a question mark. You will ultimately have to decide for yourself on which side they belong.

*"Pain is inevitable ...*
*misery is optional."*
Dalai Lama

**Exercise**

A wonderful poem/prayer created this Wisdom Chart. Most people resonate with its insight and say, "Oh this is so true..." Many repeat it as a mantra. Some have it embroidered on their walls, or as a reminder on their desk. However, they often lack the understanding of what it ***really*** means, or the ***power*** found within its simple message.

## Serenity Prayer

*God, grant me the serenity to accept the things I*
*cannot change, the courage to change the things I can,*
*and the wisdom to know the difference.*
From a poem by Reinhold Neibuhrt.

Most people agree with this simple wisdom, but until it's practically applied, it is only a dust-collecting poem mounted on their wall. So instead, let us explore this wisdom more deeply and hopefully, you can personalize it. *"...grant me the serenity to accept the things I cannot change."*

You already listed everything you ***Can't Control*** in this column. Until you accept what you ***Can't Control*** about your difficult situation, you will continue to worry, and true serenity will continue to elude you. If you accept your list as it currently exists, you may find a shortcut leading toward peace. *"...the courage to change the things I can..."*

Focusing on the ***Can*** Side of this C***an/Can't*** divide is ***Thumb-Work***. Hold your two hands out, palms down. Now bend at the elbows and point the thumbs back toward you - ***Thumb-Work***. Most people, especially in times of stress, want to engage in ***Finger-Work*** and point their finger at others, inventorying people's defects, bad-mouthing their banker, and insisting someone else change so they can be successful.

*"...and the wisdom to know the difference."*

Thank God for this wisdom. This simple awareness separates what I ***Can*** control from what I ***Can't***. The ***Wisdom Line*** distinguishes strength from weakness, chaos from peace, and discord from understanding.

What does the word serenity mean? Picture yourself as a captain on a submarine cruising on the surface of the Gulf of Mexico. Suddenly, you spot Hurricanes Katrina, Rita, Gustaf, Ike, and Ida all rolled into one gigantic storm coming right at you. You order the submarine to dive for the bottom. *Awooga! Awooga!* On the surface, there are huge, gigantic waves crashing, lightning flashing, and the thundering roar of the storm. ***Mayhem, calamity, disaster!*** Maybe this describes your life today?

Safe on the bottom, there is calmness, peacefulness, serenity, confidence, and feeling okay. Do you want those feelings deep within you, *regardless of the storm above*? Would that provide comfort? Could you better manage the stress you now feel with this serenity?

**Exercise**

When focusing on the ***Can't*** side of your identified problem, which one(s) of these are true for you:

- I'm not okay
- Worry
- Anxiety
- Stress
- Depression
- Chaos
- Mayhem
- Anger

*"A crisis is a terrible thing to waste"*
Paul Romer

## Wisdom Line

When focusing on the ***Can't Control*** side, which from the previous list do you experience? Put your answers in the **What do You Experience** box on the ***Can't Control*** side. If this describes you – check if your picture is there.

*"A problem well stated is half solved"*
Charles Kettering

However, when focusing on the ***Can***-side, you get something entirely different like:

- Peace
- Calmness
- Serenity

Now add these next words in the What do You Experience box on the ***Can Control*** side.

**Exercise**

Go back to the Wisdom Line exercises and notice at the bottom, there are two empty boxes. On the ***Can't*** side, label this side **FEAR**. In the box, on the ***Can*** side, label this side **TRUST.** Decide which side you want to be on? Not many choose the **FEAR** Side.

Key question: why do well-meaning, well-educated, good people choose to focus on what they ***Can't*** control, the **FEAR** side? Why do we do this? Why do humans focus on what they ***Can't*** control?

## Habit of Thought

Consider this theory. The reason people focus on things they ***Can't*** control (**FEAR** Side) is because of a ***habit of thought***. How people learn to think forms habits. Focusing on **FEAR** is a destructive habit that costs unnecessary anxiety and worry. This model allows you to challenge past habits of thought.

The Wisdom Line provides a challenge to thinking, a choice of focus on what you ***Can*** control (**TRUST** Side) – with the reward of peace and serenity. Or you can focus on that which you ***Can't*** control (**FEAR** Side). Your choice.

You are not a bad person if you continue to focus on the ***Can't***. However, focusing on the ***Can't*** side, creates the *Happy-Vac, Fun Sponge,* or the *Midnight Sleep Robber*. Focusing on the ***Can't*** side sucks up happiness without leaving a trace.

***"Knowing you have a choice decreases stress"***

Picture driving into a service station to buy gasoline. You pull up to the pump, stick the credit card into the slot, put the little numbers into the machine, and get the hose. You are all set, right? Instead of putting the hose into the gas tank, you start pumping gas on the ground.

The meter is running, costing you money. Tell me, is the gasoline on the ground doing your car any good? No, wasted energy! So, has any bit of your worrying…***ever*** really changed the outcome? All worry does is make the problem larger and deprive you of the energy needed to persevere, to keep on when you would rather quit.

*"If you don't like something change it;*
*if you can't change it,*
*change the way you think about it"*
Mary Engelbreit

Dividing your identified worry topic into what you ***Can't*** control from what you ***Can*** control, creates a road map, a navigation guide to help manage stress and worry. You can focus on things you ***Can*** control and have the corresponding peace and serenity, or you can focus on things you ***Can't*** control. This is your choice, your power.

If you find yourself worrying, make a declaration, "I choose to worry about_________(fill in the blank), I know this worry will cost me, and I am *willing to pay the price*." When declaring you are going to worry about something and by accepting responsibility for the outcome, you are now in a position where you can choose.

**Exercise**

Since you have completed the Wisdom Chart, your homework assignment (should you choose to accept it) is to increase your awareness about the line separating the **FEAR** side from the **TRUST** side. Look for the ***Wisdom-Line*** in all your relationships. This line exists between you and others, individually and collectively. There is one line between you and each of your kids. There is a different one with your spouse, lover, co-workers, boss, in-laws, etc. Can you control the traffic jam? No. Can you control your attitude while waiting for the traffic to clear? Yes. *Simple...not easy.*

*"85 percent of what we worry about never happens"*
Don J. Gowey

When focusing on what you ***Can't*** control, your thinking is circular. Your mind runs in circles in a squirrel cage fashion. When focusing on what you ***Can*** control, your mind becomes linear, increasing your ability to perform the next right step. When you start feeling *squirrelly* (author's term for anxiety), just ask yourself,

"Self, what are you focusing on?" You will often discover it is on the ***Can't*** side.

When you can shift your thinking from the ***Can't*** side to the ***Can*** side, a wonderful calmness is yours. What side of the Wisdom Line will you be better able to manage through your current dilemma, the ***Can't*** or ***Can*** side? ***Realizing what you can't control is a simple, yet powerful understanding.***

Rational Recovery came out of the problems some people had with Alcoholics Anonymous, so they started a different program of recovery for their addiction. Their first objection was the concept of higher power thinking it was forcing them into a religion. The other problem and what is germane to this chapter is the concept of powerless. Rational Recovery did not want to be powerless.

The first step of the 12 Steps of Alcoholic Anonymous is, "We admitted we were powerless over alcohol - that our lives had become unmanageable." Now, please understand, I'm not suggesting you have a problem with addiction but using this as an example of a powerful principle, one that has helped millions of people break the high walls of denial. For the alcoholic, it is easy to describe how unmanageable his/her life is before this exercise. That is the easy part. Do you want to be powerless? No. No one does. When thinking about your identified problem, you listed the items that were out of your control on the ***Can't*** Side of the Wisdom Line. This is what is in your circumstance that you had no control over – what you were powerless over. When working on this exercise, you reduced your stress level when you recognized all that was not in your control.

With this awareness, you now are not wasting energy on what you have no control over. You now put all that energy that used to be wasted strength into what you can control. With this simple awareness, you ***gain power from recognizing your powerlessness***! Instead of pouring gasoline on the ground, you put it into your tank where it is the catalyst necessary for change.

***Until you start to choose –***
***you do not have a choice.***

Slightly modifying the first step, *you admitted you were powerless over* (your identified problem,) *and your life had become unmanageable.* How much energy and happiness have you wasted when focused on things that you have no control over?

## Four stages of education.

What is the object of education? To learn, right? Maybe, consider this. Think of your first bicycle. Before you had one, you were envious of the other kids. You knew you could ride if you just had one. You are in the first stage of education - you are ***ignorant about what you do not know.***

For your birthday, you received a shiny new bike of your very own. You jumped on it and immediately fell. This is the second stage of education - you now ***know what you don't know***.

After many trials and errors, skinned knees, and disappointments, you successfully rode in a circle on the driveway and hollered, "Mommy, look at me." Here you are in the third stage of education: ***you are aware of what you know***.

Now that you already know how to ride, you could jump on it and ride away. This is the last stage of learning; you are ***unaware of what you really know***.

*The chief object of education is to unlearn.*
Gilbert K. Chesterton

This crisis is your company's launch pad. You just need to blast off in the rocket to places unknown. You can boldly go where you've never been before even with limited resources, experience, and suitable maps. You are ignorant about what you don't know. This journey will force you to discover new realizations, innovations, improvements, and insights.

I promise your exciting journey will unlearn you. By the time you arrive at the fourth stage of learning, what you know now will be vastly different from what you may have expected or anticipated. This learning will be in many ways unexpected, beautiful, and many times frightening.

**If you are too afraid of falling –**
***you will never learn to ride.***

You will be very board if you walk
a mile in my shoes, but terrified if
you spend 30 seconds in my head.

# Chapter 2

## Behavior Cycle

There is an easy correlation between behavior and results. If you speed on the highway, you will get a ticket …eventually. When you don't pay your taxes, Uncle Sam knocks on your door.

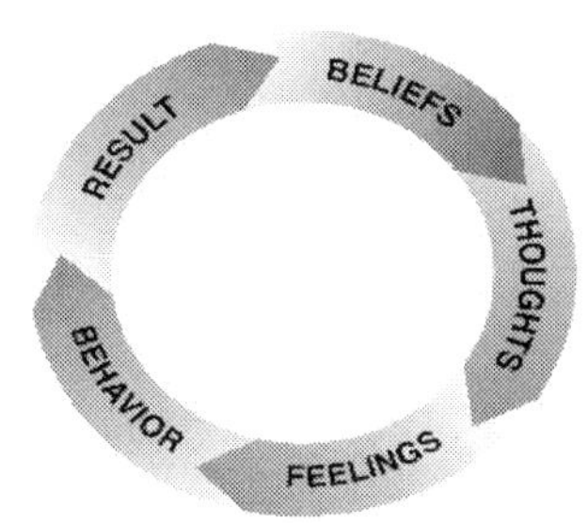


Another dynamic is how a person's beliefs dictate their thoughts. People with a belief that they are successful have thoughts of accomplishment. Correspondingly if they believe their success is in the rearview mirror, all in the past, then it is difficult to have positive thoughts about the future.

As you can see from the above Behavior Cycle diagram, everything is connected. Results tend to reinforce beliefs, and thoughts are the basis of behavior. Your company has been bombarded with negative results putting tremendous pressure on your beliefs, probably causing you to question your survival. Many difficult feelings are now yours. Explore what happens with a negative belief system.

**The Behavior Cycle**

***Beliefs***– *Examples of Negative Beliefs*:

- I am a loser.
- My company cannot overcome this crisis.

- My employees have no confidence in me.
- I must be strong and cannot show vulnerability.

***Thoughts***: *Examples of Negative Thoughts*:

- We will never get out of this.
- I will never succeed.
- Everyone is against me.
- All my employees want is a paycheck.

***Feelings:*** *Emotions based upon Negative Thoughts*

- Anger
- Inadequate
- Fearful
- Worried
- Disgusted
- Ashamed

***Behavior***: *Behavior from Negative Thoughts*

- Toss 'n turn
- Do everything myself
- Avoids decisions
- Lies / critical
- Snaps at others
- Belittle others

***Consequences:*** *Possible undesirable consequences*

- Resumes on the street
- Gloomy atmosphere
- Poor morale
- Calling the loan

When reviewing these negative consequences how might they re-inforce the belief that I am a failure?

*The world we see that seems so insane is the*
*result of a belief system that is not working.*
William James

## The Behavior Cycle – *Positive Examples*

***Beliefs*:**

- I am successful.
- I am worthwhile of a positive self-image
- I am worthy of self-respect
- My company will overcome this financial crisis.
- I have very good employees.

***Thoughts: Different thoughts comes from positive beliefs***

- I think positive thoughts about ……. (describe).
- Day by day in every way, I am getting better and better.
- I can lead this company to success.
- My employees will strive to solve this problem.

***Feelings:***

- Confident
- Enthusiastic
- Happy
- Hopeful
- Inspired
- Joy

***Behavior:***

- Eagerness to solve problems.
- Work-life balance.
- I take care of myself.
- I am honest with my banker.
- I set an example for a positive attitude of success.
- I focus on solutions not on someone to blame.

***Likely Consequences***

- Positive financial indicators
- The increased trust of my banker/ employees
- Good morale
- Willingness to take risks.

The Behavioral Cycle dynamic may sound too simplistic. ***Breaking News*** - Everything you will read in this book is simple – not rocket science. Understanding your balance sheet is more complicated than what you will read in *Outrun the Wolf.* Although simple – change is not easy. Using the Behavioral Cycle, you can challenge yourself about your current thoughts and beliefs.

*To perceive the world differently, we must be willing to change our belief system, let the past slip away, expand our sense of now, and dissolve the fear in our minds.*
William James

When a person enters detoxification treatment from alcohol addiction, they are isolated from many negative temptations and behavior immediately changes. They are no longer on the street or going to their favorite bar, so some of the consequences of addictive behavior problems changes. With this simple change of behavior, their results begin to be different – more positive. Just by controlling your cash flow, treating workers with respect, or complying with your banker's restrictive requirements, the results often produce positive change. Changing behavior is on the ***Can*** side of the Wisdom Line. Reading this book is a good example of changing behavior.

*The critical first step in any crisis is to establish control. Control of your thoughts and your reactions first. Control of cash, customers, and employees next.*
Jeff Sands

The Behavior Cycle seeks to show the interconnection between thoughts, behavior, results, and beliefs. You will discover that many suggestions found in *Outrun the Wolf* will affect various parts of this model. Much of this book focuses on thoughts, changing destructive thinking, managing emotions, and suggested behavioral changes. Some seek to challenge your worldview. Thinking differently can reduce stress and improve outcomes.

Note: In many of the following sections, you will see the Behavior Cycle depiction with one of the cycles parts in the middle relating to that section's topic.

**Exercise**

*Life is 10% what happens to us*
*and 90% is our attitude.*
Charles Swindoll

What part of the 90/10 Rule is in our control? **Attitude.** We have some small degree of control over what happens to us. If we don't go to work, we will not have a job for very long. However, we have 100% control over our attitude. The 90/10 Rule is a liberating principle. ***We all have 100% control over our attitude.***

## Thinking

This section will help you get to a magical place – *no, not with mushrooms – or Harry Potter's wand,* but just by your ability to *think about your thinking.*

In the Wisdom Line Exercise, you acknowledged on page 10 in the section entitled: "My Worry", something or someone was a concern to you, a declared worry. This exercise provides a clear realization about the power of choice- your choice. Where is your focus? Is it on the ***Can*** side, or the ***Can't*** side?

In the Wisdom Line discussion, I used *insufficient cash flow* as the worry example. Now for my next trick, I am going to read this person's mind. Here is what I assume a person who does not have enough cash flow may be thinking. *I have given up a lot of sleep and happiness because my company does not have sufficient cash flow.* If this is what you and our fictitious person are thinking, then by this declaration, they can start to ***think about their thinking***.

**Exercise**

Write your worry here as you did in the entitled Section **My Worry**"- page 7. ________________________________

**Problem:** Now comes the hard part. What has been the cost of your constantly dwelling on this problem? In the example above, the executive was *losing a lot of sleep and happiness*. Once you identify your problem, you can then determine its cost.

**Cost:** Now combine your identified problem and the associated cost in one sentence. For example, *I have been losing sleep and happiness worrying about my cash flow.* Once you have that combined sentence written, say it aloud. Now say it again. Whose problem, is it? If it's yours, then own it. Once you stated the problem and agreed it is yours, you are now at a magical place.

***You are now on the road less traveled***
***where honesty and personal power merge.***

You stated the problem; it is known. Now read the price tag hanging on your thinking. What is life is expecting you to pay?

With this awareness dig deeper. Do I want to think this way, or would it be better for me to think differently? Asking yourself questions like this is called ***Thinking About Your Thinking***. In the Wisdom Line Exercise, do you recall where you put your thinking? Was it on the ***Can*** or ***Can't*** side? You were encouraged to put it on the ***Can*** side where it belongs. If indeed, your thinking belongs on the ***Can*** side, then you have just demonstrated that you have the choice to change your thinking or not. I said this before, and will again …

***Until you start to choose –***
***you do not have a choice.***

When a problem hits us from out of the blue. ***BOOM!*** Our instinct is to react to the ***BOOM.*** Most people run away from the pain, hoping it will solve the problem. When in this problem-solving mode, it appears safer to focus on what is out of control, setting off an avalanche of extreme emotion that demands a high cost. This may be a price you may or may not be willing to pay. How much has your current problem already cost you with your family? How much sleep have you lost? Has it affected you emotionally and physically? How has it affected those you care about?

When you ***think about your thinking*** you have taken a large step towards reclaiming power you were not even aware you had lost. When you ***think about your thinking*** you are now ***living your life on purpose***. You are living with intention. Now the ***BOOM*** is no longer running through your mind, rent-free and with muddy boots! ***That's personal power!***

If for some reason this does not make sense, please consider re-reading it and doing this exercise again. Search through other worry areas. Identify what other things you can and cannot control. Once established, examine your thinking, and calculate the associated cost.

Not many people in this world ***think about their thinking***. If you get nothing else from your current crisis but the ability to ***think about their thinking***, then your relationships will be better, and you can better share the deep love in your heart. Amazing! Even your business decisions will begin to improve, and in the long run, you will be happier. ***Drastic promises, I think not.***

*Success is not final; failure is not fatal:*
*it is the courage to continue that counts.*
Winston Churchill

**Exercise**

What is the opposite of ***thinking about your thinking?***

> I didn't say it was your fault. I said I was blaming you.

What is the opposite of living your life on purpose? Good question. Try this. It is ***volunteering to be a victim.*** "Who wants to be a victim?" Raise your hand and yell, "I do! I do! Take me! Please!" Of course, no one wants to be a victim. That is ludicrous! But when exploring your thoughts, you may find many examples where you raised your hand and volunteered to be a victim. If you are alone reading this now, raise your hand and experience how uncomfortable it is when you say aloud, "I want to be a victim."

***Try it. You'll hate doing it!***

If you have not yet thrown this book across the room, here are some more thoughts about your thinking.

The following are the effects assumptions have on behavior.

- If you assume there will be a bad outcome what are your normal reactions?
- Do you become anxious, or feel paralyzed with fear?
- When the results are not what you hoped for, does this increase your fear and confirm your negative assumptions?

Fear is an often helpful and sometimes a lifesaving emotion. But it can become debilitating when we give it our steering wheel.

*...you'll be called to the carpet at your friendly neighborhood bank. This is an awful experience, but in reality, it is great news because now you have concerned and committed partners focused on your business.*
Jeff Sands

You may already have had that humiliating experience with your banker, or that day could be fast approaching. Jeff Sands' quote suggests a change of thinking. Change the perception of attack into realizing an ally. The disaster you feared can then morph into a possible solution.

**Exercise**

Words are powerful, they carry a lot of weight. When faced with a difficulty, say letting go of your former lover, the tendency is to say something like this, "I can't let her go," or "I'll never date anyone again." Don't get me wrong. Grief is real and can be quite painful. However, the pain increases dramatically when using the word ***Can't.*** Unless someone has a gun pointed at your head, the word ***Can't*** become debilitating. You have much more power if you substitute the words, "I ***choose not*** to, or I damn well am not," instead of ***Can't***. Now, I might have said this before,

***Until you start to choose –***
***you do not have a choice.***

This simple change of wording puts the power back where it belongs. In the example of the jilted lover, the decision to hang on or to move on belongs on the ***CAN*** side of the Wisdom Line. The ***Can't*** is on the **FEAR** side. Who am I without this person? This is the reason causing your grief.

*Life is like a roller coaster,*
*troubled times are part of the ride.*
Bobbi Sims

Words are so powerful. Once I mashed my thumb in the car door, it hurt like &%*#%. A nurse asked about my *discomfort level,* questioning if it were between 1 and 10 with 10 being the highest.

Later, I quizzed her about this strange *nurse-talk*. She said the word *pain* is negative and triggers an automatic reaction. *Discomfort* is a neutral term and does not carry the same power as the word *pain*. Considering your current crisis, are you now feeling pain? What is your discomfort level?

Have you ever had a night where sleep was elusive and toss and turn was the norm? Your mind is racing, worry is constant, and tomorrow you will need all your strength. With your worry, the comfort of sleep just will not come. ***TNT*** (toss 'n turn) nights often come with the position of leadership. When the ***TNT*** fuse is lit, you desperately seek a solution.

Do want to know something that works on ***TNT*** nights? Assuming you do, get up and take a sincere look at the source of your worry. Since you cannot sleep, why not make good use of this time?

*It's not possible to 'get away from it all*
*'cause everywhere I go ... there I am!*
Ziggy

Make two columns; one is what you ***Can't Control*** and the other for what you ***Can Control***. Ask yourself, will focusing on what you ***Can't Control*** solve the problem? If not, you have done enough for this evening, and no more useless energy is required. Sleep will come. And tomorrow, when you review the ***Can*** side, your to-do list has already been made.

*I've always believed that anything you vividly imagine,*
*ardently desire, sincerely believe, and enthusiastically.*
*act upon, must, absolutely must, come to pass.*
Skip Bertman, LSU baseball coach –
National Championships 1991, 1993, 1996, 1997, 2000

## Stress management

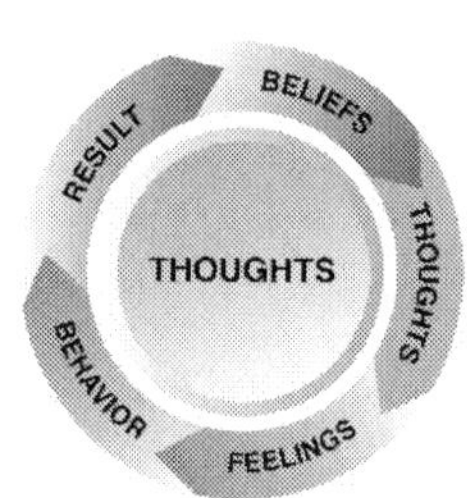


An obvious cause of stress is just living. Life can be stressful especially if you are at the helm of the ship. Did Captain Edward John Smith, the captain of the ill-fated Titanic feel any stress 30 seconds after striking the iceberg?

There is some not-so-obvious cause of stress that includes your worldview, your judgments, your expectations of others, your desire for control, etc. How the anxiety is handled becomes the difference between success and failure. Here are some ways people handle stress.

**The Ostrich:** H*ead in the sand.* By ignoring or denying the problem, maybe hoping, or wishing it will magically disappear.

**Hiding:** *Hiding from the problem* by taking drugs, alcohol, food, obsessive sex, work, or anything else to make it go away. This band-aid approach works - temporarily. It is a great example of an ***external solution to an internal problem.***

**Healthy Stress Management:** *The right proven stress management tools,* have a mitigating effect on stress, such as meditation, biofeedback, exercise, diet, breath control, attitude, and thinking about thinking.

**Reason:** *By uncovering the real problem.* Using coping skills to find and correct underlying problems, is one of the many effective tools found in *Outrun the Wolf.*

When troubles hit, many think, *why me? Why* is a great question to determine *why* the car will not start or *why* your best salesperson is not effective, or *why* the production line is down? When contemplating your identified trouble, a better question to ask is. *What am I going to do about it?*

"Why" belongs on the ***Can't*** side. "What am I going to do about it" is smack in the middle of the ***Can*** side.

My good friend and copy editor, Jack Chapman questioned me about the diagram on the next page. He asked why **Can't Control** points to **Don't Worry,** and **What needs to be done** also points to **Don't worry**.

# Can - Can't Problem Outline

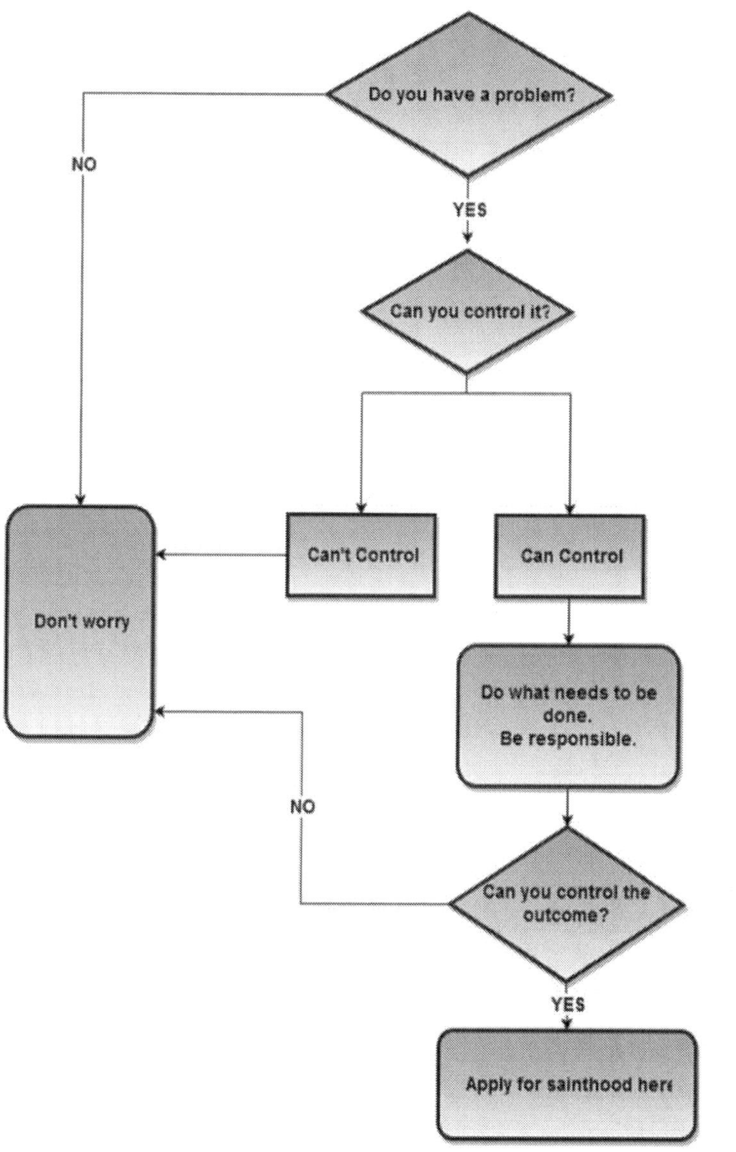


Outline modified from the work of an unknown author.

Think about this, after you complete **What needs to be done**, the outcome then is not in your hand. So, don't worry.

Note: To check your accumulative effects of stress, read the section titled "Taking Care of Your Health", in the Appendix.

I asked a lady what her husband did.

"He was a Captain in the Navy."

"Was he a captain of a ship?"

"No, he was …you know, he told the captain where to go."

"Oh, the navigator?"

"Yes, she answered."

"People are always telling me where to go," I said.

"Yeah, but I bet they don't call you a navigator!"

## Meaning

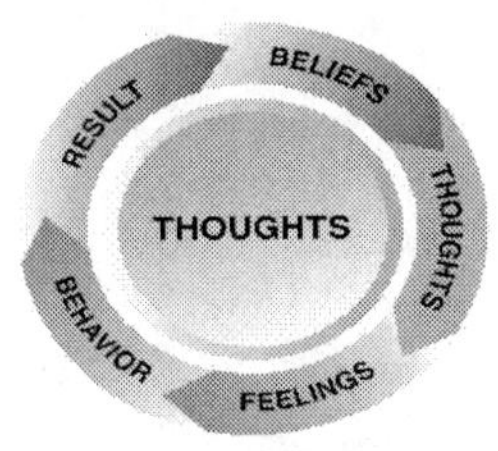


Surviving a painful event provides experiences that help navigate through the next. Are you now a better person for having survived the last crisis, maybe even thrived, and even soared? Here is a challenge, what are you going to do with this *unique opportunity* this crisis affords? Are you going to waste it, or look for emerging opportunities and innovations, and become the inspiration your company needs and deserves?

**What is pain?** When you put your hand on a hot stove, what happens? You withdraw it rapidly, along with a few expletives. What made your hand move? The pain – right? If it were not for the pain, you would not have known there was a problem until you smelt the burning flesh – way too late. So, ***pain is awareness***. Life is painful. Pain provides the awareness that ***change is necessary.***

Currently, you are in pain, your company is in crisis, your profits are hemorrhaging, and you doubt your abilities to overcome this problem. Your very economic future is threatened. All those symptoms cause pain. Part of this is personal; it hurts!

A good friend, Jimmy Cason once gave me a blessing I would like to pass on. Once when I was suffering, he smiled and said, "I wish you a lot of pain." My first reaction was anger. How insensitive of him! Here I am hurting, yet he wishes me more pain? Then I understood Jimmy's best wish for me. He hoped I would gain the awareness the pain affords. So, at the risk of your again throwing this book across the room, ***I wish you a lot of pain.*** Ah, you did throw it across the room, but good, you now returned.

In *Outrun the Wolf,* there are many lessons and quotes from *Man's Search for Meaning* - a powerful book about life. The Editors of *Encyclopedia Britannica* described Viktor Emil Frankl, (26 March 1905 – 2 September 1997) as "an Austrian Holocaust survivor, neurologist, psychiatrist and author of *Man's Search for Meaning*. He was the founder of Logotherapy (literally *healing through meaning*). In 1942 Frankl and his family were sent to Auschwitz-

Birkerau Concentration Camp, where his father perished, and his mother was exterminated. His wife died later in the Bergen-Belsen concentration camp. As Frankl observed the brutality and degradation around him, he theorized that those inmates who had some meaning in their lives were more likely to survive…"

*Healing is accomplished the instant the sufferer*
*no longer sees any value in the pain.*
A Course in Miracles

From this horrific experience, Frankl became an expert in suffering and more importantly how to survive the immense cruelty and agony. He wrote, "The Nazis took away all their earthly possessions, separating them from their families, depriving their worth as a human, took away their freedom, and changed their name for a number tattooed on their wrist. They became a number. You have your own suffering and what Frankl learned can be a touchstone for your journey.

## Locus of Control

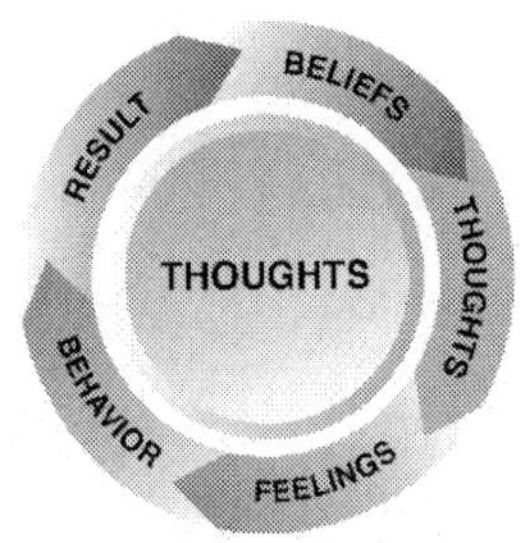


Locus of Control was developed by Julian B. Rotter, and it categorizes what people believe about their ability to influence life events. People with an external locus of control, believe external factors, such as random chance, government, or other environmental factors are responsible for their lives. People with an internal locus of control think they have a great deal of influence over what happens, and they have confidence in their own abilities. Just as Viktor Frankl was as an inmate, employees are vulnerable to various outside factors. But Frankl discovered in the most devastating of times, that the only thing that cannot be taken away is one's attitude.

Those with a more internal locus of control tend to be more successful, healthier, and happier than those with an external one. In times of high stress, many become caught in what is happening to them and what is out of their control. They allow these factors to dictate their fate to define them. They become the deer caught in the headlights unable to move away from traffic. There are many outside factors creating the pressure you feel. Locus of Control can begin to provide the basis for managing this tension. Self-efficacy, as described by psychologist Albert Bandura, refers to the belief that they are able (or not able) to accomplish tasks and achieve goals. People with high self-efficacy "...have high self-esteem, feel secure and content with themselves, and aren't overly concerned with other people's opinions of them. People with strong self-efficacy are more resilient and less likely to be destabilized by negative life events. Their locus of control is more likely to be internal than external."

The more that someone believes their actions determine their future, the more likely they are to engage in healthy behaviors, like eating well and exercising regularly. If, on the other hand, they feel like they have no control, their stress and depression validate their feeling of helplessness.

**Locus of Control**

**Internal** **External**

Frankl observed that when a prisoner "did not struggle to save his self-respect, he lost the feeling of being an individual, a being with a mind, with inner freedom and personal value. These prisoners were too frightened to make decisions and assumed that fate was their master and that one must not try to influence it in any way, but instead let it take its own course. Great apathy."

*Apathy is a communal disease and*
*can only be cured by enthusiasm.*
Penny Earle

Although Frankl did not use the term "Locus of Control," I think he was referring to it when he said about those who would not

"... submit to those powers which threatened to rob you of your very self, your inner freedom, determining whether you would become the plaything of circumstance, renouncing freedom and dignity to become molded into the form of the typical inmate." This person "accepts his fate and all the suffering it entails, the way in which he takes up his cross, gives him ample opportunity, even under the most difficult circumstances, to add a deeper meaning to his life. It may remain brave, dignified, and unselfish. Or in the bitter fight for self-preservation, he may *forget his human dignity* and become no more than an animal. Here lies the chance for a man to forgo the opportunities of attaining the moral values that a difficult situation may afford him. And this decides whether he is *worthy of his suffering or not.*".

*Hope is not a strategy.*
A Newman & Associates

## Silver Lining

Is there a silver lining in what you are experiencing? Think about the current despair you acknowledged in your Wisdom Chart. Now think about your suffering, stress, and sadness – how you are experiencing this main problem. One moment you are spreading your arms out wide, feeling the wind on your face on the bow of the

Titanic, and the next moment you are shivering in the lifeboat watching your ship sink.

Using your stated problem statement, let us use it to explain Locus of Control by using Viktor Frankl's math formula – his understanding, so painfully learned. It is a very difficult algebraic formula so hang on to your high-school math dread.

**D = S**

The **D** and the **S** are connected by the equal sign. Remember, boys and girls, if the ***D*** gets larger or smaller the ***S*** must become the same because of the equal sign, they are always equal. I warned you this could be challenging! In this formula, the ***D*** stands for despair, and the ***S*** stands for suffering. Despair equals the amount of suffering. Now, let's make this more complicated – a higher level of math.

**D = S – M**

***D*** and ***S*** are equal but when the value of ***M*** is subtracted from ***S,*** it causes the ***D*** to decrease accordingly. Is your head spinning? In this case, the ***M*** stands for meaning. The suffering is reduced by having meaning. The larger the ***M,*** the smaller the ***S.*** Using this formula, the Meaning could be so large that the suffering could be negative. If one wants to have a greater internal Locus of Control and lower despair, according to Frankl (the suffering expert), then one must find as much meaning in the situation as possible. ***Finding meaning in the suffering lowers the despair.***

The problem you acknowledge in My Worry is your current despair, so labeled it ***D.*** Your suffering is ***S***. The hard part of

Frankl's formula is to discover meaning in your current pressures. This may not immediately pop out and may take some reflection. How can your suffering have any meaning? Using this formula, the more meaning you find, the more your suffering, and despair decrease. Frankl allowed this realization to help him survive horrendous deprivation. One day, I promise, this current crisis will be behind you. You will be successful if you can say, "That was a hard time in my life with a lot of pain but because of it, I am a better person. *Thank you, crisis!"*

*Meaning seeks to find value where one*
*believes there is little or none.*
Mathew Brash

In the 1980s, a surplus of crude caused a drastic decrease in the price of oil and a severe economic downturn to the Gulf coast area. What Frankl endured was more suffering than my experience when I was fired. However, not having his equation, I was unaware of the power of finding any meaning in my suffering. During his imprisonment, Frankl would have smiled if he knew his suffering would now provide you some relief.

## Types of Behavior

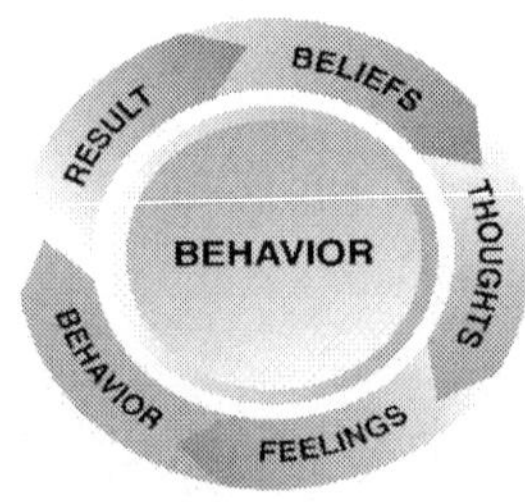


There is various behavior exhibited in the workplace and in families: aggressive, passive, passive aggression, and assertive.

***Aggressive***: Violating the rights of others by using tactics such as humiliation, domination, or belittling, and sometimes violence. These hostile actions often are the result of pent-up emotions.

***Passive:*** Going with the flow, showing little commitment, and not caring. Example: "Do my forty and then the gate."

***Passive-Aggressive**:* Indirect behavior which may be aggressive, but beneath the surface, doing just enough, barely in compliance or deceptive sabotage.

Passive aggressive is a destructive way of arguing. The very first day I worked with MacTavish Williamson in his counseling agency, the office manager, Jackie, told me her pet peeve. "I hate to come into the bathroom and see the commode seats up. Will you remember to lower it?"

In this office, we had only one bathroom, so I understood her concern. I like it when people tell me what they need. For three years, I faithfully lowered the commode seat. I was proud of myself!

One day when I finished, my usual practice after washing my hands was to lower the commode seat, but I was mad at her. I thought, "I'm never going to lower the toilet seat again. In fact, I'll go in after others and raise the commode seat!" Fortunately, a little sentence flashed through my mind, *"If you don't speak it out, you'll tend to act it out."*

Once I heard my own words, I lowered the seat, went into her office, and said, "I have a problem." Using this wisdom, I did not act it out! When I related that story to a teenage girl, she looked at me, smiled, and said, "I've been lifting a lot of commode seats!" Lifting commode seats is passive-aggressive behavior and is an indirect expression of strong emotions.

***If you don't speak it out, you'll tend to act it out.***

***Assertive:*** Standing up for one's rights respectfully, honestly, and directly while also respecting the rights of others. This form is often sadly lacking but direct communication creates an atmosphere of trust.

**Exercise**

Been lifting any commode seats lately?

# Chapter 4

## Mood Chart

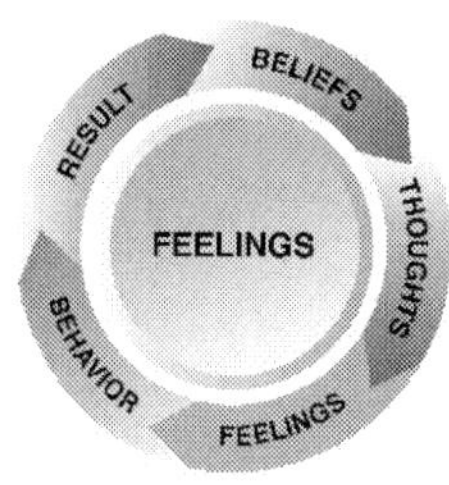


We all have had an argument that seems to go round and round. You know it is something stupid, petty, or maybe you are not even sure what the argument is about, but it has a life of its own. When couples come in for marriage counseling, they ***ALL*** have a similar complaint: "We don't communicate." Many continue the same old destructive patterns *even when they do not work!* The Mood Chart, found in this chapter, can change things. When we learn to understand our emotions and then that of others, we have a better chance of knowing what is driving the disagreement.

***When honest feelings are shared,***
***positive change is now possible.***

Permit yourself be emotionally honest. This seems like magic but when clearing the air with honesty, a resolution is now possible. *The Mood Chart has magical qualities. Magical? Yes!*

Once a client was in my office and madder than anyone I've ever experienced. He was so angry that he could not sit in the chair. Standing and pointing, he berated his wife with horrible accusatory terms. He was so emotionally violent; I thought I was going to have to restrain him. I gave him the Mood Chart and asked, "Tell me what you are feeling?" He pushed my hand away and continued his horrible tirade. I again put the Mood Chart in his face and demanded to know his feelings. He pushed my hand away and cuss me out. Well, I put the Mood Chart back in his face, and yelled back at him, "*&^%%* ! Tell me what you are feeling! *I called this therapeutic cussing!*

He grabbed the chart and started yelling his feelings. As he said these words, you could see the energy-draining and he finally sat in his chair, obviously much calmer. I thanked him for his honesty. I am unsure why just saying the words releases the emotional energy, *but it does*.

*Employers do not provide a hook for employees to hang their emotional lives as they enter through the workplace door.*
Peter Connelly

The management team of Valero's Krotz Springs plant was discussing workforce empowerment, and most were left-brain engineers. So, when I asked them to express their feelings, most gave superficial answers until one manager exclaimed, "Stark raving fear! Once that was said, other managers were able to share their innermost fears. With this honesty, solutions were not going to be hindered by unexpressed emotions.

Keep a copy of the Mood Chart (next page) in your office or home. Shock your staff by starting the next manager's meeting by expressing your current emotions from this chart, and then asking your team to do the same.

You will have limited buy-in to start, but if you continue you may be surprised how valuable it is. During the meeting, when you feel an emotional undercurrent, solicit feelings. Most are reluctant to express anger, disappointment, fear, and/or worry, but with time they will. This level of communication is not common in our world, but it is so necessary for understanding. Keep a copy at home. Teach those you love to use this simple wonderful tool. Families who have followed this advice ALL reported positive results!

Your current difficulty is a threat to your economic viability, how you feed your family, your reputation, and/or who you are. These are just a few of the myriad of possibilities now heavily resting on your shoulders. When the threat ends, strong emotions arise.

**David Walton Earle**
A key coping skill necessary for survival is the ability to manage emotions and have them work for you - *not against you.*

*All Progress is Change but*
*All Change is not Progress.*
Dean Lindsey

It probably is not far from the truth to think of your current problem as a threat. When most people think about conflict, anger is the vision most often coming to mind. Learning anger management is critical to your mission.

*Manage your choices and*
*you will manage your life.*
Shad Helmstetter

# Mood Chart

| MAD | GLAD | SAD | FEAR | HURT |
|---|---|---|---|---|
| Agitation | Admiration | Abandoned | Alarm | Aloof |
| Angry | Affection | Agonized | Anxious | Ashamed |
| Annoyed | Ardor | Bored | Apprehension | Belittled |
| Antagonism | Calm | Crushed | Bashful | Burdened |
| Arrogant | Confident | Deflated | Bewildered | Cheated |
| Bitter | Curiosity | Depressed | Cautious | Contempt |
| Contempt | Delight | Disconnected | Confused | Denied |
| Defiant | Desire | Distant | Distraction | Deserted |
| Disapproving | Ecstasy | Distraught | Dread | Disappointed |
| Disdain | Ecstatic | Distressed | Embarrassed | Dismay |
| Disgust | Elation | Downcast | Envious | Embarrassed |
| Enraged | Enthusiasm | Forlorn | Evasive | Guilty |
| Frustrated | Excitement | Gloomy | Fearful | Humiliated |
| Furious | Fervor | Grieving | Frightened | Insulted |
| Hateful | Flush | Helpless | Horrified | Lonely |
| Irritated | Generosity | Hopeless | Inadequate | Pain |
| Pissed | Happy | Ignored | Insecure | Regret |
| Rage | Hope | Isolated | Overwhelmed | Shame |
| Resentful | Hopeful | Jealous | Worry | Shocked |

*What comes from the heart reaches the heart.*
anonymous

# Breathing

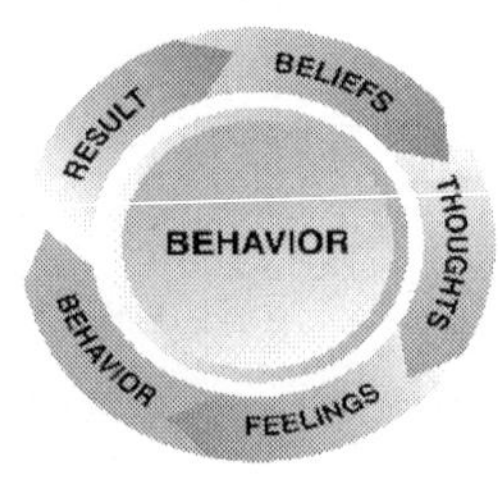


How do you breathe when you are angry or anxious? Short and rapid. Put your hands on your stomach and begin breathing. Breathe deeply and slowly. Breathe deeply so your stomach rises with every breath you take. Get your stomach to pooch out every time you breathe in.

Try it now. This is how you breathe when you were born. Babies come into this world doing deep breathing. I checked this out when my grandson, Cody was born. I watched his little stomach as he breathed (He is now much bigger than I am.). Birthing is very stressful on the mother, but it is also traumatic for the baby. When suddenly thrust into this bright and terrifying world, Mother Nature gives children this natural stress reducer – *deep breathing*.

**Exercise**

Practice this simple breathing exercise. Do deep breathing while sitting at your desk, watching TV, and the next staff meeting. You will need this when you again face your banker. When you are as frustrated as a Golden Retriever at a tennis match, breathe. The banker just called your loan, breathe. You are awaiting the outcome of an important bid, breathe.

*There must be another way to go through life*
*besides being pulled through kicking and screaming.*
Hugh Prather

# Chapter 5

## Anger

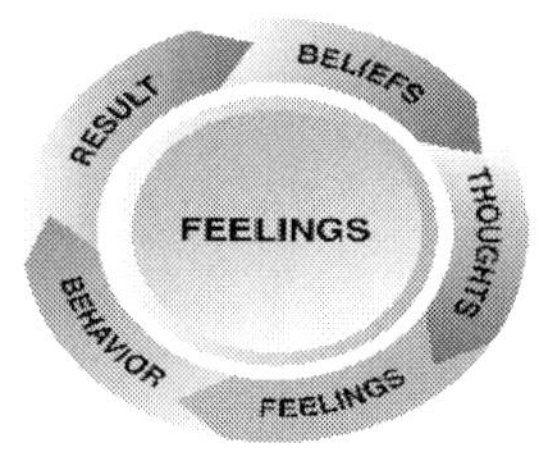


Are there benefits to anger? Yes. Anger does two things for us. For us? First, the emotion of anger provides a warning. It could be an attack of disrespect or an actual physical assault. Anger is your early radar system, designed to provide a signal of potential harm. The second benefit of anger is that it provides the energy we need for change. It was the fight or flight syndrome that kept us alive on the African Savanna when we descended from trees and walked among hungry beasts looking for lunch. The anger gives us the energy we need to take care of ourselves. Anger's energy comes from our adrenal system, the energy you would not have without it. Sometimes you need this energy to escape physical danger, end a painful relationship, stand up for injustice, or assert your rights to your banker.

This is not a trick question, but could you get along without anger? Without this emotion, there would be no warning, making you vulnerable to others taking advantage of you, and the energy to defend yourself would be missing. Anger and conflict seem to be one of those absolute associations, like peanut butter and jelly, having one without the other is what is unusual. Before the psychotropic drugs of modern medicine, doctors could not do much for angry, violent patients, other than strait jackets and padded rooms. In severe cases, the doctors would perform an operation called a Frontal Lobotomy where they cut the nerves to the frontal lobes of the brain (the frontal lobe is where all the emotions are processed).

After the operation, you could slap the patient and there would be no anger reaction. Without emotions, they were much easier to deal with in the mental health hospital. Could these patients stay on the street? People without the benefit of emotions do not have the necessary ability to defend themselves, thus requiring life-long hospitalization. On the street, they would be too vulnerable.

**Exercise**

What would happen if instead of going off on someone, you just expressed your feelings from the Mood Chart? "I'm angry! I'm hurt! I'm disappointed!" Expressing your feelings is a true form of honesty. Try this magical method of regaining your emotional sobriety.

*Lessons don't go away. They keep presenting themselves until we learn them.*
Cherie Carter

The power of anger cuts two ways, one constructive and the other harmful. Dr. Martin Luther King, Jr provided a wonderful example of the effective use of anger. King was a civil rights advocate in the late '50s until his assassination in 1968. He sought to change the oppressive Jim Crow Laws, all designed to keep black people subservient, poor, without power, and living as second-class citizens. He led civil rights marches to change the unjust and harmful laws by actively disobeying them but without violence. Mahatma Gandhi used this same non-violent anger in the fight to gain independence from Great Britain after the Second World War. Dr. King learned civil disobedience from studying Gandhi.

In the early sixties, people witnessed King and his followers marching in Selma, Alabama on small black and white TV sets. The nation watched in hushed horror as King led a group off the bridge into a sea of angry heavily armed white cops, townspeople, firemen with fire hoses, and guard dogs. At the foot of this bridge, the riot began.

The City of Selma refused Dr. King's parade permit to march to Montgomery, the state capital. Technically he was breaking the law. I am white and back then had a high degree of ignorance, so initially, I aligned with the white authorities. As we witnessed the courage exhibited by those "law-breakers" and "rioters", "them uppity-n-word" (as they were called) our perspective began to change.

Although we did not immediately realize it, our contempt for "those people" began to turn into respect, and "those people" became our brothers and sisters, Dr. King's dream. You cannot limit someone, judge them, or make a slave of anyone without being part of the same system. If you enslave someone, you must be there as their overseer. When you judge someone, you defend your judgment even with evidence to the contrary. Minds can play tricks on us when we want our reality to match our perception. The opposite is also true. When we are willing to accept others with their perceived differences and allow them the same rights we enjoy, then change starts to happen. This is the universal law of love.

Can you imagine the courage to walk arm-in-arm across this bridge, singing "We Shall Overcome," into all those hostile, white law-enforcement people? Where did that courage come from? The energy propelling these courageous people was their collective anger. Black people experienced hundreds of years of slavery, abuse, discrimination, and murders. It was their anger energy that provided the necessary courage to correct an injustice so long endured.

The Civil Rights movement helped remove the blinders of inequality, injustice, and begin the process of change. Unlike the heavily armed whites guarding the bottom of the bridge, these marchers were only armed with the conviction of the cause and the courage in their hearts. They did not wish to inflict harm on those who tormented them but sought the respect and the equality already granted by the US Constitution. They used their anger to summon the courage and strength to stand up for what was right, to forgive their enemies, and attempt to express love to those who had so much hate.

*This is an excellent example of anger used constructively.*

The civil rights protesters, who marched off the Pettis Bridge on March 7, 1965, into history, demanding equality, and respect. We are all now better off for their courage. Thank you, my black brothers, and sisters. Despite the guns aimed at these marchers, their courage changed history. Freedom does not come from the number of guns in a person's basement but from the courage to stand up against injustice. Our country is now better off for their march.

***Justice will always prevail…eventually.***

**Exercise**

Can you think of a time your anger worked for you? When did you need the power of anger? Did it give you the strength to stand up for justice? Is anger a choice? Can you choose to be angry or not? Contrary to most people's beliefs, ***anger is a choice***.

When I first learned this profound wisdom, I did not believe it! Anger had been my constant companion for over forty-two years, so thinking I had some degree of control was completely alien to my experiences. The fact that my constant state of irritation was not effective but was working against me. This realization just might have occurred to me had I the knowledge found in this book. But back then, "I didn't want or need any $&%@ psycho-babble!" (See how much wiser you are than me!)

*The choices we make in the heat of emotion would be better left for some other day."*
Shad Helmstetter

Even though I did not believe my anger was a choice, I was fortunate I did not discount the hope of managing my constant companion, anger.

> Expectations are resentments under construction.

As life would have it, very shortly afterward I had the chance to prove it for myself (God has a sense of humor). I locked my keys in the car! I remember standing in a hot Houston, Texas parking lot. My ever-present slow-burning anger started to simmer then boil into situational rage and without much thought, I was looking for something to beat my car up with. With a cooler head, breaking that window did not make sense, but at the time, it was exactly my plan. My best thinking was to look for a weapon to inflict my rage on my car. Then I remembered, I had a choice. I asked, "Self, do you want to get angry about this or not?" Surprisingly, I responded, "No," and I didn't. I was pleasantly surprised when I stopped being angry! I was then free. I knew then, I could choose to be angry, and that the power of choice belonged to me. I could choose not to rage or continue my old behavior. What a lesson! What freedom!

*So, can anyone make you mad?* In response to this question, I know you may be saying, "If you had to live with my wife, you'd understand. She's Darth Vader's evil twin sister," or "My husband is always putting me down. He's always saying negative things. Saint Peter would be cussing if he lived with that man." You may be living with a man with two horns and a pointed tail or with a wife who flies on a broom, but the truth is, *anger is always a choice*. No one can make you angry - without your *permission*. Do not get me wrong, some people give us great opportunities when they know exactly how to push our buttons, especially our loved ones. When pushing our buttons, they receive our predictable reaction. Despite all the button-pushers of the world, you still get to *choose* - to be angry or not.

Who and what is ruling your life? Is it you or is it your emotions? Does your inner-tantrum-throwing-toddler come out at the most inappropriate times? When our emotions control our lives, we get ***emotionally drunk***. When we automatically react, we may be guilty of RUI - ***Reacting Under the Influence***.

People drinking alcohol do not make good decisions. Alcohol decreases intellect and suppresses natural intelligence, so the only thing remains is the person's emotions. The more a person drinks, the stupider they get. This is why drunken people often make poor decisions, because it is all emotional reasoning.

*If we don't change the direction soon,*<br>*we'll end up where we are heading*<br>Unknown

Emotionally drunk people are like a person drunk on alcohol. Since, like the drunk, their emotions have taken over, often with unintended consequences. These emotions can turn ugly, hurtful, and sometimes deadly.

**Exercise**

Do you frequently work out in the Tantrum Gym? The bad news is, reacting with emotions is a learned behavior. Want to know the good news? Reacting with emotions is a learned behavior and *any learned behavior can be changed.*

***All emotions can be managed.***

Do you say or do hurtful things that you later regret? Are you ***emotionally drunk***? On the Gulf Coast there are many petrochemical plants where steam is a necessary commodity for driving pumps, turbines, and other process equipment. Picture a pressure vessel where steam is continually being added but never released. If the steam continues to build without release, what do you think will happen? A catastrophic rupture! However, there is a safety device on each pressure vessel called a pop-off valve. It is designed to rupture at a certain predetermined pressure allowing the steam to escape long before the structural integrity of the vessel is breached.

***Change is usually a painful process,***
***but it is the building blocks of growth.***

Humans are like a pressure vessel where the emotions (especially anger) are like steam. When life causes a person to be upset, where is the anger energy stored? In this example, it is stored in their emotional pressure vessel. The stockpiling of strong emotions creates overwhelming pressure. So, when this pressure is released, it becomes emotional vomiting, often directly on our loved ones. Accumulated anger, like too much pressure, turns into rage. When this explosive anger is directed toward loved ones, it pushes them away. When directed inwardly, it has a corrosive effect on lowering our self-worth, with possible ulcers, or other physical ailments.

Disaster occurs when stored anger energy is combined with a faulty pop-off valve. Here, this sudden release of pressure can result in an explosion either outward or inward. The ultimate expression of an outward explosion is going *postal.* A terrible inward explosion and suicide is a probability. When ***emotionally drunk***,

When wearing a bikini, women reveal 90% of their bodies. Men are so polite; they only focus on the covered parts.

just expressing feelings from the Mood Chart releases pent-up energy. Continuing the pressure vessel metaphor, instead of storing this energy, release it into harmless water vapor by expressing what you are feeling.

Have you ever experienced road-rage? My friend Charles Mayeux swore at other drivers who cut in front of him. That was, until he realized that for all these years, he had been giving free driving lessons to people who could not hear him. He could not control them, and they never paid him or even thanked him for his thoughtful driving lessons! You can cuss out the other driver, or you can say your feelings out loud, thus allowing the energy to be released.

***Your windshield is a wonderful listener.***

You cannot control other people, but you can control how you respond to their behavior. With unexpressed emotions, there is a great tendency to act it out, often with negative behavior.

***Remember: If you do not speak it out, you tend to act it out.***

**Exercise**

Think about your pressure vessel. Have you been storing your emotions and allowing them to accumulate? Can you go from neutral to super-charged manic in seconds? Think about the harmful effects and what it does to you. If your anger is working against you, maybe you need to explore another coping skill.

Picture an iceberg. As you learned in the third grade, 90% of the iceberg is under the water. The Mad column represents the tip of the iceberg on the Mood Chart. Your anger is what others observe. But until you identify what emotions are supporting your "pissivity," you are unaware of what is under the iceberg. Until those feelings are acknowledged, you are often oblivious of the forces dictating your behavior. The Mood Chart is a useful tool in identifying and managing your emotions.

Now think of the ***Three What's***...."What?"...The ***Three What's***.

**First *What: What*** am I feeling? Explore your emotions and question just what you are feeling? ... ANGER? Good! Now what else are you feeling? Use the Mood Chart's to scan the other columns under the Hurt, Sad, and Fear columns. What else you may be feeling? What other feelings are supporting the anger you feel?

**Second *What: What*** are the thoughts driving those feelings. ***All feelings are based upon thoughts.*** It is hard to identify the thoughts until you discover the actual feelings. Pinpointing the emotions, makes discovering thoughts easier. ***Your feelings do not lie to you.*** However, they may be based upon faulty thinking so challenge them. Are they true? Are they False? Do you have all the information necessary? Is this healthy thinking or stinking thinking? Is this thought going to build or destroy?

**Think about your thinking**.

**Third *What*** - ***What*** am I going to do about it? It is hard to know how to solve a problem until you know the thoughts behind it. Most of us desperately fumble around trying to get our needs met. We are often unsuccessful. The ***Three What's*** can help in this quest.

***Just because your feelings do not lie to you, understand that- your feelings are not facts.***

Anyone not yet a master of arguing, raise your hand. Nicholas Abraham, PhD, LPC-S said: "Arguments are about one party trying to convince the other party to convert a happening that rarely, if ever happens. By their very nature, arguments end in one of two ways: there is either a winner and a loser or both will lose. From an unscientific perspective, I would conclude that the numbers of the latter far outweigh the former.

Arguments erupt when the pressure is on, when; insecurities are high and when we feel the urgency of maintaining some small degree of power. We react with oppositional and defiant energy, both of which seek conversion instead of the common good."

***A civil conversation is only possible when the anger energy is dissipated.***

## Difficult Event

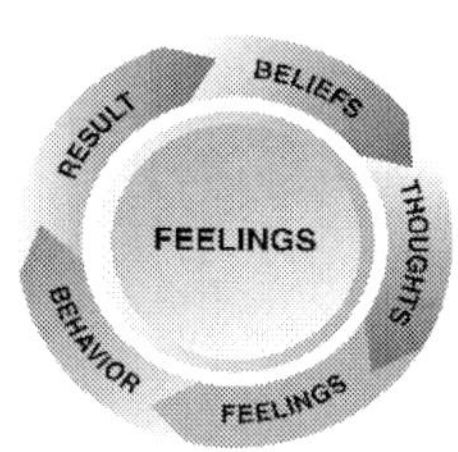


Think about an argument you had with someone you care about when your anger was out of control, and you said things or did something you later regret. (Pick out a memorable one for you will need to refer to it several times and call this your **difficult event**.)

***Anger can enslave us, or it can set us free,
all depending upon how it is used.***

During this **difficult event**, list your mad feelings found on the Mood Chart, then list your feelings from the Hurt, Fear, and Sad columns. Pick out the most significant emotions, the one(s) best describing your feelings, the one(s) with the most energy (no more than three but only one from the mad column). You were upset for a reason. What was the thought(s) driving these energized emotions? What needs of yours were not being filled? What expectations were not met? What was the problem and whose problem was it?

***Unmet expectations are often expressed in anger.***

I started my consulting career in graduate school with a wonderful contract. The Brock Group sent me to Tennessee to help prepare an estimate for a conveyor system in a coal-powered power plant. I worked all day Saturday making the measurements and exploring the conditions required for our bid. Our plans were to put the estimate together the following Monday with the bid due on Tuesday.

When I finished the measurements, I was hot, sweaty, and full of coal dust. I went in the men's room, laid my notebook down with all the measurements, and washed off. I was excited about returning to Memphis to have a nice meal and maybe catch a movie.

Upon returning to Memphis, I discovered, *I had left my notebook in the restroom!* I threw my briefcase on the ground and said a few not polite words (Mother would have been shocked). Then a little voice said to me, "David, you can get as mad as you want to, but you're still going to have to go back and get your notebook." This gentle statement allowed me to regain my emotional sobriety.

*Feel your feelings.*
*Control your behavior.*
Bobbi Sims.

I drove three hours back to the plant with the windows rolled down singing country and western songs, picked up the notebook, and arrive with only enough time to catch a few hours' sleep before my Sunday flight.

**Exercise**

Do you ever wonder if your anger is legitimate? Do you question if you have the right to be angry? Do you doubt if your anger will do any good? Some people are fearful of expressing anger because of their tendency of hurting others. Some fear their honesty will cause others to abandon them, cause resentments, or make the problem larger.

This just in...*Breaking News*: Your anger is legitimate! You have the right to your anger. Remember, ***anger is designed to create change***. However, you do not have the right to hurt others with your wrath. Do others have the right to hurt you? Again, the answer is no. Anger is not the cause of the problem. Results come from how this transformative emotion is used.

Anger is just a feeling and feelings are ***just that – feelings.*** Feelings are neither good nor bad. When you feel anger, it is legitimate.

Have you ever had anyone try to control you with their anger? Have you tried using anger to control another? Do you anger upon others or upon yourself? When around angry people, many revert to feeling like a kid when their parents would explode, frightening them into compliance. As an adult, we are not that scared 8-year-old kid anymore. Unless the anger is accompanied by a physical threat, you do not have to fear another's anger.

***It is okay to be angry, but it is not okay to anger upon someone else.***

**Exercise**

Think about some experiences you had as a child when adults controlled you with anger. As an adult, you can respond appropriately instead of cowering like a little child.

Currently, there are many outside people, events, and situations requiring your attention. Maybe you feel like Willie E. Coyote who just ran off a cliff - suspended in midair –and just realizing what will happen next. These problems are coming at you, most belonging on the ***Can't*** side. What makes this harder is the unmanaged emotions controlling you and all your team/family. However, instead of disaster coming out of the shadows to stab you in the back, using the tools found between the covers, you now can manage the various emotions that used to control you. This awareness is freedom, and it belongs on the ***Can*** side.

*"...every time you open your mouth to talk, your mind walks out and parades up and down the words"*
Edwin H. Stuart

# Chapter 6

## Communications

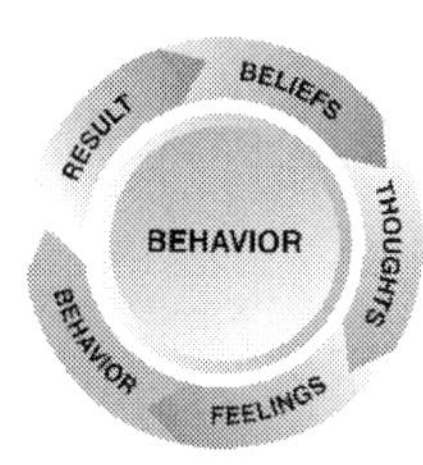


Without successful communication, the chances of escaping this crisis are severely handicapped. *All leaders* can improve their message. This section provides an overview of the key ingredient of successful communication – ***listening***. You may be the best communicator in your company, but crisis requires even more.

Most people listen through their own sometimes unaware filters of personal experiences and sorted by their worldview. Jumping to a hasty conclusion and reacting personally often causes incorrect conclusions. People presume they understand when they often do not. Problems increase by the cubed square when the results are only the illusion of understanding. All humans have a great hunger, a tremendous ache to be understood. As you experienced when someone listens, your hunger is satisfied. When not, this need can be manifested in anger, rage, or other types of acting out behavior.

*You are the message.*
Bob Pries

Understanding greatly increases the chance for a successful outcome. When I trained substance abuse counselors for the Evangeline School, Effective Listening was part of the curriculum. For each different course, we would be in class for one entire weekend and return in two weeks to finish the course. I presented Effective Listening skills the first weekend. Upon returning for the second weekend, one student, Dallas told this story.

"As I was driving home two weeks ago, I thought about what we learned in class and realized that I had been married for 37 years and in all those years, I had never listened to my wife. I decided to try out these principles to see the results."

"I want to tell the class that it was the best two weeks of my life. I didn't know she was so interesting. I didn't know I could feel so close to her, and I can't wait for this weekend to be over so I can listen to her some more."

A couple of years later, I asked him, "Dallas, are you still listening to your wife?"

He responded, "You bet."

I taught management principles to state employees when I worked for Louisiana State University. On the first day of the training program, we did a listening exercise. On the following day, one of the participants told the class, "I tried those listening skills on my wife, and they worked wonderfully."

"You did? How fantastic," I responded.

"Yeah, but I'm not going to do them anymore." In shocked horror, I asked him, "Why?" "If I continue to listen to her, she will think I'm having an affair!"

*If speaking is silver, then listening is gold.*
Turkish Proverb

## Effective Listening

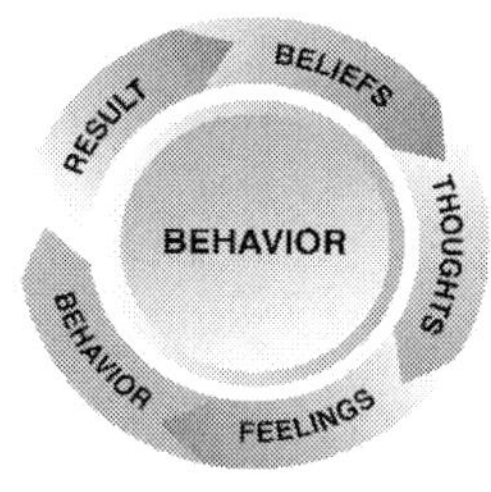


***Good communication is an absolute must***. You are the chief message carrier, so any improvement greatly enhances the outcome. Improving always starts with a decision *to choose to improve.* Life changes when we make a concerted effort to listen – to really hear the other person. Even the best communicator can improve their listening skills. This is especially true when navigating through a financial burp in your company's history.

### *Competitive Listening*

At a party, three or four people are engaged in a conversation with one telling a story that reminds you of a wonderful tale you are dying to tell. While they are talking, you are thinking of your story and eagerly wanting to speak. We have all done this type of communicating - *Competitive Listening*. You want them to finish quickly so you can tell your story, and while waiting you only half-listen. *My story is more interesting, and I want to tell it, so quickly shut up!* This attitude is anything *but* effective listening. A good listener makes the other person feel understood, and there is a connection between the sender and receiver that is lacking in *Competitive Listening.*

I just need
you to
understand!
The employee would stand on his head in order to be heard.

### *Decrease talking*

When you practice effective listening, the other person usually talks more than you do; 5-20 more words compared to you. You cannot *receive* while you are *sending.* Monitor your own conversation. *Who's doing the talking and who's listening?* This is not easy, especially if you are not used to it.

When Bob Hambright was president of J. A. Jones Construction, it was a stern atmosphere. At his next position at Centex Construction Company, he wanted it different, so for example, he made the break room to be spacious with lots of windows. He encouraged his employee to enjoy each other's company and often participated in their small talk. He wanted a relaxed, fun culture, and where he could do more listening than talking. "Many useful discussions often take place in this relaxed atmosphere." This comfortable environment helped him decrease his talking and improved his listening.

***Seek First***

Being understood is a need we all have. When understood, people feel different about themselves and the listener. If someone does not listen, this callous disregard breeds negativity when the listener appears not to care. As a leader, you communicate with many people. Some do not understand your message. They seem to only care about their own. This can be extremely frustrating but could be a signal to increase your listening. One of the *Seven Habits of Highly Effective People* by Steven Covey is, **seek first to understand than to be understood**. Anger is a demand to be heard. A well-tuned ear increases interpersonal connection and the reason for anger fades. Calmness is the reward.

***You can out-listen most others' anger.***

When you put aside your legitimate need for understanding, a couple of things will happen. First, at least one person will know both sides of the conversation. Second, if the other person perceives you are trying to hear them, they might reciprocate.

Flip the coin. Think our designated antagonist, the banker. She is not listening to you when you desperately want to understand. Do you compound the felony by tuning her out? Mark Goulston, a psychiatrist, business consultant, executive coach, and hostage-negotiation trainer for the FBI wrote, *Just Listen.* His rules of listening are:

- Be more interested than interesting.
- Make people feel valuable.
- Help people exhale mentally and emotionally.

# The Good Listener -

Let the worker do the working
and the shirker do the shirking,
each, no doubt, will reach his proper end.

Let the talker do the talking,
and the mocker do the mocking,
beware, for both are easy to offend.

But the man whose halo glistens
is the man who sits and listens,
for everyone will always call him friend.

Let him be the entertainer
when you listen, you're the gainer,
you can borrow, if he has a thing to lend,
keep your lips a little smiling
and your eyes, perhaps, beguiling
if you haven't any interest, just pretend.

For the saint whose halo glistens
is the guy who sits and listens
and it's funny, but he really is a friend.

Written by my grandfather, Eli Walton Earle –
January 31, 1948

## Listening Traps

| Author unknown | 1 | 2 | 3 | 4 | 5 |
|---|---|---|---|---|---|
| | Innocent | | | | Guilty |
| Do you tune the other person "out" to prepare your response? | | | | | |
| Are you often so wrapped up in your own feelings that it is impossible to "get outside yourself" to really listen to another person? | | | | | |
| Do you tend to "jump ahead" of the speaker and reach conclusions before you have heard the person out? | | | | | |
| Are you anxious to contribute your ideas to the conversation, or relate your experience while another person is trying to talk? | | | | | |
| Do you have tendency to finish sentences or supply words for the other person? | | | | | |
| Do you get caught up with insignificant facts and details and miss the emotional tone of the conversation? | | | | | |
| Do you listen with half your attention tuned toward giving advice, solving the problem, or figuring out what to say to make the other person feel better? | | | | | |
| Does your mind tend to "wander" and think about something else when you are supposedly listening? | | | | | |
| Are you human? | | | | | |

| | Total Score |
|---|---|
| | |
| Below 20 | Great listener, keep it up. |
| 21 – 30 | Far above average, strive for excellence. |
| 31 – 40 | Improvement needed |
| 40 – 50 | Improve your score and your associates and loved ones will be happier. |

## *Preparing to Respond*

My best listener is the windshield.

When focusing on what we want to say, we are mentally forming our response. Occupied minds can only half-listen. Listening is not necessarily agreeing, but the willingness to know someone else's mind. Instead of putting the focus on how to respond, ***blank your mind to your agenda and listen.***

*"...develop a big ear rather than a big mouth"*
Howard G. Hendricks

## *Increase Patience*

Some people are harder to listen to than others. They may have an irritating mannerism, and/or have difficulty getting to the point. *Listening is hard work.* Dedication, focus, and practice build concentration ability. It will not come easy, but patience pays dividends.

## *Listening Environment*

Distracted by noise, other people, confusing backgrounds, or if you are in an uncomfortable situation, you may have difficulty *receiving* effectively. Listening in a noisy plant or a crowded restaurant can be challenging. Finding a place where words are effectively exchanged is necessary for successful communication. When distracted, ask for a change of environment. Other situations may affect listening, such as the pressure from the latté you recently enjoyed. When that happens, ask to be excused with a twinkle in your eye. Say, "I'm losing my focus." If encountering a puzzled look. explain, "I need to relieve myself of some negativity."

## *Divided Attention*

In everyone's home, there is an electronic instrument interfering with good communication. You guessed it, the TV.

In 1967, the Dallas Cowboys played the Green Bay Packers in a championship game later called the Ice Bowl. Although Dallas lost, I have been a fan of the Cowboys ever since. I always followed their pre-season wondering who they were going to draft, which player was going to make the team, and worried how they were going to beat the dreaded Washington Redskins.

It was the fourth quarter, and we were playing the Redskins. The Cowboys had no time-outs and were behind by 4 points. A field goal will not bring them victory. Quarterback, "Dandy" Don Meredith hits Lance Rentzel for a twenty-yard gain. As he stepped out of bounds. I screamed, "Go Cowboys," at the TV. On the next play, Meredith throws to Bob Hays for a 30-yard gain, *We're gonna score!* Just then, my kids came in. "Daddy, Daddy!" they exclaimed. "Get away, be quiet, the game is on!" I responded. I am ashamed to acknowledge this but what message was I sending my kids? You guessed it; they were not as important as the game.

In 1987, my life was a wreck, my kids were doing drugs, my marriage had failed, and my business was in free fall towards complete failure. In my deepest and darkest time of need, not one of those Cowboys called, offered any condolences, or sent any money. Too late for my kids, it then dawned on me what was important.

**David Walton Earle**

A few years ago, I was watching the Cowboy game and my now-grown daughter walked in. I turned off the TV. "Go ahead, Daddy I know you love the Cowboys," she told me. "No," I happily responded, "you are more important than they are." It was wonderful to give my daughter something valuable.

I learned the hard lesson to turn off the TV, turn off the computer, and put down the paper - they will always be there. People and relationships are what is important! By sitting across from other people when conversing with them without external distractions, the reception improves. What message do you send to your employees when they are trying to talk and most of your concentration is elsewhere?

*Your current condition is as unpleasant and frightening as it may be, provides the chance to achieve human greatness even an accomplishment which in ordinary circumstances you would never have achieved.*
Viktor Frankl

## *Criticism*

It is so easy to be critical. People often focus on the sender's poor grammar, clothing, style of presentation, level of intelligence, etc. or, judge them when they have different views. What is important is what is being said, not how it is articulated. Good listeners focus on what the person is trying to say, instead of interpreting what or how they are saying it.

**Exercise**

Criticism skips your normal defense system, and its energy attacks your self-esteem. We often internalize the rebuke, then magnify it, and take it personally. Often, we end up compounding the problem with our attack statements.

Go to your medicine box and find a ***Q-TIP***. Run it across this page on both ends to get the magic the publisher embedded. Finished? This ***Q-TIP*** is special.

It stands for ...***Quit*** ... ***Taking*** ... ***It*** ... ***Personally*** ... ***Q-TIP!*** Instead of a lightning rod where criticism goes right into our self-worth, having a ***Q-TIP*** becomes a shield.

Now put this magical ***Q-TIP*** in a place you can often see it. Some taped this reminder to the car's headliner or on the plastic covering the speedometer. Some tape it on their bathroom mirror or computer. One woman asked me, "Do you have a string, so I can tie it around my neck?"

Before a maintenance turnaround at REG plant, I gave everyone a ***Q-TIP*** with instructions about its purpose. On a hot afternoon in June, I came across three millwrights who were tired and frustrated trying to fix a pump. There were heated voices and expressive hand gestures. I noticed the supervisor, Mike Hoyt, was calm. When he saw me, he smiled and pointed to his ***Q-TIP*** taped on his hardhat.

*The trouble with the world is that the stupid are*
*Cocksure and the intelligent are full of doubt.*
Bertrand Russell

**David Walton Earle**

## *Silence*

Immature people are often insecure, so becoming the talker becomes their overriding concern. When they spend all their time telling others what they know, they learn very little.

A nurse described my new client at the Lady of the Lake Hospital as *excessively verbal*. She was indeed verbal– very verbal! She talked, talked, and talked. I listened, listened, and listened for 45 minutes! At the end of her ranting, she caught her breath and asked, “they say I talk too much. Do you think I talk too much?” I gently answered, “I think you are uncomfortable with silence.” My diagnosis turned out to be true.

She did not get along well with others but tried to communicate by her obsessive chitchat. I observed her frustration trying to connect with others with her verbal assault. At first, other people would politely try to get away with an excuse. However, politeness did not stop her, and her verbal vomiting continued, even when others backed away. In desperation, she grabbed them physically demanding their attention making a healthy connection improbable.

We practiced listening for understanding and allowing others to respond. I saw her several years later and she came running up with a bright smile. She immediately began to talk but then caught herself and said, “And how is your family?” We then had an appropriate and pleasant conversation. Maybe not as pronounced as my client, but many people are uncomfortable with silence. How comfortable are you?

The president and vice president of Gulf Tech and I made a sales presentation to Boise Cascade in Deridder, LA. Our sale plan was for the president to present the overall company values and history, and the vice president to explain our capabilities and safety record. I was to negotiate the deal.

Boise already had our proposal (Plan A) and before this meeting, called saying they wanted to meet and also discuss the cost. I prepared two other proposals each with a lower price than Plan A. I had Plan B in one jacket pocket and Plan C in the other.

Boise asked questions regarding how many people did we think were necessary for this plant, how much space we needed for our portable buildings and equipment yard, and the most telling, "When can you start?" What I heard was buying signals- not objections. At the end of the meeting, we shook hands on Plan A, and I never mentioned the backup plans in my pockets.

Walking out of the meeting with Boise-cascade, the president turned to me, "David that was the best sales presentation I ever heard."

The vice president was incensed, "He didn't say anything!"

The president smiled and said, "Exactly!"

It seemed to me they had already made up their minds, so I was not about to muddy the waters with discussing price.

***Sometimes the peace of silence can increase communication and improve the outcome.***

**Exercise**

Can your silence help improve listening?

## *Fatigue*

When you are unable to give your full attention to a conversation, politely ask for another time. People respect this honesty much more than half-listening.

In Lake Charles, Louisiana, we employed unionized painters. When the contract expired, we negotiated a new one. Often these meetings were emotionally packed, sometimes bitter exchanges of different needs, perceptions, and values.

One year we were at an impasse for many weeks and the atmosphere had become quite tense. The international union was asked to attend in the hope that new energy would turn the tide. After we negotiated most of the day, we were all exhausted, discouraged, and ready to give up. We agreed to a much-needed recess. In the men's restroom, I saw this international unions representative take off his shirt, wash his body, and put on a clean fresh one. When we returned to the bargaining table, he was invigorated. His body language reflected his renewed spirit as he listened to the nuances of what we were saying. We ultimately settled the contract.

## *Body Language*

Most communications are non-verbal. It is not the words that are said so much as what others read into our body language, such as posture, eye contact, and or the inflections in our voice. For example, when a person hesitates, looks away, or stammers, it often means something if we are observant enough to understand the message.

When conducting mediation for the EEOC at Exxon Refinery in Baton Rouge, Louisiana, Exxon's attorney sat almost sideways to the opposing counsel. He had his arms crossed and his legs turned away. Contrary to this posture, his opening statement was, "We are going to be very open in this mediation. Everything is on the table."

After separating the parties, the plaintiff counsel said, "Did you see that attorney's body language? I responded, "Yeah, it's going to be a long day." His body language said the opposite of his words. This dispute did not settle in mediation and went to court.

Fully focusing on body language, expressions, eye contact, and other non-verbal clues takes a high degree of concentration. When negotiating a contract with Olin, my associate, Ken Istre and I would alternate being the observer and the presenter. The observer looked for telltale signs when the presenter was speaking, gaining a few valuable clues as to Olin's thoughts. We won the contract.

**Exercise**

Focus on reading other people's body language. What is their posture saying? Observe their eyes and the inflections in their voice. Suggestions for improving your body language:

- Face the person eye to eye. A smile is inviting.
- Develop good eye contact. Do not stare. Just look them in their eye.
- A forward body lean indicates attention.

- Open your arms instead of crossing them over your chest.
- Nodding the head indicates connection.

**Exercise**

Be aware of what your body is saying.

## *Judging*

Not judging another is a very difficult thing to do. We all judge others to some degree. Some people judge so much that it becomes a disconcerting habit. Whenever someone shares a contrary opinion, or has a different religion, or supports the "wrong" political party, the tendency is to think of them in black and white terms: "I'm right and you are wrong."

Because of our judgement, we may think them ignorant and lack credibility. Our interaction then often becomes a struggle for who's right. Of course, and it's me!

During a discussion with a good friend, our political views agreed, and we connected. However, on another topic, his view was opposite mine. "He was wrong!" I felt my attitude change from warmth to distance when I judged him.

In the cartoon Haggar the Horrible, his sidekick asks him, "Why are we fighting so hard?" Haggar emphatically answered this ridiculous question, "Because we are right!" With childlike innocence, the sidekick asked, "And they are fighting because they are wrong?"

When an employee suggests a solution, no matter how stupid, search for what part could be correct. Great wisdom may be there. If this idea is discounted, your organization may be deprived of the next one, a long-sought solution. Be aware of your judgment tendencies. Think about your thinking during, *I'm right and you're wrong* arguments. Ask yourself, why do I need to be right?

***When judging, effective listening suffers.***

**Exercise**

Listening without judging is very hard, and that is the reason Effective Listeners are so valuable. Observe your tendency to judge.

## *Absolute Statements*

If you want to start an argument, use absolute statements containing "*always*" or "*never*". For example, "You *never* take out the trash. You *never* listen to me. You *always* interrupt me."

Penny, my wife of over 30 years, once commented, "I always find your laundry tags from the cleaners scattered everywhere all over the house." I know an absolute statement when I hear one, so with a twinkle in my eye,

I responded, "Always?" "Everywhere?"

"Yes," she answered, "always!"

Well, I was going to show her "*always.*" I started saving laundry tags. When I told my friends what I was doing, they bought into the mission and saved them, and the laundry gave me a fist full. My inventory grew and grew. Then on March 31 when she went to bed, I took those tags and put them *everywhere*. I put one in the cookie jar, one in her laundry basket, one with her teabags, rolled two up in the toilet paper, and spread the rest through the house in very creative places. I put them *everywhere.* Her *always* became true!

The next morning, she woke to see tags everywhere and quickly understood my gag. "You know, that is a wonderful April Fool's Joke. It really is." I was beaming with pulling one over on her. "You know that joke was so good. *It was so good,* let's make love tonight." My heart jumped, my cheeks flushed, and instantly my anticipation grew. After a few moments of savoring my expectation, she sprung her trap, "April Fools!" I'd been had.

Wedding vows should include a promise to eliminate ever saying *always* or *never.* Happier marriages would result.

Exercise

Be aware when you use absolute statements.

## ***Should***

There is another form of an absolute statement that comes packaged as a "*should*". An inappropriate "*should*" is a judgment. It means, "I know better than you, so follow my advice." When judging others, you are not a good companion or listener; you are judging and not listening with acceptance. You do not have to agree, but others have the right to be understood.

Control statements come in several forms: "*should/should not*", "*ought/ought not*", "*must/must not*", and sometimes even without these words, the implication is a "*should*". At one time, others called me, *Mister Should-Ought*. Now when someone trusts me enough to share a problem, I consider it a sacred honor that I must not abuse it with *SHOULDS.* Man, sometimes it is incredibly hard.

What works much better than *SHOULDS* is by asking, "What options do you see?" If stuck, ask if you could present a few choices. If they do not want your possibilities, do not inflict them with your wisdom.

***Misused demand statements are counterproductive and increase conflict.***

After learning this wonderful coping skill, my son asked my advice, so I helped him develop three or four options with the pro and con of each. I knew what I thought best, but these were his choices, not mine. I had to laugh when he reverted to our old dysfunctional pattern and asked, "Okay, Dad, what should I do?"

I responded, "Well you got option one, option two, and option three, which one are you going to choose?"

"No dad, what shall I do?"

"Well, you got this option, then this one and the other choice is this, which one are you going to choose?"

In frustration, he exclaimed, "Dad, you've been telling me what to do for 18 years. What shall I do?"

"Well, son, as I see it, you got option one, option two, and the third other option is this.

Parents need their children to fail. Wow, what a horrific statement! Having them fall short when you are around to pick them up, provides a teachable moment. Children learned to walk by falling. If we do not let them fall, they will never learn to walk. When unsuccessful, it is so easy to reinforce the *SHOULD* we previously gave them, with judgmental statements, like, "See, I told you so."

Instead, when others face failure, try this wonderful question: "What did you learn?"

*Appreciate people. Nothing gives*
*more joy than appreciation"*
Ruth Smeltzer

When my twenty-year marriage ended, my dad called and told me, "David, this is what you should do. Get down on a bended knee and beg her forgiveness." After that conversation, I was in a two-day depression until I figured out what happened. My father, who I respected more than anyone in the world, just told me I was not living my life based upon what he thought. I was not okay. In his effort to show love, he put me in a depression with his judgmental statement.

*If you don't take some risks, you won't get the chance*
*to succeed. While you are trying, you are winning.*
Jack Chapman

Later I told him, "Dad that is not what I need from you. What I need is understanding and acceptance not telling me what to do." He understood, and for the rest of his life, he tried very hard to give me understanding and acceptance. Sometimes he would preface his comments by, "David, this is not *a should,* but..." Sometimes they were, but his acknowledgment made all the difference in the world.

Albert Ellis, the famous psychologist, has a wonderful way of conveying this message in a way *you will never forget*. When you tell someone, what he or she should do, know what you are doing? ***Musterbation!*** And you are ***SHOULDING*** on them.

Uck, you just ***SHOULD*** on me.

So, do not ***SHOULD*** on people!

Instead of *SHOULD* statements, what do you do when someone has a problem, and you just know the answer? You do not want to SHOULD on them, but want to help. Instead of the *SHOULD*, you can ask them, "I have some experience that may benefit, want to hear it?" If they say "no", honor their request and just shut up. This gives them the right to say no. Human nature being what it is, their curiosity usually will overcome any resistance and they will come back to you, on their terms. This is how we show respect to others.

***When you give someone the option of saying No, they just might say Yes.***

**Exercise**

Study this word *SHOULD* in three different situations.

- Observe other people trying to control others with *SHOULD* statements.
- Identify what you feel when someone gives you an inappropriate S*HOULD.*
- Then the biggest *SHOULD* of them all. The *SHOULDS* you give yourself.

There is a correct place for *SHOULD* statements, such as, "You should be at work at 8:00 AM, or "You should get this order to the customer quickly." There is less conflict when the sender is aware of when to use *SHOULD* statements and when not to. Used correctly, should statements do not have the same negative connotation in the workplace or when instructing your children to clean their room.

## *Fixing It*

What do you want when someone is listening to you? Do you want their undivided attention, their understanding, and acceptance? Sure. If you are lucky enough to receive the gift of Effective Listening, do you want them to ruin it by telling you how to "fix" your problem? Fixing it often can be an expression of love, but unsolicited wisdom comes out sideways.

Men do three things well, build things, fix things, and blow things up! When our significant other has a problem, we men want to show love by solving it for her, showing off how smart we are, and receiving her undying appreciation. Often this love comes out as a *SHOULD* statement.

My first wife had a job at Weingarten Real Estate and often shared her frustrations. "You tell that boss …" or, "You should do this or that …" These were samples of the love I wished to extend.

Finally, she quit. And in my great capacity for understanding (sic) I said, "Well, it's about time." The look in her eyes could not hide her fury. Unmanaged rage of which I was completely unaware!

"I would have quit six months ago if it weren't for you!" Because of my sideways love, I inflicted pain and suffering on my mate, not what I intended. Supervisors fall into this trap when they jump to solutions too quickly. Instead, ask, "How are you going to solve this problem?" This simple pause allows the employee to think. Insisting employees use their brains is a necessary component in their development. This respect helps to allow workers to own their job and be the type of employee needed. Isn't this a desired trait that better serves your organization?

*We shall hew out of the mountain*
*of despair, a stone of hope.*
Martin Luther King, Jr

## *Emotional Communication*

It is difficult to Effective Listen when in physical or emotional pain. When emotions run riot, effective communications are compromised. When *emotionally drunk,* many unintended consequences happen. Postpone what your unmanaged emotions are telling you. Wait until your cool returns, be *emotionally sober* when disciplining.

*Discipline yourself, before you*
*discipline your children.*
Ross McElwee

Correcting your children or employees when *emotionally drunk,* comes out as punishment, not discipline. What children see their role model being out of control. Children with anger problems often have parents who also lack restraint. This dynamic is similar in the workforce where anger is experienced as hostility, sarcastic comments, humiliation, and/or overreaction. When employees experience punishment, they think they are being treated like children. People feel respected when the discipline is applied with learning as the objective.

## *Interested vs. Interesting*

Humans have a basic need for attention. When someone is interested in what we say, it makes us feel intelligent and worthwhile.

*Be more interested than interesting.*
Mark Goulston

Children do not have the language ability of adults or abstract reasoning abilities, so a child's language is their play and toys are their words. Adults talk about the horrible experiences and children play out their trauma. Your willingness to allow employees to fully express what is bothering them will pay immense dividends of respect.

At the REG plant, two very valuable operators were also keenly aware of injustice. That awareness - when realized - is an asset to successful management. However, they both allowed their emotions to control them and ultimately doomed both their futures. Successful management would have allowed this full venting, acknowledged their perception of the injustice - making changes where necessary, and then later coached them on better methods of expression. Easier said than done. In this case, when the supervisor expresses genuine interest, the employee appreciates the attention, and resolution is then easier to obtain.

## *Value People*

The requirements for healthy people are *to love and be loved and to feel worthwhile to ourselves and others.* When the listener cares about what is said, the receiver feels worthwhile, appreciated, and valuable.

> I asked God for a bike, but I know He doesn't work that way. So, I stole a bike and then asked for forgiveness.

Is there room for love (not romance) in the workplace? How great it would be to have such strong feelings for a coworker and felt love? Brad Albin is a no-nonsense executive who has managed over 70 manufacturing sites and does not mind lobbing a few F-bombs. He and I developed a close relationship when we worked together during some very difficult times. Many times, this man, whom I have the utmost respect for, would tell me that he loves me. Love can exist in the workplace, and it takes a strong person to be honest about this degree of care.

*Make people feel valuable.*
Mark Goulston

## *Exhaling*

A man lost the love of his life and cried through his entire first counseling session. In this environment, it was safe for him to be REAL because he knew someone was listening.

*Help people exhale mentally and emotionally.*
Mark Goulston

An 11-year-old girl would not talk to me but rolled up in my blanket on the floor. I allowed her to express her misery in silence.

Our last time together, she wrote on my grease board, "Thank you for everything," and decorated it with hearts and flowers. I treasure her message and have never erased it. What would it be like if we allowed others to "…exhale mentally and emotionally?"

## *Angry / Listening*

Anger decreases communication. It is hard to listen to someone drunk with rage, yet this is exactly what is needed.

***You cannot have a successful relationship without anger!***

My son, Garrett learned to assess his anger by assigning a point value. He ranks each situation from 1 to 10 with 10, being the most severe. What he discovered, he was expressing anger at twos and threes! Humans spend a lot of energy on small numbers!

**Exercise**

Think about a time when anger caused problems in your relationships. Can you remember another time when you used anger as a building tool instead of an explosive? Was anger a problem in the difficult event you previously declared? When emotions run strong and there is limited common ground, try preemptive humility by saying, "I need to take a break because I can't think of anything constructive to say. I don't want to add to the problem, so, I'm going to stop here, sleep on it and take if from the top tomorrow."

***Anger is like dynamite;***
***we can use it to build or destroy.***

Mark Goulston shared his experience as an FBI Hostage trainer. Below are his thoughts:

- "When people are behaving at their worst in a way that scares the heck out of everybody else, it is because they have felt so powerless for so long and are now reacting to it."

***You can out-listen most people's anger.***

- You can help someone move "... from their acting out lower brain up through their emotional middle brain and into their upper rational brain." Listening to others helps them sober up emotionally.
- When people know they are understood, there is little need for anger. This allows others out of their emotions and into their intellect.
- By mirroring what the other person is thinking, "... they will be drawn to your understanding and empathic caring and away from their agitation which is mainly a reaction to feeling misunderstood and not cared about."

When you need to get emotionally sober, try saying, "I need to be quiet for a while." This alerts the need for quiet introspection. Later when you are emotionally sober, the discord can continue, but with an improved chance of success.

## *Triangulation*

When one person complains to another person about the behavior of a third person, this communication style is *triangulation*. Picture a triangle formed between three people. Person A has an issue with Person B, but complains to Person C about Person B. See the triangle?

It is easy to see this dynamic in the work environment. One coworker complains to another about the boss. When coworkers vent emotions between coworkers, the issue is never resolved because the problem is between the coworker and the boss. Triangulation is learned in dysfunctional families then brought into the workplace.

Using this example, expressing this verbal energy to the neutral person does not work. The issue is between the employee and the boss. The thinking is: if I complain long enough or hard enough, magically resolution will happen. It does not.

A local credit union hired me to help them with teamwork and communication skills. I conducted a written survey about their view of company problems. One main issue that stood out was "Back-biting and gossip". In a company-wide meeting, I debriefed the team on their survey answers. Armed with this information we met with the employees and discussed how we can communicate better in the future. "Back-biting and gossiping were high on the list of your concerns." I checked with the group if indeed this was a problem. They all emphatically agreed it was a major problem, and how they hated it.

I asked, "Well, I'm confused, everyone has told me that this is something they hate, correct?" Heads nodded like bobblehead dolls. "We have everyone here, right? Again, the bobbleheads responded, "If everyone is here, and everyone hates this, I have to assume whoever is doing the back-biting is right here in this room.

*Are all you here part of the problem?"* Immediately there was then profound silence, then slowly the bobbleheads returned. From this understanding, we could now discuss triangulation.

***Direct feedback to the proper person at the proper time and in a respectful manner is an essential key to problem-solving.***

Feedback does not belong to the neutral person. Get out of the dysfunctional family rules and get honest with the correct person. Then resolution has a possibility, and they no longer must carry the resentment. Freedom! Leaders complain to other supervisors about their employees. Unless this concern is directly addressed, how can the employee know of your dissatisfaction?

My therapist says I am obsessed with vengeance. We'll, just see about that!

It is another thing to seek suggestions from a third party on how to handle a problem. The intent must be getting ready to discuss the issue with the proper person. In healthy companies, the employee can say, "Boss, I have a problem."

**Exercise**

Think about times when you vented on one person when your anger really belonged to another. Did your venting achieve resolution?

## *Decision Question*

*You can get furious ... or ... you can get curious.* Kerry Patterson, co-author of the book, *Crucial Conversations* presents a wonderful question to ask yourself whenever deciding how to respond to a difficult situation:

Most of us when *emotionally drunk* are furious. Having this simple reminder provides the space to breathe and to consider your response. "How come this person is so upset? I wonder what they are feeling. Is this about me or is it about the other person? What am I feeling? What thoughts are driving my feelings?" Getting curious is an awareness often lacking in good communication. All it took is to become … *curious*.

When in conflict, the tendency is to ask, *Why*-type questions. Such as: why are they saying this? Why are they so angry? Why are they doing this to me? Sometimes, *Why* is the exact question to ask, such as: "Why wasn't the contract signed? Why is this system not working?" But in human relationships, *Why* is a very limiting question. *Why* engenders *Because*. Unknown reasons create emotions that reinforce the *Why* question, becoming a squirrel cage of mind chatter. A better question provides the key to escape from your self-induced cage. A more useful question is, "*What am I going to do about it?*" Why questions often belong on the ***Can't*** side. "*What am I going to do about it?*" belongs on the ***Can*** side.

When all else fails, being furious may become the correct action. When this rare occasion is necessary, plan to do it, and be emotionally sober when you do.

## Gratitude

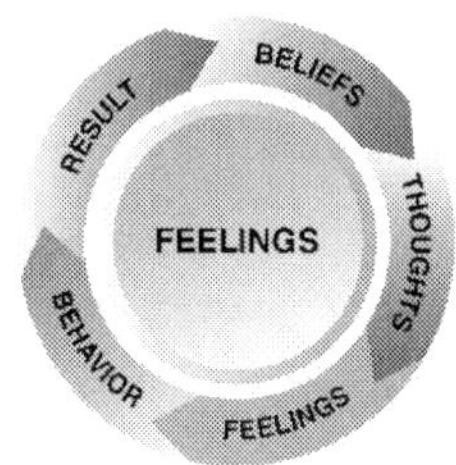


What are you grateful for? In these depressing times, it may be difficult to see anything at all to be grateful for. Consider struggling with identifying your gratitude – especially now. Most of us often complain with our mouths full.

**Exercise**

Write a gratitude list. This exercise puts a fractured life in proper perspective. And when searching you will discover that there is a lot to be grateful for. Keep adding to your list.

*The hummingbird and the buzzard both search for food.*

*The hummingbird looks for nectar and the buzzard for rotten meat.*

*Both are successful in their quest.*

**You find what you are looking for.**

## Author's Note:

This completes the Survival section. Quick review, the Wisdom Line exercise provides an effective tool to manage stress and improve thinking. If you just read your way through this exercise, please stop and give yourself the gift of writing it out. I promise this will be a key tool you need to withstand the wolf's hot breath.

Through Viktor Frankl's experience, finding meaning will decrease today's suffering. Find enough meaning and joy replaces despair. With improved listening skills, you are an even more effective leader who can now understand situations so baffling before. The more you improve on these skills the greater your chance of survival. Without you, your company chances greatly diminish. If your family is the concern, they need you, not your dysfunction.

Since you started this book. you have been battling on two fronts. One is your current reality and two, your inward journey, what you personally need to know.

*I feel like we all have two battles or enemies going on. One with the man across from you. The second is the man inside of you. I think once you control the one inside of you, the one across from you really doesn't matter. I think that is what are all trying to do.*

Tony Romo
Dallas Cowboys

I run like the winded.

# Thriving

## Staying ahead of the wolf

# Chapter 7

## Monsters under the Bed

Solutions require change. Since change involves people, change *is messy,* and *people is people*. We all have emotions and often neglect them when making decisions. Change …*any change* … causes some degree of anxiety, fear, worry, doubt, and often panic. *Outrun the Wolf* provides suggestions on how to take care of oneself during periods of high stress, how to develop personal resiliency to a crisis, and how to help your team members.

As a leader, you are a living, breathing human being and not your balance sheet, your personal guarantee, or the banker calling your loan. As the hero in this book facing a crisis in your business, you will ultimately have to make many decisions in this recovery process. However, when also taking care of yourself, your decisions will be made in your rational mind, not consumed by unmanaged emotions and unmitigated stress.

***Embrace the pain.***

## Change Postures

There are various postures people take when being confronted with change: Active Resistance, Passive Resistance, Compliance, and Willingness to Support.

**Active Resistance:** Any change will always have distractors, and some will openly fight what is new.

**Passive Resistance:** Some will not openly resist but will sabotage the process without making enough waves to bring attention to themselves.

**Compliance:** This person looks at change as *Change Du jour* as just part of the job. "I'll just do my 40, it all pays the same."

**Willingness to Support:** There will always be (except for cutting wages) a percentage of followers that jumps right on board and readily incorporates the change.

Managers love the enthusiastic support. However, the active resister may prove the most valuable. Their concerns often have considerable validity. When these concerns are validated, negativity can change to support and even enthusiastic compliance. A person with passive resistance is the most difficult to deal with since their concerns are underground, often hidden, - and can stab change in the back.

Jack Chapman poses this question: "What do most people do when they encounter resistance? They tend to rail against resistance, and if not successful in their arguments, they often give up, and then shut down." He concluded; "nothing becomes great without overcoming great resistance."

## Change Mindsets

There are various mindsets taken when being confronted with change: Denial, Blame, Poor Me, Game Over, Status Quo, and Thrive.

**Denial:** The obvious need for change is discounted as unnecessary.

**Blame:** There is a certain comfort in finding someone or something to blame.

**Poor Me:** The pity party – *Why do all bad things happen to me?*

**Game over:** Some end up checking out, quitting, resisting authority, and often making others miserable.

**Status Quo:** Give up control of the current reality. *It's not so bad – why change*?

**Thrive:** Some love the challenge and want to make changes, even when unnecessary.

Employers should be aware of all mindsets and employees have to decide to participate in the change, or stubbornly resist and become a victim. Leaders must determine how to challenge each mindset to best encourage and drive the transformation.

*I am a firm believer that success or failure*
*begins and ends with leadership.*
Bob Pries

In the face of possible death from a medical condition, people seldom change their lives to a healthier lifestyle. Why? Alan Deutschman explains that people facing life or death decisions involving drastic lifestyle changes face tremendous odds for failure. Nine out of ten people go back to their old destructive behavior within two years. Heart attack, stroke, or cancer victims face shorten life spans unless they make significant changes in their lives. Most vow to change, but only a small few succeed. Why? There is a hard truth about the soft part of changing. Business projects seldom fail because of the hard components, but rather they often fail because of the soft part - *the people*.

My neighbor keeps stalking me. I know that 'cause I looked through my telescope and she was Googling my name

Change Wright Consulting thinks that the common reasons for change resistance are "inadequate sponsorship, unrealistic expectations, problems with training, and poor adoption of change." All these reasons are important, but often the human nature part of the equation is disregarded, creating *very large monsters under the bed.*

*Competitors spend most waking moments planning your demise. To survive /prosper, you must change.*
Michael Manes

Hendrie Weisinger, Ph.D. stated in his book *Emotional Intelligence at Work,* "… you intentionally make your emotions work for you by using them to help guide your behavior and by thinking in ways that enhance your results." If the emotional side is not recognized and successfully dealt with, the change process often hits a wall of resistance. Glen Bucholtz the General Manager of the Shell Chemicals plant in Geismar, Louisianan plant told me, "In my years of industrial experience, I have observed that we tend to hire people on their technical skills and lose them because of their social, or interpersonal skills!"

## Change Premises

> *The teacher asked the class to write an unusual event.*
> *One little boy read his essay, "Daddy fell into the well last week ..."*
> *"My goodness!" the teacher exclaimed. "Is he all right?"*
> *"He must be, "said the boy. "He stopped yelling yesterday."*
> Jerry Lieberman

Bob Pries, the senior manager in the Human Resources of Procter & Gamble has a series of premises regarding the change process.

### Premise # 1 – Change is Messy

Change is like breaking an egg for breakfast; the egg will never be the same, the cooking process transforms the egg, and upon eating it, the human body will change the egg once again into fuel. The shattering of the shell begins this chain reaction. Egg breaking is always messy and so is the change process. According to Pries, leaders need to be "both flexible and firm". Planning for unplanned events is a key component of change management. During the evacuation of the British and French forces from the beaches of Dunkirk during WWII, Churchill sent everything that could float to rescue the surrounded troops. He was wise enough to give orders with wide latitude to carry out this desperate rescue.

*Things do not change; we change.*
Henry David Thoreau

I was hired as a culture change catalyst in Valero Energy's plant in Krotz Springs, Louisiana. I told the plant manager, Ralph Youngblood, "I am going to be the needle and you the doctor. Together we are going to puncture this infected boil. We will get a lot of pus, but this wound would start to heal." This proved an accurate description. In the middle of the "pus-stage", a large operator looked down at me and said, "We have a new nickname for you." When I questioned what was the latest of a series of names inflicted on me, some of which were humorous and some quite unrepeatable, he simply said, "Troublemaker". I knew then we were on the right track. ***Change is messy***

*Our only security is*
*our ability to change.*
John Lilly

## Premise # 2 –Change in the absence of context is chaos.

What is the reason for the change? What meaning does it have? And most of all, what is in it for me? These are the key questions that need to be explored. Viktor Frankel developed a theory that "...human beings can suffer any loss, make any change, and endure any hardship if there is meaning ... the hopelessness of our struggle did not detract from its dignity and meaning."

A leader must be able to know the context of the change and articulate it clearly to those who have yet to accept this new reality. Not doing so is what Pries calls a "failure of leadership".

John Kotter has hit on a crucial insight. "Behavior change happens mostly by speaking to people's feelings," he says. "This is true even in organizations that are very focused on analysis and quantitative measurement, even to people who think of themselves as intelligent in an MBA sense. In highly successful change efforts, people find ways to help others see the problems or solutions in ways that influence emotions, not just thought."

*To meet the demands of the fast-changing competitive scene, we must simply learn to love change as much as we have hated it in the past.*
Tom Peters

Dr. Dean Ornish, the founder of the Preventative Medicine Research Institute, realizes the importance of the emotional component that co-exists with the data driving the change. "Providing information is important but not always sufficient. We also need to bring in the psychological, emotional, and spiritual dimensions that are so often ignored."

Ornish thinks that the reason lifestyle changes have such a dismal record is that motivation by fear is not enough to sustain the change. Change can be too frightening to think about. Denial is a trick our brain successfully plays unless the emotional component is solved. It is similar in alcoholism. Most patients will not quit their drinking out of fear of imprisonment, death, or significant loss. Their powerful denial system protects the addiction. When addressing personal feelings people start to think differently and recovery begins. They discover coping skills that work better than drinking. The more they practice, the more the *need* for drinking goes away.

Ornish thinks that"...telling unhealthy people who are lonely and depressed that they're going to live longer if they quit smoking, change their diet, and lifestyle is not that motivating. Who wants to live longer when in chronic emotional pain?" Who wants to give up alcohol, a cherished habit?

***The Joy of living is a much more powerful motivator than fear.***

Ornish reframes the issue from "fear of dying" to "joy of living!" AA helps to change thoughts from "restless, irritable, and discontented" to "happy, joyous, and free". Both attitudinal shifts put context into the chaos of change.

## Premise # 3- No such thing as too much communication.

Alan Deutschman said, "CEOs are supposedly the prime change agents for their companies, but they're often as resistant to change as anyone - and as prone to backsliding." George Lake often echoes Deutschman, "Concepts are not things that can be changed just by someone telling us a fact. We may be presented with facts, but for us to make sense of them, they have to fit what is already in the synapses of the brain." Alanson Van Fleet, a human resource professional, thinks the leader's message should be, "To challenge the status quo, a leader must be perceived different, not too complex, shortsighted, or out of reach".

*The only difference between a rut and a grave is their dimensions"*
Ellen Glasgow

The petrochemical industry has a phenomenal safety record, considering the amount of material and the nature of what is manufactured. "It's not chocolate pudding," one crusty safety engineer told me. This industry has a good record because there is a direct correlation between the emphasis on safety and the results achieved. Safety is talked about every day. Everyone has a high degree of awareness.

*Change your thoughts and you change your world.*
Norman Vicent Peale

Lee Trusty, the Site Leader at Dow Chemical's Plaquemine, Louisiana plant went to all departments with this one question: "Cite examples of where you have cost Dow money being safe?" From that question, he wanted them to know that safety is more important than profits. Powerful message!

Bob Pries thinks "...when many people may be in the denial phase it is imperative that the leader communicates as often as possible. The message needs to be consistent in providing the context so necessary for success."

*It is not necessary to change.*
*Survival is not mandatory.*
W. Edwards Deming

Howard Gardner, a professor at Harvard's Graduate School of Education, studies what is most effective for leaders. He stated, "When one is addressing a diverse or heterogeneous audience the story must be simple, easy to identify with, emotionally resonant, and evocative of positive experiences. Incorporate different communication methods with diverse groups, where each gets the core message but tailored to the various audiences." This coupled with the advice from Pries, "A message heard several times a day for 8 days is virtually memorized".

**Premise # 4- Nothing substitutes for face-to-face dialogue.**

Scientists calculated that 93% of communication is nonverbal. With face-to-face communication, reading of facial expressions, body language, voice inflections, tone, and eye contact is important for successful communication.

An associate, John Reed, and I got into a disagreement and began a series of email debates over this issue. Since John and I often teach communication skills, I was surprised when we engaged in the exact behavior, we warn our clients about, expressing emotions via email/text. When this finally dawned on us, we swapped this electronic exchange with face-to-face dialogue over a hot cup of coffee. Resolution soon followed. There is no substitution "for face-to-face dialogue." What happens if the leader cannot physically provide this in-person dialogue? In the darkest days of WWII, Winston Churchill would walk the recently bombed out parts of London. The people of England witnessed their leader walking the streets of rubble with a look of concern, but also one of determination. In his radio broadcasts, Churchill was eloquent as he provided honest assessments and inspiration keeping the fragile British morale from succumbing to despair.

> My problems began when I tried to leap a twenty-foot crater in two ten-foot jumps.

No matter the company's size, for increased effectiveness, face-to-face communication is necessary. Pries advocates that any form of communication that is not face-to-face "…makes the leader removed from the organization and inaccessible. Communication is then one way."

In the aftermath of Hurricane Katrina, Procter & Gamble wanted to convey concern and belief in the future to their employees at their New Orleans Folger's Coffee plant. The management conveyed this in the interaction with the employees but knew this was not enough. Although this plant itself was not flooded, the hurricane created considerable damage that they were desperately trying to repair.

After Katrina ravished New Orleans, Folger's market share dropped from 42% to almost half of that overnight. There was tremendous corporate pressure to get the plant back into production. Compounding that, almost 70% of these workers lost most of their worldly processions in the floodwaters. Losing their homes forced many family members to migrate to different locations; some as far away as Maine and then having to return for their shift to rebuild the plant. Overnight Folgers had a traumatized workforce, without the succor of their families, as they attempted to rebuild a heavily damaged plant. These employees faced the uncertainty of rebuilding their homes. Many tried to buy a home in higher ground with the housing market suddenly turned upside down. This was a workforce facing tremendous trauma.

P&G's message was one of calmness and hope, one that showed that the company cared, and that the future would be brighter someday. They wanted to decrease the traumatic effect of the hurricane, so they hired mental health counselors specially trained in Critical Incident Stress Debriefing. These professionals provided employees the opportunity for open and safe dialogue.

I spent many days walking the plant and listening to every employee. Sometimes we discussed the latest woes of the New Orleans Saints, but most conversations involved what they were feeling. From an area map that illustrated the extent and depth of the floodwaters, I asked, "Show me the location of your house." They would point their home and then elaborate where their relatives lived, the house of their high-school best friend, and where they launched their fishing boat. This exercise encouraged the open expression of their pain, sorrow, and frustration that was in danger of consuming them.

*The rate of change is directly proportional to*
*the rate of change information passed.*
Bob Pries

One employee told me that I could not understand unless I could see his house in Chalmette, in St. Bernard Parish. The plant manager said, "Go," so he and I crossed the bridge to *The Parish*, as the locals fondly called the area. Here we entered a world of destruction I could have only imagined. A war zone would have been a good description. Within three hours of returning to the plant, all 500 employees of the plant knew of this trip. Immediately, many people called me and wanted to talk. Somehow my new awareness represented a deeper level of understanding, the same message Winston Churchill conveyed when walking the bombed-out streets of London. Being sensitive to their employees' disrupted lives was a message carried face to face, and it helped them adjust to this tragic reality. It was an active method of concern.

There are no substitutes for face-to-face dialogue. After the fires at REG, Peter Guay would spend time in the smoke booth and control room answering questions and providing reassurance. This principle is called *management by walking around.*

## Premise # 6- You are the message.

My mother repeated slogans during my formative years, many of which served me well. One of *Jean's Commandments* was, "Don't be afraid to get your hands dirty." Nothing connects employees to management better than a leader who is willing to "…get her hands dirty", especially when the project calls for extreme effort. In 50 A.D., when Julius Caesar was marching his troops over the Alps to attack his enemy from the rear, he took his turn shoveling snow to clear a path for the troops to follow. Caesar was respected by his troops for his dedication to duty.

*For every change initiative, there is a golden thread,*
*woven together of logic and ownership.*
Ivan Overton, MD

Lacking this golden thread connecting the employees with the message, Pries accurately labelled this, "a failure of leadership". James Firestone, president of Xerox North America said,"People need a sense of confidence that the processes will be aligned internally."

***When not aligned, change is chaos.***

People who believe in the change behave differently than those who do not. Employees look to their leaders, especially in the chaos of change, for inspiration, direction, and confidence. The leader's words, body language, and behavior all must have the same message.

Doctor Ivan Overton sees several potential areas for failure if this alignment is not established and maintained. A leader needs to seek many opportunities for interaction and not rely on one-way communication. Overton agrees with Pries that good communication needs to be said many times and in many ways. Mass communication channels should not be relied upon as the exclusive medium. Overton thinks that employees "... expect to hear about change directly from their leaders, and do not generally place much stock in messages that come from other sources." Important messages need to be directly conveyed by the leader and then reinforced.

*Successful leaders know this and are very deliberate about what message they want to send and consider that in every action they take. It is dangerous for the leader to think that once it is said the communication is complete.*
Bob Pries

**Premise # 7 -Do not expect of others that which you do not expect of yourself.**

On the morning of May 6th, 1864, during the Battle of the Wilderness, Robert E. Lee faced a hopeless situation; the enemy suddenly attacked with overwhelming numbers. In desperation, General Lee rode to the head of his troops preparing to lead them in a charge. To a man, they all shouted, "Lee to the rear! Lee to the rear!" He was willing to lead his troops, but he was so loved by his men and deemed so valuable that, these soldiers would not allow their general to expose himself to deadly Yankee fire.

*The question is not whether we are able to change*
*but whether we are changing fast enough.*
Angela Merkel

So, inspired by this act of Lee's, their counterattack changed the course of the battle. Lee would have led that charge and his men knew it. By his willingness, he communicated the importance of this battle and his men responded accordingly. Pries believes an organization act "exactly like the leader. He reasons it is because the leader is "their model of success.

*An organization will take on*
*the personality of its top leader.*
Abraham Lincoln

Leaders who try to change an organization without first changing themselves flirts with failure. Many times, different managers have told me, "We have a *us and them* mentality in this plant." Management often has the illusion that I can change their workers into exceptional employees. At a seminar for the first-line supervisors, I asked why there was a *us* and *them* mentality in this plant. The attendees answered, "*Us* is here, where is *Them*?" When hired as a business coach, I ask the top executive to provide a list of candidates for leadership development. Rarely is their name included. I then ask the undefendable question, "Why are you not on the top of the list?" Think of the difference in these two thoughts: "I'm sending you to the business coach," or, "I have a business coach who has helped me. I'd like to share him with you.".

*Done deeds are done deeds.*
*They cannot be undone.*
*Learn from them and move on.*
Bobbie Sims

For many years, I taught a court-ordered anger management class for Baton Rouge City Court. You can imagine some of the attitudes of my court-ordered students. Some classes were good, so I labeled them to myself as an ***A***-Class. Some would be considered ***B***' and some I labeled Z ***double O!*** At the end of each class, I gave each attendee a little card with the Earle Company motto:

***My Life Will Change ...***
***When I Change!***

After one class, in the men's room, I found my motto card discarded on top of the dirty paper towels. Here this person was attending a *court-ordered anger management course.* Obviously, something in his life was not working, and he throws away the one important message that could change his life. What a Freudian message to himself!

***You cannot be a victim and believe that motto!***

## Premise # 8 - Lead the change

Doctor Overton thinks that leaders often make a fatal assumption when they assume, they intuitively know what is needed to support the initiative. Overton thinks "…much of the success of the change initiative is dependent on them as leaders". The result will be ineffectual unless they understand the "change leadership roles they will be expected to perform". Leaders should know the game plan including a "… timeline and detailed approach" to know "… when and how they should participate".

There are some parts of the change process leaders cannot delegate. Having someone else carry this vital message is inefficient and possibly makes the leader a barrier to the desired change. When teams work in a vacuum without leadership input, their results may not match the original objectives. They may work long and hard but come up with the wrong answer.

***The change belongs to the leader.***

## Premise # 9 - Simple Model

When human behavior is routine, predictable, and safe, it can become increasingly more dangerous. If the known danger becomes commonplace, some of the normal fear protecting workers is lessened by familiarity. Gone is the fear that used to once promote caution. For example, some people stay in abusive relationships or in dead-end jobs even when knowing the extent of the abuse or drudgery.

Thinking of moving away from what is known involves dealing with the unknown and that triggers fear, the fear of the uncertainties of the future. Without external stimuli, routine processes increase rigidity. This is how we've always done it, why change? One advantage of your current crisis is more of your employees than you think, are now willing to change.

Change requires something to be different. If that difference is unknown, it is often perceived as unsafe. I have often asked people in dire circumstances if they would trade their problems for mine. The vast majority declined my offer. They know the extent of their problems but mine are unknown.

When people feel unsafe, it is the unknown that creates fear, and it is this strong emotion that causes them to dig in their heels and resist change. This Fear when coupled with a vivid imagination produces the ***monsters under the bed*** **-** a reality that must be dealt with. This is the point where leadership becomes vital. The more complex the change seems, the greater the fear, and this increases the difficulty– all of which impacts the results. The simplicity of The K.I.S.S. Theory works well here. ***Keep It Simple, Stupid!***

*Ownership must flow unbroken from the most senior source down through the organizational structure.*
Bob Pries

## Premise # 10 - If it looks screwy, *it probably is.*

Ever have a great idea, but when sharing it, realized how stupid it is? This is not because we are foolish, but we do not have a well-defined frame of reference inside our heads. A reference is missing until expressed aloud. We need a touchstone or perspective that can externally calibrate our thinking.

I have made some of my most brilliant decisions without sharing my thoughts. However, some thoughts that seem so splendid alone in my head turn out to be the most ill-conceived. From my many negative experiences, I now know that sharing my thoughts improves results. Having a trusted advisor - preferably outside the organization - that understands business but has no vested ties with the company, usually makes a good sounding board. This collaboration increases awareness and provides a non-biased point of reference by which all ideas can be evaluated. Magical thinking is wishing for a superhero in a flowing cape to rescue you, to save you from the reality of the day, or just wishing it would go away is. Some claim they are not in denial but are very selective with the reality they accept. Understanding the true reality of your situation is the difference between successful change and failure. By understanding the dynamics of change, you vanquish ***the monsters under your bed,*** and then ***Change becomes your ally.***

Do you recall the quote by Gilbert K. Chesterton: "*The chief object of education is to unlearn?*" Now that change has become your ally it is time to be "*unlearned*"! Picture you and your team stranded on a deserted and barren island. Do the people in this example seem depressed about their circumstances and resigned to their fate or are they excited about the future and motivated? According to Merriam-Webster dictionary, motivation means "the act or process of giving someone a reason for doing something." In this example, is everyone motivated to build a boat? Unless they like bleak landscapes and coconuts or perhaps are wanted for murder at home, most are eager to return.

*The good news is that it doesn't cost much money to change your thinking. In fact, it can be done for free.*
Robert Kiyosaki

So, in your best management style, you declare, "People, in order to get off this island we need to change." That probably is the most obvious understatement a manager ever made, and it just came out of your mouth. Undaunted, you lead your team on what needs to be done, agree on a deadline, assign team members to various tasks, oversee the boat's design, and finally inspect the construction. At the end of the day, you are satisfied, proud that the voyage is ready to begin. See, Bob Pries, no failure of leadership here!

Now here comes the unlearning part I promised. According to Owen McCall with Owen McCall Consulting, "most organizations do not lack for change, they change all the time. New people, new structures, new strategies, new products, markets and customers, and a never-ending stream of projects.

*Sacred cows make the best hamburgers.*
Robert J. Brandt

They don't lack for change, what they lack is a coherent direction. When you have a lack of direction the cumulative effect of a series of changes is at best random." McCall believes it is not just the change that we need, but more direction, more progress. Change tends to be directionless but "progress has direction." Change is difficult and it is made more difficult because we think of change in a negative fashion. Now compare *change* with *progress*.

Change creates certain emotions, fear being the most common. Is it less fearful when we discuss progress? "This company has to change, or we will not survive!" That might be accurate, but now compare it to a progress statement: "We will be successful and be achieve profitability when we …."

What motivates your team more: the fear of never leaving the island or the desire of returning to the safety of home and loved ones?

| ***CHANGE*** | ***PROGRESS*** |
|---|---|
| Usually starts with where we are now and how undesirable this is – (STRESS &PAIN). | Starts by defining where we want to be and how desirable is our goal. |
| Often directionless - the impetus for change is to move from an undesirable current state –(PAIN). | Directed - the impetus for change is to get to the goal or at least progress towards the goal. |
| Often initiated by FEAR, escape from PAIN, and/or STRESS. | Driven by aspiration, a desire to improve, moving towards a shared goal. |
| "Success" may not be clear as the desired outcome is often a double negative (i.e., don't be disrupted. (CONFUSION dominates) | Success is clear, it is a goal achieved or progress towards the goal. |
| Can happen "to you" (FEAR driven) | A deliberate choice to move in the direction of the goal. |

Owen McCall graciously allowed the inclusion of emotions to the change side of his wonderful description of Change vs Progress.

| ***Change Drivers*** | ***Progress Drivers*** |
|---|---|
| Pain | Pleasure |
| Fear | Peace of Mind |
| Uncertainty | Reward |
| Confusion | Goals |
| Need | Prestige |
| Worry | Desire |

*Life can be pulled by goals as well*
*as it can be pushed by drive.*
Viktor E. Frankl

After working at Folgers' Chantilly plant for over four months, Bob Pries and I had completed our respective missions. Folgers had around 500 employees and another 200 contractors, but Bob chose just five people to award beautiful blue sweaters inscribed with the 9th Infantry Division – Vietnam insignia. Bob was an NCO and served two tours in Vietnam. The worth of this sweater became invaluable to me when he told us why we were selected. Bob looked each one of us in the eye and said,

"I would go to combat with you." My heart filled with pride and love. We, among many, were the people he trusted enough to risk his life. Since that day, I too identified a few, "I would go to combat with." People I trusted enough to have my back. I have a special relationship with those who fit this description.

***Be deemed trustworthy enough that your***
***teammates want you in their foxhole.***

# Chapter 8

## Emotional Tai Chi

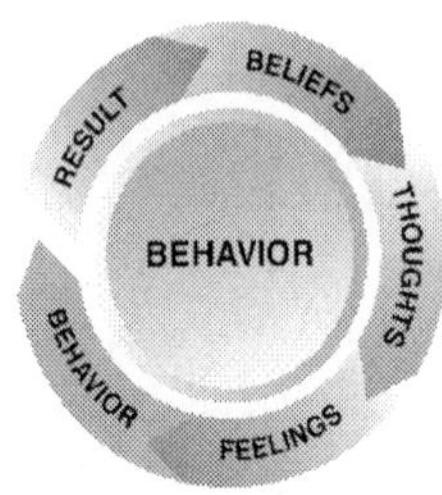


Tai-Chi is a martial arts discipline requiring considerable practice and training. Its principles include avoidance, deflection, and a counterattack to neutralize an opponent. Tai Chi students feel more powerful. They know they can, if required, protect themselves and their loved ones. Emotional Tai Chi creates the same confidence in the ability to avoid, defend, and correct inequalities. The following are Emotional Tai-Chi principals.

### *Attitude*

When attacked, anger becomes the early warning system; someone has crossed your boundaries. The common reaction is to attack back, flee, or defend, and in an instant - if not careful - we are ***emotionally drunk.*** Emotional Tai Chi provides for more successful reactions. When someone is perceived as a doormat, others treat them accordingly. Does Casper Milquetoast get the same respect as an assertive person? Casper talks softly and gets hit by big sticks. By behavior, attitudes, and communication, we teach others. Emotional Tai Chi is declaring the attitude, ***Doormat No More***. If this doormat definition fits, why are you surprised, hurt, and depressed when other people wipe their muddy shoes on you, *the doormat*?

My friend, John Williams wrote many thought-provoking songs; my favorites is *Wickie-Woo*. You should thank your lucky stars you are not hearing my singing. John wrote, "Turn around and it might be you, making you sad, making you blue... *Wickie-Woo*." The best line is "...get yourself off the floor, and I won't have to step on you... *Wickie-Woo*."

***We tend to train others how we want to be treated.***

Visualize your picture on a doormat. Following the *Wickie-Woo* wisdom, pick up your doormat - soiled by encrusted mud from many feet for many years – and scrub it clean. You now have a choice, leave it on the floor for others to walk on, or hang it on the wall as an *objet d'art* for others to appreciate its beauty.

***Introspection is scary for it often requires change - your changing.***

Pick out a person you would label a ***challenging person*** to listen to. What would happen if you chose to see this person - instead of ***challenging*** - as your...***teacher***? "What could they possibly teach me," you ask? Nothing, if you hold that attitude, but a tremendous amount if you choose to enter their classroom and allow them to be your ***teacher.*** This monumental shift in perception from a ***challenging*** person to a ***teacher*** requires rewiring your brain called, ***Thumb Work.***

***Finger-Work*** is pointing the accusatory finger and taking another person's inventory of their obvious imperfections – is much less threatening. If you explored this perception from ***challenging***

to ***teacher,*** would you die? Would you be indicted then convicted? Say hello to your teacher.

*Every wrong attempt is another step forward.*
*People who make no mistakes don't make anything.*
Jack Chapman

**Exercise**

When thinking about changing your attitude toward this difficult person, what are your feelings you identified found on the Mood Chart.

*Your courage will protect and immunize you from the*
*wearying psychological grind of a turnaround.*
Jeff Sands

Jerry Lane Stovall played college football **at** Louisiana State University **(LSU),** where he was a unanimous selection to the 1962 College Football All-America Team **as a** halfback. He was the number one NFL draft pick (1963) where he was 3 times selected to the NFL Pro Bowl. Stovall served as the head football coach at LSU, from 1980 to 1983. He and I shared our experiences of being fired, Jerry from his head coach in 1983, and mine from Sline Industrial Painters in 1982.

Jerry said something that has always stuck with me. "David, I wouldn't hire anyone who has not been fired!" I looked at him in pure amazement when he said, "***I want to see if they land on their feet or their head!***"

## *Words*

When you say, "I can't do any better," or, "I can't forgive…," or "I can't learn that," those words are powerful. When you make a "can't" statement, you are right. You "can't." Instead, substitute the word "can't," for "choose". The "I can't" statement means someone has a gun to your head and in that case, you "can't." Using self-limiting words decreases your options. Saying "I choose not to" returns power to where it belongs.

***Stress decreases with options.***

**Exercise**

How does ***can't*** affect your attitude? Are you going to land on your feet or on your head?

## *Deflection*

When surprised or confused from a personal attack, instead of responding or standing with your mouth wide open, simply say, "***Tell me more***." This quiet response does several things. First, it provides some breathing space between the attack and your reaction. You have time to think, center yourself, get emotionally sober, and not react. It also tells the other person you are willing to listen.

*If you think you can, or if you think*
*you can't – you are right.*
Henry Ford

South Louisiana experienced a tremendous rainfall in 2016 that created floods. One of the hardest-hit areas was around the REG plant in Geismar. Some employees could not return home. Some were surrounded by water, and some had to stay manning a skeleton crew. I told the Executive Vice President, that we would explore setting up a FEMA village for the employees to live as they rebuilt their homes. P&G did this at the Folgers plant during Hurricane Katrina. "Go to the site and explore this option."

The corporate engineer and I had just sat down with all the operators when one of them jumped up. "You're taking our PTO away! You cannot do that! It's illegal!" He was way out of line with his intensity and the engineer wanted to get in his face. To prevent escalating this tension, I grabbed his shirt and said to the operator, "Tell me more." The operator soon calmed down when he knew we were listening. At that time REG did not have a PTO policy, but by the end of the day, we did. "Tell me more" worked well, for we resolved this problem. (Confession: Then I did not know PTO stood for personal time off.) This operator is very conscientious and someone I greatly respect. The next week when we were alone, I asked him if he could have presented his very valid concern another way. He kicked the dirt and said, "Yeah, I need to work on that."

***If you have a bull's eye on your chest, who is in control?***

If I kicked you in the shins and it hurt, what would be the first thing you would say? Probably, "Ouch", right? And then some other choice words. Saying "*Ouch*" when physically hurt, provides immediate feedback. Then if someone hurts your feelings with just words, can we respond with *ouch*? Would this feedback about emotional pain be valuable?

*Education is the most powerful weapon which you can use to change the world.*
Nelson Mandela

During an LSU seminar on *Creative Conflict:* How to Get Along with Difficult People, a woman raised her hand and said, "My husband is always saying negative things. He's always putting me down. What can I do?" I told her about "*Ouch.*" She looked at me and said, "Ouch…ouch, I can say, "ouch."" Several weeks later, she called about another topic. When we finished, I asked, "Have you been telling your husband, "Ouch?""

She responded, "I sure have…every day!"

"How does it feel?"

"It feels good!" she answered.

Saying "*ouch*" is an immediate, non-attacking communication indicating another's behavior has caused pain. Saying "ouch" does not add to the problem, but like the woman in my class, it "feels good." It feels good because you are being honest, defending yourself…***doormat no more.***

**Exercise**

Recall a time where someone you card about abused you. What would have happened if you just said, "*ouch*"?

*… when we maintain our joy, we rob circumstances of any power to disturb us.*
Anonymous

Sometimes the attack is disguised as a joke, humorous arrows tipped with painful barbs. If what is said is painful, it is not a joke. And saying "ouch" lets the other person know about your pain. When confronted by your *ouch*, they may defend themselves by saying, "I was only teasing," or "Can't you take a joke?"

If their actions hurt, your straightforward reply could be, "What you said hurt, it did not seem like a joke to me, and I need you to stop." To make the statement even more powerful, say it quietly but with force. People often hear a quiet response better than a shout.

***Many people - especially men–***
***hear fewer words better than many.***

> **Be decisive**. Right or wrong, decide. The road of life is paved with flattened squirrels who could not make

In this example, if you worry about hurting their feelings, think this through. You have just been hurt enough to say, "*ouch*". However, now you rush in and rescue them from ***their*** feelings, maybe even saying, "*ouch*" for them! It was their behavior that was unacceptable, but it is you who are worrying about their feelings. Doormat?

Sometimes people may not listen, and you may need to say it several times before they know you are serious. Repeating it is the *Broken Record Method.* Be quietly assertive, and if they still have not understood your meaning or lack the proper response, repeating it several times will eventually penetrate their reality. Change some of the words, but do not deviate from the message. Broken Record: repeat it *quietly, forcefully, reiterating your message.*

## *Physical Threats*

At the weigh-in, the two boxers get nose-to-nose trying to intimidate each other with their hard stares. When physically confronted, just like the boxers, some people step towards the threatening person, escalating the tension. If you wish to provide a reason for disengagement, instead of stepping forward, take a step back. The increased distance does not leave you vulnerable but lets the other person know, negotiations are possible.

*You cannot pull yourself up by your*
*bootstraps unless you are bent over.*
Penny Earle

Have you ever been consumed with anger? Are you human? Instead of standing red-faced and out of control - sit down. Strangely, you get less angry when sitting than standing. As a possible escape from pending conflict, try this: "Okay, this is what I think you are telling me." This statement conveys understanding but not necessarily agreement. Rephrasing demonstrates your trying to understand them - seeing life as they see it.

**Exercise**

Look in the mirror and put both of your hands up with your palms away. Quietly but emphatically say "no". Practice this until you get this image in your mind. What do you see in the mirror? A doormat? Or do you see a confident person making a powerful statement? This reflection is *YOU!*

*It is impossible for a man to learn*
*what he thinks he already knows.*
Epictetus

You decided to remove your doormat. This is the same doormat you allowed people to walk on so long. Nobody can step on it anymore for it is no longer on the floor...*Wickie Woo*. Now it hangs on the wall to be admired. The image is *YOU.* You teach others how *YOU* want to be treated. *Doormat no more!*

Do you ever consider what your wants are? When consumed by the fiery flames of conflict, are your needs at the bottom of your thoughts, or are they so paramount you are unwilling to see what others may need? What others may want, and need are important, but what about your wants and needs? Are they not also important? When not valuing yourself, you lose your voice. You may be so consumed by what others want; you ***over-love*** them. This is the Martyr Complex, which ultimately dooms your self-respect.

***If you are more than fair to another person, you are often less than fair to yourself.***

Families and companies have recognizable patterns of interacting with one another. She says this and you do that, or you do this, and he says that. This is a predictable pattern; like two dancers who both know the steps so well, they do them unconsciously. If you were watching this dance, it would be very graceful because both partners have danced together for so long, they know the steps. Watching them glide across the dance floor, no one knows if the dance is painful or not. This illustration came from the book, *The Dance of Anger* by Dr. Harriet Lerner

***The cornerstone of conflict resolution is understanding.***

When people need mediation in their marriage or business, it is because their dance steps have become too painful. If the hot breath of the wolf is your reason, continue reading. ***I wish you a lot of pain.***

Many enter the change process but often flee when action is required. ***Change is hard***. The process of learning to act in different ways can be overwhelming. There is a strong tendency to go back to old dance steps rather than to change, especially when the progress we want seems to be far beyond the horizon.

Continuing with Dr. Lerner's descriptive story, when a person recognizes they are in a painful dance, they have three choices. One is to continue the old painful but familiar dance steps. The second choice is to develop new dance steps. Now if your partner continues the old steps, and you are now dancing differently, the dance has now become awkward, and not smooth, or graceful. At the risk of redundancy ...***Only when you start to choose, do you have a choice.***

When a person in a relationship enters treatment, attends a 12-Step program, and makes significant changes, and the other one does not, it puts tremendous pressure on the relationship. Most relationships – business or personal - are very rigid. Most marriages break up when one changes, and the other does not. Changing how your company operates puts tremendous pressure on employees. Some will respond, some will not, and you will have to walk some to the gate.

The third choice of this Dance is to *stop dancing.* This sometimes is necessary. When one dancer has changed their dance steps, their partner now has three choices: continue the old dance steps, develop less painful new ones, or quit dancing. When you change, there is no guarantee that your partner/employees will learn new ones. You have the power to look at your dance, discover which steps cause pain, and adjust. One person can have a tremendous effect on changing relationships.

**Exercise**

Review your identified conflict with your significant other. What percentage of the problem was theirs? What was yours? Let's say your part was forty percent. If you worked on solving your part, what happens to the size of the problem? Your partner may not have changed a bit, but your efforts have made the problem much smaller. Smaller problems are often easier to deal with.

***Changing your dance steps forces others to consider how they dance.***

## *TV Remote*

In your hand, is a TV remote. Give the remote to an employee/spouse with whom you are often at cross-purposes, someone who rubs you the wrong way. Watch them push your buttons and enjoy your predictable reactions. Consider this image: you gave your TV Remote to someone else, then you taught them what buttons to push to get certain reactions (your dance). So why Symbolically do you get upset when they treat you exactly as ***you taught them!*** These reactions are patterns developed over time in close relationships.

**Exercise**

Would you care to take back the power you gave others? Let's be sure of a couple of things: (1)You are responsible for your happiness, (2) The TV remote belongs to you. Both correct? Symbolically, we give our remote away with an unexpressed message. "Treat me as you wish but *just don't leave me,*" (Humm, sounds like a doormat to me). As John Williams sings, "*Turn around and it might be you…making you sad…making you blue…* ***Wickie-Woo***.

Reclaiming your remote does not mean ending the relationship or firing the employee - although that could be a byproduct - it does mean your remote is in your hands – now you can choose your behavior. Think about your remote while humming ***Wickie-Woo.***

## *Depression*

Hopefully, you have already looked at the Depression Questionnaire in the Appendix. If not, maybe this would be a good time to inventory yourself. A high correlation on the Depression Scale indicates a need for self-intervention. Call a professional counselor if these problems persist. If you are thinking of hurting yourself or someone else, please take this seriously and find someone who will help you, or call the appropriate crisis hotline, or call 911. You are valuable! *Does it feel like you just won four days and three nights in historic downtown Chernobyl?*

Let's assume the Questionnaire indicated a degree of depression. Many people suffer from depression, and some have a chemical imbalance requiring medication. Medication changes brain chemistry and they are effective. Even when the medication changes the imbalance and the person feels better, the medication has not solved many of the underlining problems contributing to depression. This next section provides some suggestions to manage your melancholy. Changing how a person thinks also changes brain chemistry. ***An attitudinal adjustment increases effectiveness***.

What does the depression tell you? What are the symptoms? Example: Isolation, lack of focus, curling up in a ball, feeling sorry for yourself, or thinking about what you don't have. When a person dwells on this lack, this focus tends to decrease concentration, cut off communication, change eating and sleeping patterns, and can increase the possibility of giving up on life, fostering emotional or physical self-abuse.

**Example**

| *Symptoms* | *Remedies* |
|---|---|
| Isolation | Go out with friends |
| Curling up in a ball | Exercise |
| Focus on lack | Focus on gratitude |
| Eating comfort food | Eat healthy food |
| Decreased appetite | Eat small amounts regularly |
| Giving up on life | Find new meaning |
| Physical self-abuse | Talk it out |
| Not talking | Seek an understanding ear |
| Being rigid | Look for the grey |
| Hate your current reality | Seek new opportunities |

## *Managing Depression*

What is the opposite of your depression symptom? Write a personal intervention in the Remedies Column creating a road map for dealing with your sadness. After you listed your symptoms, create your antidote in the column listed Remedies.

**Exercise**

Think of how depression affects you now. List your symptoms in the left-hand column.

| *Symptoms* | *Remedies* |
|---|---|
| | |
| | |
| | |
| | |
| | |
| | |
| | |

*"We can't solve problems by using the same kind of thinking, we used when we created them."*
Albert Einstein

A depressed dad was CEO of a troubled construction company and would hide in his office failing to make the critical decisions. In this leadership vacuum, he did not seek help or appoint a leader to take his place. His two sons physically fought for control of the sinking ship. Thank goodness, there was an opportunity for one to escape to build another company. He gladly jumped in the lifeboat and escaped from this sinking ship.

***A depressed leader severely limits any success that outside interventions can provide.***

Fred, a counseling client, would come in for 2 or 3 sessions then would disappear for 6-9 months. Over several years when he returned, he always had the same complaint: "Nobody loves me. I'm worthless. I can't change." He would isolate himself in his apartment, smoke marijuana, drink beer, and feel sorry for himself. His only friend was his drug pusher who would play cards after each delivery. When finishing his litany of woes, he would ask for possible solutions. I suggested he attend Narcotics Anonymous, join a single group, do volunteer work, get another job, or do something else productive. Fred's answer was always the same, "No, no, and hell no."

*The more you focus on what you don't have*
*The more you get what you don't want.*
Anonymous

At the end of August 2005, Fred made an appointment. When he arrived, I said, "I am glad to see you again, but maybe this time we need to do it my way." He responded positively, "Well, my way is not working." (Maybe someone wished him a lot of pain.)?

Upon arriving, he went through his standard recitation of woes. I asked, "Want suggestions?" And when he said yes, I would repeat my own well-worn and suggestions. Fred gave me the same answer as before, "No, no, and hell no."

In frustration, I said, "Since you admitted YOUR way is not working, Fred, you've got to do something different."

He hung his head. "Okay, I'll volunteer at the Food Bank." Shocked, I wanted to believe him, but with his history, I had my doubts. He shocked me when he started working at the Food Bank, then Hurricane Katrina struck! Lower Louisiana was devastated, New Orleans was flooded, and Baton Rouge was packed with refugees. I can only imagine the pressure this event put on the food bank.

On September 3, 2005, I received an email from Fred:

> "Ya know…the next time you run across somebody kind a like me…stuck in a deep hopeless rut…and they don't have a clue how to be happy in their pitiful little life…tell them that the absolute best thing in this world they can ever do, is to just give to somebody they don't even know…not a friend, not a relative…a total stranger…"
>
> "I'm not quite sure how this all works, but I can tell you one thing…I ain't about to quit this…it's such a good feeling inside. Just in two days and I can feel it's something I really needed to do, and it really feels good…I can't wait to start another volunteer job."
>
> "I'm so glad I'm finally out of the horrible life I was living… thank you so much for pointing me in this direction just when I needed it the most…and all the alcohol, pot, anti-depressants,

counseling (sorry!) couldn't do what this is doing for me…"

Fred did the opposite of what his depression told him. He took positive action and in doing so, he regained some control over his life. Several months later, Baton Rouge Detox asked if I would help serve food at their fund-raising luncheon. I said, "Sure, can I bring a friend?" They hardly agreed, so I invited Fred.

How do you know when a thief is not a thief anymore? Of course, when he stops stealing. No, when he starts giving!

I arrived a little late and walked up behind the serving line. There was Fred between two women. Each person would pass a Styrofoam plate down the line and a different server put part of the lunch and passed the plate down the line. Fred was joking with the woman on his left and flirting with the one on his right, having a ball. I marveled at what I was seeing. Here was *poor-pitiful-me-Fred* enjoying life and all he had to do was change. *Eureka!*

Before Fred started volunteering, his life lacked meaning. Once he allowed himself to get beyond his misery, he discovered something more important. No one knew what he was doing at the Food Bank. No one ever knew who touched those food containers shipped to the hungry people of New Orleans, but he did. His life now had meaning. Fred was happy.

A combat veteran with Post-Traumatic Stress Disorder (PTSD) volunteered in the recovery efforts from Hurricane Isaac and said, "This is a great experience, I'm helping people who need me, and it has sure helped my PTSD!"

**Exercise**

What brings meaning to your life? What excites you enough to get out of bed in the morning? What would you want your loved ones to write on your tombstone? How would they describe you? This is a hard exercise. Not having meaning in life is a sad way to live, existing in the drab shadows of a black and white world without much happiness or joy.

What inspires me to get out of bed in the morning is my bladder.

You have the power to change a bleak, colorless life into bright Technicolor! Is the struggle you experience in your business or your life not only your threatening livelihood but ripping holes in your meaning – taking you into the pit of despair. *Who am I without this business? How can I live without this person?* These questions can strike fear in the most hard-crusted hearts. Will you sound the alarm and close the watertight doors to save the ship? Or will you join the Titanic on her journey to the bottom?

***If you are what you do, and then you don't – you ain't!***

## *Pain*

In 1987, when my 20-year marriage ended, I experienced a great deal of emotional pain. Fortunately, I learned something that helped a lot. Before recovery, I would have turned to my mistress, "Ethel" as in Ethyl Alcohol. Ethel would have numbed the pain, at least temporarily.

The first thing that dissolves in alcohol is dignity.

Feeling the rejection from a 20-year mate, I needed some help to manage this terrible awareness. *What could I do?* Luckily, someone gave me some advice, a method to heal instead of a place to hide. "*When the grief threatens to overwhelm you, set aside some time to be alone with your grief. Have your pity party and honor that commitment to yourself.*"

Shortly after learning this wonderful coping skill – personal pity-party - I was in Mexico on a very difficult business contract. Many years later I found out I was negotiating with the Mexican Mafia. In a meeting across the border, I felt alone and abandoned. I felt like crying. This was unacceptable, especially with all the machismo in the room. I was glad I remembered this suggestion and then set aside time that evening to be alone. With that declaration, I was then able to put off the tears until later and concentrate on the business at hand.

Three nights in a row when I returned to my room in the Mexican motel, I allowed myself to get in touch with the pain, roll on the floor, got snotty-nosed, and threw up in the commode. Instead of allowing the grief to control me, I allowed my feelings to come to the surface where I could properly deal with my sadness. I did not stuff it, I did not ignore it, and more importantly, I did not fail to respond to its demanding call. Today when sadness threatens to overwhelm me, I now know how to manage grief. I personalized my anxiety with the name, ***Professor of Pain***. Invite the Professor to your next pity party. Somehow, his presence provides comfort during the high trauma of a grief session.

If the management of difficult events is critical to healthy living, my good friend, David Abbott has a unique way of embracing pain. He looks for uniqueness in difficult or painful experiences. Life has taught him that, someday he could retell this event and by embracing the experience, he will eventually bring understanding and/or joy to others. As he says, "The stories are revealing, and when in competition with good friends, who can tell the funniest, saddest, or scariest stories, I will have my family and friend rolling on the floor. No one will be able to top it for the most horrible day!" He also admits to allowing himself license to embellish the story to make it more entertaining.

David taught his sons about his life's difficult "events". No matter how horrific, all experiences contain an element of humor. Through this laughter, we all learn valuable lessons and about how to put the pain behind us.

My friend, Jan Zeringue, lives in Carencro, Louisiana and during a particularly bad storm, her house was flooded with 38 inches of water. Having your house flooded creates real damage, emotionally as well as financially. She was greatly surprised by how many friends helped her gut her house and rebuild it.

One tiring day, she asked one of her friends to put something in her car and instantly felt embarrassed. Her car was full of whatever she could salvage from her flooded house, her clean clothes, and building supplies for the next day. There was, barely room for her to drive. It was a mess.

She looked at the ground. "Oh, John, my car is such a disaster."

John smiled and softly said, "Jan, your entire house is a disaster."

She giggled and then continued to laugh every time she felt overwhelmed with the magnitude of her disastrous circumstances. John's light-heartiness provided her with a humor touchstone. She could always count on this wonderful phrase to laugh away her current misery.

A great question to ask yourself in a crisis is, ***I wonder what I will learn.*** Life is a continuing learning experience, and any calamity provides a wonderful opportunity for understanding and growth. A crisis is a terrible thing to squander. ***You can waste it or learn from it***.

*Humor was another of the soul's weapons*
*in the fight for self-preservation*
Viktor Frankl

When receiving a flu shot, you experience a different pain level when you are relaxed compared to being tense. You embraced the pain when you relax your arm, and it hurts much less. Embracing the pain is a fantastic stress reducer. Laughter is a wonderful way of relaxing, so life stings are manageable.

*The pain will cease, the instant the sufferer*
*no longer sees any value in the pain.*
A Course in Miracles

When grieving a loss, invite the ***Professor of Pain.*** Hug him, embrace your anguish. By doing this, the suffering will become less painful, and it won't last as long or go as deep. Embracing the pain helps accelerates the miracle of healing. The ***Professor*** has wonderful gifts of knowledge. When embracing the Professor's lessons, eventually your anguish will not be necessary. When the value of the pain is identified, addressed, and assimilated, the memories decrease their ability to inflict great pain.

## Professor of Pain

The large steel doors slowly opened.
A sinister professor dressed in long black robes
smiled and bowed, as I entered.
His smile was returned by me, then the bow
and to his great surprise … *a hug!*
The hard lines on his face
became suddenly softer, gentler, even fatherly.
"*You gave me an embrace?*" he asked.
"You gave me knowledge."

I went to the front of the classroom,
took a front-row seat,
awaiting his lecture.
For a moment in silence he pondered,
he sat at the edge of his desk,
looking at me over his bifocals.
"*You embraced me, the Professor of Pain!*"
"Yes, sir, I respect you."
"*Do you know who I am?*"
"You're on the payroll. You are on my side."

A large grin appeared on his face.
"*You have just passed your final exam.
You have now graduated.
What are your plans, my son?*"

"I came here to celebrate life.
You are part of living,
and I want to continue my education."

He took off his robe.
A glow appeared over his head,
his angel wings were exposed.
He looked at me, winked, and spoke:
"*You can now see me as I am.*
*underclassmen are not allowed to know.*"
He shuffled his papers,
cleared his throat,
and began to lecture.

Give the Professor a Hug, he knows me well.

***I wish you a lot of pain.***

## *REAL*

People using Emotional Tai Chi strive to live authentic lives. Their insides match their outsides. They do not have a false front or worry about what others may think. They are true to themselves; they are authentic. This creates an element of trust. People trust *REAL* people. People are more trustworthy once they person become *REAL*. People who are not *REAL* are illusions – not who they appear to be and difficult to trust.

*No one man can, for any considerable time, wear one*
*face to himself, and another to the multitude, without finally*
*getting bewildered as to which is the true one.*
Nathaniel Hawthorne

When *REAL* people make promises, they work hard to live up to their commitments. *REAL* people do not have to lie, exaggerate, or brag for they are self-contained in being okay with themselves. Pretense is not necessary. This is who I am, and *I am good enough*. Being *REAL* is being honest with yourself and others. It is a choice. It is incredibly hard to be *REAL* or honest especially when receiving or delivering bad news. When talking to your banker, you so much want to paint a rosy picture about what she wants to hear. With this fear, you hide the reality of the real facts. The banker will find out eventually and one of your greatest assets - *trust* – will be gone.

***Other's perception is the reality you must deal with.***

Your honesty at least gives her a *chance* to continue the business relationship and a reason to reassure the uncertain banking loan committee. When *REAL* you do not have to live with a lie, eliminating one more reason keeping you awake when sleep is so precious. Instead of running away, part of your ability to *Outrun the Wolf* is facing the difficulty head-on. There is a time for you to be vulnerable and a time to put lipstick on the pig. I usually regret the times I've tried to make the pig anything else than what it really is. *REAL* is being comfortable in your own skin. Liking who you are. As Fred Dent said, "Souls don't grow in sunlight." In the depressing night of your current experience, allow your soul to find and reconnect with you. This beautiful journey is worth all the darkness you suffer.

A young person I am very close to was raped. I cried thinking of the pain and humiliation she suffered. After the jury convicted Jason St. Romain (5 life sentences at Angola state prison), the judge let us make family victim statements to this convicted child rapist. I told him, "You tried to teach her pain and love are the same. You tried to take her spirit. You failed!" She told him, "Despite the pain, the suffering, and everything I've been through, I want you to know I've forgiven you – for myself."

Several weeks later I apologized for not being more aware of what was happening. She amazed me. She told me, "I've thought about that. If all the bad things that happened to me had not, I would not be the person I am. And I like who I am!" At eighteen, she was far on her journey towards self-love. She is my hero.

Although forgiveness is difficult, ***resentments are toxic to the soul.*** Even so-called justified resentments can become very expensive to the beauty of life.

**Exercise**

Are you *REAL*? Are you living your life and not someone else's? If you were drowning and came to the surface for the third time, the final time just before death, whose life would pass in front of you? Yours or someone else's?

Are you *REAL*? Can you forgive those who have harmed you? Are you *REAL*? Can you forgive yourself? Are you *REAL*? Can you love yourself – ***again***?

## *Awareness*

When the truth is too painful to acknowledge, denial is a trick of the mind. Without the awareness from introspection and feedback, a person can lose a lot of serenity when blocked from reality. In denial, we do not have to be responsible, and hiding provides great opportunities for blaming others, often taking potshots at them from our protected position.

The best method – *and often most painful* - of finding what needs changing is the feedback we get from others. In quiet introspection, sometimes other people's behavior is really what we do not like about ourselves. Awareness is one of the advantages of a self-help group, attending therapy, hiring a business coach, and/or developing a circle of friends who are also dedicated to self-improvement.

*Awareness is not for the faint of heart.*

Lately, you have been besieged about everything that is wrong with your company and your management. Quite frankly, it hurts! New awareness and discoveries is your path forward. Perhaps the hardest part of all this awareness is that your best thinking got you into this situation. If that thought was not bad enough, your employees, banker, and other stakeholders begin to doubt you. "The same person who got us into this mess is the same one who's supposed to get us out?" Acknowledge those thoughts and put them away. They are just Swampy attempting to sabotage your progress and pull you into the Swamp of Despair.

> The ability to speak several languages is valuable. The ability to keep your mouth shut is priceless.

Being aware of personal feelings is the key to this process. Picture two people (forgive me for this sexist illustration), the stoic man and the overly emotional woman. The man shows no emotions, has a flat affect with no expression - the strong and silent type. On the other hand, the woman is all over the board, physically displaying emotions with histrionics, loud waling, and the accompanying river of tears. What characteristics do they have in common? Both are not in touch with their emotions! The man hides inwardly, and the woman hides externally. Both their emotions are out of control. Both are *emotionally drunk.* One holds his drunkenness under an expressionless face while the other is histrionic with her overexpression. Healthy awareness (some call mindfulness) is obtained by using the Mood Chart and identifying strong emotions.

*You can do this!*

**Exercise**

I just hit you hard with two disturbing thoughts:

- Your best thinking got you into this situation.
- The same person who got us into this mess is supposed to get us out.

Most leaders doubt themselves in crisis. Probably these thoughts have been in the back of your mind for some time. I brought them to the forefront forcing their exploration. Read both difficult sentences again. Now from the Mood Chart, acknowledge your emotions. Pick one or two of the strongest, except from the Mad column. What thoughts are making you feel this way? I would be willing to bet they have some degree of insecurity. When you are satisfied with knowing the thought(s), then go to the magic place - think about your thinking. Examine these thoughts in the light of day. Are they true, false, or do you need more information? Are they healthy thoughts or stinking thinking? Are they helping you get through this crisis, or is Swampy pulling you down into the Swamp of Despair? Knowing the actual thoughts by thinking about your thinking, is emotional management, putting you back in charge. When thinking about your thinking *...you are now living your life on purpose.*

## *Ax in the Attic*

Tai-Chi students are prepared to defend themselves. *Emotional Tai-Chi* works the same way. Do you have an Ax in your attic? Hurricane Katrina caused several New Orleans levees to fail, and suddenly floodwaters inundated neighborhoods causing many people to be trapped in their attics.

Picture this, your house is suddenly flooded up to the eves, and you and your family barely escaped into the attic. It's over 95 degrees outside and much hotter in the attic. Snakes, mice, and rats also seek refuge with you in your attic. You have no way out, you are helpless, trapped, with no drinking water or food. Can you imagine this immense suffering? These people had no escape except praying for outside intervention. However, some people who had a similar experience during Hurricane Betsey (1965) knew to keep an ax in their attic. They were able to escape by knocking a hole in the roof.

Tai-Chi is also a meditation where the mind can relax and rejuvenate. Can you relax your mind, by calming your thoughts, letting them go for a few moments, thus quieting your mind? Blanking your mind is difficult and requires practice. Some people go to the Buddhist Temple to meditate, some do YOGA, some say the Rosary, and some quiet their mind in the solitude of their morning shower.

Meditation is practicing for the pressures of life. I am a morning shower advocate. This is where I often take time to relax my mind. After I blank my mind for a few peaceful moments, I say aloud a series of statements.

- *Today, I will judge nothing I observe.*
- *Today, I will detach from outcomes.*
- *Today, I will give to everyone I meet.*
- *Today, I will practice peace.*
- *Today, I have everything I need.*
- *I choose to be happy.*

As you face the day, struggling to save your company, the more prepared you are, the better you can withstand the unseen disappointments around the corner. Think about the meditation, ***Today, I have everything I need.*** Your current reality with your bank, your customers, and your employees has all been about ***lack*** – what you need but do not have. In the quiet of your mind, yes, you have everything you need. Quite a radical thought!

I also encourage you to affirm, ***I choose to be happy.*** Even though it may be contrary to your current circumstances, say it with conviction. Making this daily declaration does not mean good things will happen, for the rest of the day, but since you set your attitude, you and you alone can determine how long any negative events are going to suck you into the swamp of despair. Choose to be happy, ***fake it until you make it,*** and will become your reality. Simple, but it does take retraining your tired and battered brain.

If you will learn to be happy, even in these dire circumstances, you will discover nothing can take away your joy, without your permission. Meditation is on the ***Can*** side and can reprogram your subconscious. It is much easier to choose your attitude in the soothing calmness of a relaxed mind.

***Quiet minds are much more powerful, peaceful, and happier.***

I live in Baton Rouge, Louisiana, more than 70 miles north of New Orleans levees. After hearing these horrific stories from the survivors of Hurricane Katrina, I now have ***an ax in my attic.*** What attitudes cause you problems?

*It's the most unhappy people*
*who most fear change.*
Mignon McLaughlin

## *Monkeys*

Everyone loves monkeys. You are a responsible person who gets ready every morning and does what needs to be done. You are responsible for being a good citizen, productive employee, and your own happiness. These are examples of *your monkeys*.

Other people have their monkeys that they are responsible for achieving. Are you responsible for your spouse's monkeys?

Your employees' monkeys? Your children's monkeys? As much as you may want to, and as much as your early learning taught you, *other people are responsible for their happiness - even those we love and share our name.*

Problems increase when we take other people's responsibilities. Carrying other people's monkeys puts a tremendous burden upon us such as stress, feeling overwhelmed, and eventual burnout. It also teaches others they are weak without us, we become so important, others cannot function without us. Is this the message we want them to think? How can they abandon us if we are so indispensable?

In dealing with many sad, horrific events happening to others, I practice the O.P.P. exercise (*Other People's Problems).* Being an overly caring person, I want to fix it for them. After all, this is the reason people seek my counsel. O.P.P. defines my objectivity and provides the awareness of knowing whose monkey belongs to whom. As soon as I cross this line, my effectiveness immediately declines, I lose my objectivity, and a fiery crash and burnout are right around the corner.

Check your shoulders for other people's monkeys; return their monkeys to the proper owner. "This is not my monkey!" You will be lighter when you are rid of those monkeys that are not yours.

How about the 600-pound gorilla you now carry, breathing in your ear. Does he belong to you?

**Exercise**

Ask yourself this simple question: Whose ***monkey is it?*** What *monkeys* do you need to return to their rightful owner? Are some of those 600-pound gorillas? Once you know whose monkey belongs to whom, you are free of another's responsibilities. Although this is essential, it is usually difficult and contrary to our past thinking and behavior.

## In Praise of ***NO***

Author unknown

***NO*** may be the most difficult time saver
in the English Language.

What it lacks in grace is more

than offset by its brevity.

You do not equivocate when you say ***NO,***

though you may risk offense.

Used with discretion and appropriate garnishes,

***NO*** can save you hours of time.

***NO*** returns responsibility to its rightful owner.

***NO*** enables you to focus on your own priorities.

***NO*** protects you from your own good heart.

**Do not scorn the pungent clarity of *NO***

***It can be your ticket to success.***

## *Confidence*

Do some people make you feel insecure? What is required for someone to create this feeling of insecurity with you?

***Your permission***.

Your permission must be obtained for you to feel insecure. Other people's behavior might be causing the discomfort but again we retain the *trigger of choice,* regarding our response. It is all about who has the power. When we give our power to another person the ability to make us insecure or angry or guilty or shame … we give our power away and we become … this is hard to hear … the *victim*.

> The reason Mayberry was so peaceful and quiet was because nobody was married. Andy, Aunt Bea, Barney, Floyd, Howard, Goober, Gomer, Sam, Earnest T Bass, Helen, Thelma Lou, Clara and, of course, Opie were all single. The only married person was Otis, & he was a drunk.

Being a victim is a learned behavior and like any coping skill, a new, alternative behavior can also be learned. This change returns power to the rightful person – *you.* Simple - not easy. *Again, can someone else make you feel insecure?* Yes, but only with your permission and the world already has too many victims.

Alternatively, do you take responsibility for other people's feelings? For example, do you have the "What did I do wrong" or, "What can I say to make it better" attitude? Do not get me wrong, there are times when those questions are appropriate, but assuming that something is always our fault just magnifies the problem.

A defining statement is to ask yourself: *"Whose problem is this?"* If the issue does not belong to you, do you have to take responsibility for it? If so, your focus is now on something over which you have no control. So, when carrying another's monkey, be prepared to pay the price. How does that monkey feel?

**Exercise**

Think of a time where you took responsibility, but it belonged to someone else. Did you say "yes" when you meant "no"? What price did you pay? Did your assumption help or hurt? Did you deprive another person of learning a valuable lesson?

*Right thinking makes for right acting.*
Dr. George Simon

# Chapter 9

## Control Drama

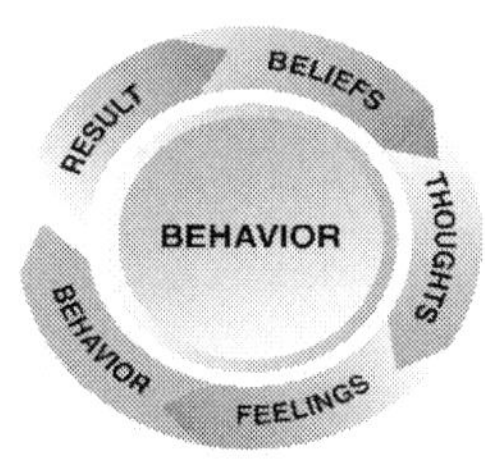


When trying to control others, defensive coping skills can lead to harmful and destructive outcomes. Picture a seesaw on a playground. When the seesaw is balanced, both people are at the same level. When one is on the high side of the seesaw, the other person must be in the opposite low position, ***not equal***.

Inequality is perceived as being in an inferior position. The only method to seek balance is to pull down on the other side of the seesaw. Using this illustration, when experiencing this downward force, the natural reaction is to resist. These diametrically opposing forces create the tension found in conflict. Many seek to control with techniques such as Intimidation, Interrogation, Aloof-Distance, Poor-Me/Martyr, Rescuer, and Attack/Blame. These are what we know and often use, even if they seldom work as intended. Oh yes, it must be *their* fault.

*Life shrinks or expands in proportion to one's courage.*
Anais Nin

***Intimidator***

This person gets in your face. It may be a gun to your head, shouting, yelling, slamming doors, shouting obscenities, hard stares, shaming comments, and/or a fist through the wall. The intimidating employee has a chip on his shoulder, tends to be prickly, often loud, always demanding, and is seldom pleased. Sometimes this person has a position of authority or assumes one. When on a playground seesaw, how much balance do you think an Intimidator allows in a relationship?

Think of a kid acting out in church. The mother turns and gives the offending child the "evil eye," the Intimidation Stare. She speaks no words, but the child corrects the behavior. Mothers all agree that they are issued their Intimidation Stares at childbirth. The example of a mother's intimidation stare can be used correctly, but so often this type of coping skill causes pain and hurt.

### *Interrogator*

"Why did you do that? Why don't you do it my way? How can you say you love me? What did you mean? These are examples of some of the questions often asked by the interrogator. It is a powerful method of controlling another.

*When you harbor bitterness,*
*happiness will dock elsewhere.*
Andy Rooney

It is hard to believe but there are case histories of suspects confessing to murders they never committed. Picture the suspect under the white light, two detectives tag-teaming him with a torrent of questions, hour after hour. Under this intense pressure, people have folded and confessed to murders they never committed. They will say anything just to stop the inquisition and have some peace. In a relationship with an interrogator, over time this intensive questing becomes like the Chinese-water torture, and the only escape is running, capitulation, or false confession. Many times, interrogators have this obsessive need to be right.

### *Aloof - Distant*

When in conflict, this person gets quiet and clams up. Not the quietness of deep reflection often occurs in a healthy debate. Walking into a room, sensing the tension that can be cut with a butter knife, you ask, "What's wrong?" The response is either silence or a faint, "Nothing," but you *know* there is something behind the blank expression and silence.

My wife of over thirty years, Penny, and I got mad at each other in Austin, Texas, and we both did the aloof-distant drama to Baton Rouge … nine hours. I told her after this horrible trip, "I never want to experience that again! We agreed to do one of two things. Either we stop the car, get out, scream, or do whatever it takes to resolve the conflict, or we would flip a coin to see who rides the bus home."

***Poor Me/ Martyr***

Picture a person with a sad expression, downturned lips, or tears. These are examples of the *Poor-Me* response method. If the person can appear sad enough, pitiful enough, or needy enough, they can establish a degree of control. Picture a beggar sitting on the street with his tin cup asking for a handout. If this beggar were wearing a three-piece Brooks Brother suit, shined wingtips, and a Rolex watch on his wrist, how successful of a beggar would he be? The beggar must look the part to invoke sympathy, or they are dismissed as unworthy of help. The *Poor-Me* response method is similar, and it is their means of controlling by acting as if they are being treated unfairly or unjustly.

*To be fully seen by somebody, and be loved anyhow –*
*this is a human offering ...bordering on miraculous.*
Elisabeth Gilbert

Everyone referred to one employee as, "Victoria-Victim." When choosing a restaurant, everyone agreed except one, "We can't go there; the restaurant is too small." Everyone looked at him in amazement until he explains, "The restaurant will be too small;

Victoria will never be able to get through the door *carrying her cross*!"

According to Kelly Bashtanyk in her article, The Martyr Complex, a Martyr needs validation and exhibits behavior that is "…selfless to the point of consistently denying one's own needs and desires and seeming to put others' needs first. The Martyr feels "…noble and self-sacrificing and, in some way, however trivial, conveys this feeling to the recipient of the good deed."

Martyrs' method of control is by always focusing on others. They seek the moral high ground as in "…look what all I do for you", or "…if you really loved me you…", or "…I give and give, and no one appreciates me…" A Martyr's best weapon is guilt. "I suffer for you, so you owe me."

*If you are tired of suffering, try eliminating*
*two phrases: to me and on me.*
Bobbie Sims

***Rescuer***

This person controls by appearing overly responsible for others' problems and insisting on fixing them, whether they were invited or not. Their message is: "I'm strong and you are weak," or, "You need me," or "You cannot survive without me." Put 100 single people in a high-school gym for a dance, and in that group is an alcoholic and codependent. The alcoholic needs someone to take responsibility for them and magically finds someone else with a need to rescue. Conversely, the codependent seeks a person that needs someone they can be responsible for, to rescue. In this example, the alcoholic becomes the Rescuer's *drug of choice.* The rescuer feels needed and useful, at least temporarily. Future "infusions" of this false self-worth are needed as they are intertwined in each other's chaos.

Parents are hardwired to protect their children, so if not careful, parents can become rescuers inflicting unintentional learning on their children. For example, the parents just found out about the science project due tomorrow and scramble to have something to turn in. They do not want their precious little one to fail. Instead of allowing the child to experience the natural consequences of failure - the embarrassment of a bad grade - well-meaning and loving parents rescue the child. He learns that he does not have to be responsible. She learns being overly responsible is how to express love, and one day brings home an alcoholic from the high-school dance!

When employers do not insist on accountability and fail to expect adequate performance, they find a designated scapegoat to blame. This employee cannot be fired for then who would the employer have to blame? In the comic strip Blondie, Dagwood is Mr. Withers's designated scapegoat.

Sometimes supervisors protect employees by doing their work, hoping to be appreciated and be well-liked. He covers this with, "It is easier to do this myself."

***A justified firing is a morale builder.***

***Attack/ Blame***

Attacking keeps people off balance and creates a perception of control over situations where the attacker feels vulnerable. The best defense is a good offense - attack first before you are attacked. Using Control Drama, the attacker does not accept responsibility for their part of the problem.

***Attack is the sharp spear of judgment designed to inflict wounds.***

Blaming protects the blamer. People with low self-esteem run from criticism. Introspection is too risky and painful to face. They find someone to blame, just anyone, so they do not have to be responsible. Blaming provides an illusion of control and creates a hiding place to protect a poor self-image. The message is, “Thank you for allowing me to focus on your imperfections, so I do not have to feel my pain.”

When employees feel they have to cover their asses, the Attack/Blame game is festering behind control room doors.

**David Walton Earle**

# Soring

**The hunted is now the hunter**

# Chapter 10

## Mind-Talk

Remember Swampy? Does this malevolent little man belong on your shoulder or smashed on the ground? For several years, I shared a practice with a wonderful counselor, MacTavis Williamson, Ph.D. When a client was leaving a session, Mac and I would give the client, the ***double whammy***. He would whisper positive statements in one ear and I in the other. At the same time, this client received two different reaffirming messages. Maybe after the beating life has been inflicting on you, what you need is a good ***double-whammy***, an overload of positive messages.

Have you ever told yourself, *this is unfair?* Does the perceived unfairness seem to become increasingly real by repetition? By repeating this perception, it becomes embedded in your mind, and every time you have this thought your stress level increases. When we perceive the world is plotting against us (real or imagined), we say, *"I can't take it,"* or "*This is so unfair,"* or "*I'm so stressed out"*. With this self-inflicted barrage of negativity, it becomes much easier to see ourselves as a victim.

On your Bingo-Card-of-Life, in the free space, picture these two statements: "***Life is Hard,"*** and "***Life ain't fair***." Being aware of these realities decreases stress. Yes indeed, ***life is not fair*** and

***life is hard.*** Accepting these two facts helps change negative thinking into positive, or at least neutral.

If you received horrible emails, all containing contempt, anger, bitterness, and criticism, how would you feel about yourself? If you are not careful, your own self-talk can be the messenger of negativity.

When one door closes and if another opens – you are probably in prison.

During the aftermath of Hurricane Katrina in the Folgers Plant, I spent 45 minutes with two of the most negative men I ever met. They complained about everything. "The company is not doing … our union is screwing us … FEMA has done nothing for us… they shouldn't pay you but instead…"

I tried to interject some positivity. "Isn't there anything good happening in your life?" "No, nothing…" as they continued with vigorous condemnation. When I walked out, looked up into the beautiful night sky, the lesson hit me.

***Negativity and happiness cannot exist in the same person at the same time.***

Thank you, unhappy men.

## Sample

Compare the negative thoughts on the left to the positive thoughts on the right.

| *Negative* | *Positive* |
|---|---|
| People upset me all the time. | I have the power of choice and can respond in any way I want. I can choose to allow others to up-set me or not. |
| I have no control over my feelings, or how long those feelings last. | I manage my feelings, and it is I who decides how long this will affect me. |
| Things never happen the way I want them to; I am jinxed. | Sometimes bad things happen to me, and sometimes good. Life is hard. I can deal with both. |
| This is terrible. I doubt if anyone else would put up with this! | Yes, this is a bad situation and one I wish I did not have to deal with, but the truth is, this too shall pass. |
| I am a terrible manager. | I have made some bad decisions. I am learning to make better ones. I am much more than the deci-sions I have made. |
| My company will never get out of this mess. | This is very difficult, but we will figure a way out of this. |

Using the example above, rewrite the following negative statements into positive antidotes.

| ***Negative*** | ***Positive*** |
|---|---|
| How can anyone treat me this badly, especially when I have tried so hard to please them? | |
| Things will never change; it is a hopeless situation. | |
| I am good for nothing; I can't achieve anything. | |

Use the next space to identify the specific negative thoughts you may have, and then substitute something positive.

| ***Negative*** | ***Positive*** |
|---|---|
| | |
| | |
| | |
| | |

*And the day came when the risk to remain tight in a bud*
*was more painful than the risk to it took to blossom.*
Anais Nin

# Subconscious

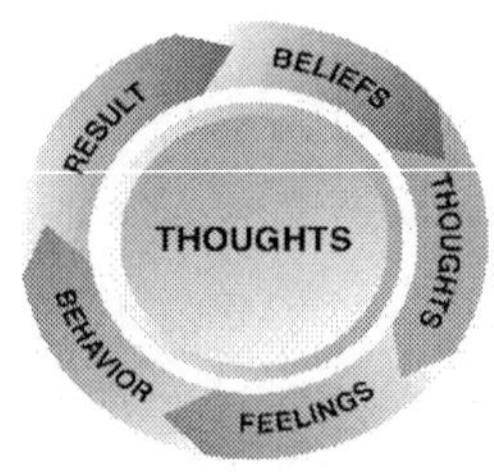


Are you the only person who did not see the movie Titanic? When the captain on the bridge saw the iceberg, he swung the big wheel hard-over, all the way to the port side away from the iceberg (left- to all you landlubbers). He then ran to the engine telegraphs and increase the starboard engine to All-Ahead Full, and then the port engine Reverse-Full.

The next scene is in the engine room where the men frantically increase the starboard engine to full speed ahead, and the port engine full reverse. Having the ship's screws moving in the opposite direction creates a twisting motion that complements the emergency turn away from the dangerous iceberg.

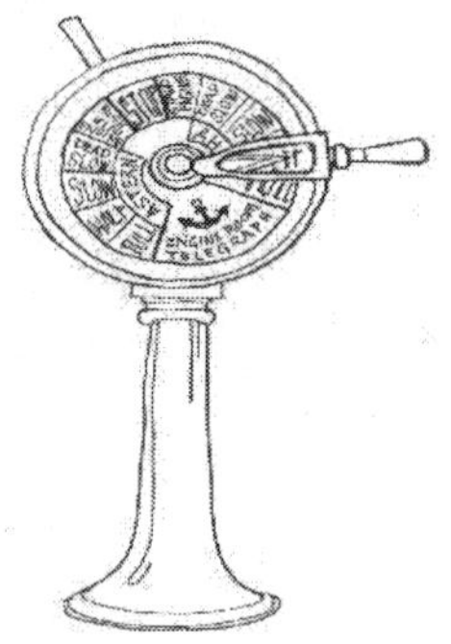

This is how our brains work. The captain was looking out and could see the looming danger. He had a frame of reference that the engine room did not. The engine room instantly followed orders and changed the speed and direction of the engines. In the dark confines of the engine room, they had no frame of reference to know if this was a good decision or a bad one. They had to believe what they were told.

Your conscious brain is like the captain with an outward view. Your subconscious brain is the engine room with no frame of reference and has to believe what it is told. From childhood onward, the big people in your life gave you messages. Some messages were very positive, and some were not. All of which were stored in your subconscious mind as truths about yourself. When your subconscious brain hears negative messages, it writes them down as facts. Maybe it is your banker giving you negative messages. Your subconscious brain accepts all messages as true, especially the ones you give yourself. "I'll never get my company profitable," or "I'm too stressed out." or "No one wants to do the right thing." or "My employees only want a paycheck." The more the message is repeated, the more deep-seated it becomes, and the more difficult things are to change.

Your subconscious mind records all negative messages in stone – that's the bad news. For many years, you, and many others have been blasting your subconscious mind with negative responses. Is it no wonder why – especially now – it has been difficult for you to get up every morning and *Outrun the Wolf?*

The bad news is: *Your subconscious mind believes what it is told.* If you were not feeling depressed before this fact, you probably are now! Want to hear the good news? *Your subconscious mind believes what it is told.*

***You can reprogram your subconscious mind.***

**Exercise**

Here are some suggested affirmations to reprogram your subconscious brain.

- I am a good leader
- I will lead my company through this current crisis.
- I am successful.
- I have good employees.
- I believe in me.
- I am productive and happy.

Okay, you just picked this book back up, after throwing it again across the room. You would not have picked it up and continued, had you not wanted to believe this truth. Re-read the above-suggested truths. Notice they are all stated in the here and now, not *I will be.* If you wrote this list as your affirmations, and even if they are not true at this moment, they are all positive and are what you want to believe.

Make your list of what *you want to believe*. Make them all positive and as if they are currently true. Additional examples of affirmations are found in the Appendix. Choose statements you wish were true for you. Write them in your handwriting and tape them to your mirror at home. Say them out loud every morning and every night before bed. By doing this exercise repeatedly, you are reprograming your subconscious mind. It takes time to change a habit, so keep on. How old are you now? Well, it took that many years to develop your current belief system, so do not be impatient. Too simple? *Yes, but it works!*

***You are worthy of love and being loved.***
***You are worthy of feeling worthwhile***
***to yourself and others.***

May I suggest one more? *I love me.* When I did this exercise and came to the affirmation, "David, I love you," my heart skipped a beat for I knew it was a lie! At that time, I did not like myself, but

I wanted to regain my self-love, so I persevered. After doing this exercise for many days and nights, one day as I looked into the mirror, those green eyes looked back at me and I felt loved and worthy.

## Self-worth

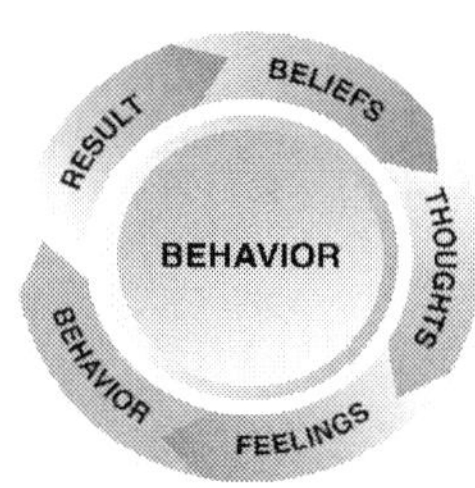


Make a list of three things you like about yourself. Considering all the negativity you've received lately, *especially from yourself*; this may be difficult. Do not fret if your beginning list is small. Listing our character faults is often much easier. After all, are we not our own best judge, jury, and prosecutor?

Even if your first attempt is limited, add a positive one every day. Eventually, you will discover a good number of great things you like about yourself. This exercise can seem counterintuitive. For so long, you listened to Swampy and didn't think positively.

***Some people have such self-limiting habits, they stay caterpillars, instead of believing they can become a butterfly!***

Acknowledging any positive affirmation violates entrenched family rules, about *tooting our own hor*n. How can I be a successful victim if I think good things about myself? By thinking differently is reprograming your battered and bruised subconscious mind. Give yourself a ***double whammy.*** Do not be surprised about all the wonderful things you will now be willing to believe about yourself.

When hearing an ***I can't*** attitude, I show a picture of Muggsy Bogues, a player on the Charlotte professional basketball team. Muggsy is standing next to his 7-foot teammate, Robert Parish. Muggsy is 5-foot-3! He was the smallest player to play in the NBA! How many times in Muggsy's life do you think people have told him what he ***can't*** do? I'll bet many. He constantly had to shrug off the negative messages surrounding him to live his dream of playing professional basketball. ***Way to go, Muggsy!***

In 1987 in amidst tremendous emotional pain, I knew I had to change. Fortunately, I began to learn improved ways of living and loving. From many years of discovery, I condensed everything I have learned about how to live a successful life into one word. One word. A word that divides successful living from living as an also-ran. Intrigued?

***The word is …***

**Drumroll please ……**

# Ready?

**David Walton Earle**

# *CHOOSE*

Picture a stop-sign every time you begin negative self-talk, thinking negatively, and/or listening to Swampy. Say the word ***STOP!*** Saying it out loud works even better. The point is to confront the negative self-talk when it happens. ***STOP,*** alerts you to a false message.

My wife and I were installing a new back door. The door company fitted new hinges to match perfectly with the old, but it seemed not to fit. I immediately became frustrated and cursed at myself.

Getting frustrated is an old habit. I immediately said aloud in the same hard tone as the cussing, "***STOP!***" I took a deep breath, apologized to myself out loud (my wife giggled behind my back), and then relaxed. Magically we were then able to fit the new door into the frame.

## *My Life will Change … When I Change*! ™

Some people use a rubber band to snap themselves as a reminder. In Valero's Krotz Springs plant, a senior supervisor was making great improvements in managing his anger. When he started to feel overwhelmed with strong emotions, he would snap that well-used rubber band, reminding himself to calm down. He hid this rubber band on the same wrist as his watch, so if you did not know it was there you might miss it. Years later at a plant retirement party, I gently snapped his rubber band. "Still got it, I see."
"Yes, but I seldom have to use it."

# Visualization

A man wanted to overcome his fear of heights, so he attended an Outward-Bound learning experience. He completed all the exercises except the last one, the one he feared. Now he had to climb a 100-foot sheer cliff. He watched all his teammates climbed to the top. Then it was his turn, as the instructor then buckled him in the safety harness and gave his last-minute instructions. "Don't look down." And "Visualize yourself at the top."

He was halfway up when he made the mistake of looking down. Terrified he froze. He could not find a toe hold for his left foot and his right foot started to shake with the increased stress it was experiencing.

All his fears overwhelmed his mind with thoughts of falling. Then he remembered the instructor's second message – *Visualize yourself at the top*. He closed his eyes and started this mental exercise. Visualizing how victorious he would feel when he felt the strong arms of his classmates pulling him over the top of the cliff to safety!

Astonishingly his left foot found a toehold and he successfully climbed to the top. He allowed this new mental image to reprogram his subconscious mind and immediately overcame his fear.

**Exercise**

Recall this quote from Skip Bertman: *I've always believed that anything you vividly imagine, ardently desire, sincerely believe, and enthusiastically act upon, must absolutely must, come to pass.* His baseball teams were very successful when using this wisdom.

**Vividly Imagine** - ***Visualize yourself at the top.***

Picture yourself as being successful. Take change and define success. Visualize that image. The more of these messages by the ship's captain delivered to your engine room, the greater the chance your subconscious will find ways to deliver your wishes.

**Ardently Desire** – ***Burning desires are hard to quench.***

Even with the trauma, you may be experiencing, you still have goals. Your hopes and aspirations are much greater than making the pain disappear. By aiming at the stars, you may just hit the moon. These are healthy desires you are entitled to have.

**Sincerely Belief –** ***You are what you believe.***

Skip Bertman's motto can lead you and your company out of the swamp of despair and to the safety of the firm ground and even to climb cliffs of great heights!

In the Behavior Model, ***beliefs*** are at the top of this circle, and it is beliefs that dictate thoughts. Believe your company will be successful. Believe you will lead them out of this problem. Believe your family will be happy. Believe everyone will be stronger and better people from this experience.

**Enthusiastically Act Upon -*Your enthusiasm is contagious.***

It is difficult to have an enthusiastic team without a leader generating enthusiasm. Ho-hum attitudes are not inspiring and do not encourage a Gung-Ho attitude. Uninspiring leaders can extinguish even great waves of enthusiasm. Writing our wildest dream downs with black ink on white paper allows your subconscious to lead you in the right direction. ***Be the change you wish to see in your team***.

*I am a firm believer that success or failure*
*begins and ends with leadership.*
Bob Pries

When working with REG helping them improve their culture, our rallying cry was, "We are going to be a first-class plant." Contrast that to the fear we all had about the possibilities of another fire, OSHA forcing us out of business, or underlying our greatest fear if we would have a job tomorrow. All our anxieties were based upon real possibilities and provided a great motivation to change.

However, they would not have the same sustaining drive without the shared vision of becoming a first-class plant. Fear-driven change is not the same as visualizing success. They are opposite mindsets. Visualization is progress added to change.

## Resentments

It takes an enormous amount of mental and physical energy to hold and store resentments. Harboring memories of past transgressions or wrongs puts the focus in the wrong direction.

Jacob Goldsmith originally published a theory of personality in the 1950s, commonly called **Type-A / Type-B.** A person with a **Type-A** personality is characterized by one who is ambitious, organized, proactive, often with a high self-opinion, and with an accelerated sense of urgency. A person with **Type-B** personality has a somewhat opposite set of characteristics. They work steadily, do not worry too much when their goals are not achieved and seem to have lower stress levels. Although this theory does not have wide credibility in the scientific communities, it serves as a good reference for understanding resentments.

Picture yourself in a white lab coat; you're a Ph.D. scientist studying heart attacks. You have unkempt grey hair, bespeckled, and are holding a clipboard. Your research is to find out which one of these groups has the greatest increased heart problems. Your original hypothesis was **Type-A.** However, your research did not prove a direct link as you expected.

*If you seek revenge...*
*dig two graves.*
Chinese Proverb

Your next theory is that heart conditions are not linked to **Type-A** or **Type-B** but some other factors. With further research, you discovered a direct link to heart problems, and you labeled this **Type-H.** The **H** in **Type-H** stands for *Hostility.* For people who do not forgive easily, hold resentments, and/or ponder on how to get even, their physical bodies pay a price. Holding resentments of past hurts, slights or outright abuse causes a high toll on the mind as well as their body. The miracle of forgiveness allows for the release of this debilitating burden.

**Exercise**

> Holding on to resentments is like drinking poison expecting another to die.

Are you a Type H? Is it hard to forgive? Instead, try this. When someone has *done you wrong* and you feel the weight of your resentment robbing you of your serenity, your peace of mind, try something different. Think good thoughts about this person, and consciously wish them good health, prosperity, and happiness. A novel idea: changing your thoughts will not bring resolution to the injustice but allows you the freedom from the high cost of resentment.

***Getting rid of resentments is a detoxification of the soul.***

## Do – Have – Be

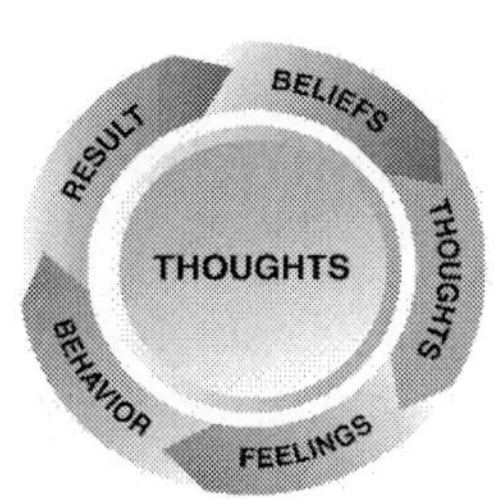


***Do-Have-Be*** people think a certain way. Every day they face the world with a desperate need to ***Do***. If they can just ***Do*** enough, get the next promotion, graduate from college, get the right person to love them, or get the banker on their side, life would be just *duckie*. This becomes an obsessive drive. If I can just ***Do*** enough, then and only then, I can ***Have*** feelings of success, peace, and satisfaction. We all want to achieve this utopian dream, the promised land, the golden days of high contentment as our just rewards.

Our society tells us the ***Do-Have-Be*** is the formula for success. When the moment arrives when we ***Have*** enough, then we can finally relax and ***Be*** okay. Many follow this pattern religiously, always pursuing the future like the donkey chasing the carrot - a relentless pursuit - a squirrel cage, a relentless struggle to achieve. When we achieve the promotion, obtain a specific degree, or marry the right person, we think we can bask in the safe harbor safe from the storm of discontentment.

However, these highly desirable events are fleeting, a temporary refuge until our natural state of "***not okayness***" arrives again, exposing our hollowness, and discontentment that only amplifies our delusions. Not being okay is scary, so it is natural to return to what is best known, the ***Do-Have-Be.*** This ***Do-Have-Be*** is what we have been taught before conscious memory. Not knowing any difference, we repeat the cycle.

My family of origin were all high achievers. They demonstrated their best map for my future, and my success path was outlined by high and often-unrealistic expectations. Our religion was ***Do … Do … Do.*** Give to the poor, believe this way, say the right thing, climb the ladder of success, always compete, and expected to win. Success was measured by awards, bragging rights, and of course money. Everyone practiced the unwritten rule that if we ***Do*** enough, then we can ***Have*** it; and once arrived, we sigh with relief, we are ***okay.*** When on this track, I attempted to manipulate life into rewarding me with peace and serenity. I ***Do*** - so I can ***Have*** - so I can ***Be*** okay. This obsession became a nightmare coated with a thin veneer of promised peace serenity but always ended with the frightening reality of knowing, I had to play the game yet another day. Contrasted with the ***Do-Have-Be*** approach is the opposite view, the ***Be-Have-Do*** method. By successfully working on ourselves, doing ***Thumb Work***, we arrive at a state of ***okay-ness.*** A place of serenity where we are independent of false external trappings of the world's definition of success. This is when my illusive ***Be*** okay (so long sought after) becomes mine. Once at this magical point, then I ***Have*** peace and serenity - my birthright – and what I searched for and fought for is now mine Here, success is obtained by changing the direction of the search by traveling inward, ***Thumb Work***.

Once I *Have* peace and serenity, what I ***Do*** becomes an expression of love rather than a demand for something or some other person to fix my brokenness – to rescue me - to make me *okay*. Once this "***okayness***" is achieved, life is much more peaceful, calmer, and the compulsive drive to achieve more and more is substituted with Joy-of-Job. Then life is more fun, and work becomes enjoyable. When I am Okay, I ***Have*** peace and serenity - so what I ***Do*** become expressions of the real me, and my victimhood is in the rearview mirror – martyr no more!

> Superman on the therapist's couch: "When is it my turn to be rescued?"

The saddest and most painful time in my life was when I was doing everything, I thought I was supposed to do for success, running on the treadmill of ***Do-Have-Be***. Today I am much happier on the road less traveled, the highway of ***Be – Have – Do.***

## Self-Kindness

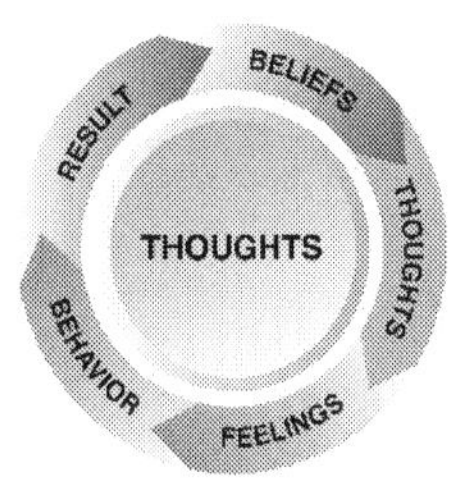


Buddhists focus on ideas that are often in conflict with Western Culture: *self-compassion, self-kindness, awareness,* and *acceptance.* Western culture teaches us to work hard, strive for perfection, and when not perfect be hard on ourselves, ***Do-Have-Be***. Self-Kindness is contrary to how many of us were raised and is often different from what we learned at our parent's knee.

There is nothing wrong with working hard and striving to be better, but when not achieving the must-sought plateau of perfection, does self-abuse serve us well? We learned that when we had good thoughts about extending love, kindness; and acceptance to ourselves, well, we just might get the *bighead.* What would the neighbors think? We learned to live based upon what we thought other people may think. We judge ourselves accordingly and always came out second best – often to those we did not like! We learned to self-bash, find fault, criticize, and judge ourselves – most of the time harshly. Many of us become Olympic-grade self-abusers winning well-earned metals of shame, loathing, and contempt.

Do you beat yourself up with, your *Why-Whip*? Why did I do that! Why can't I make a profit! Why can't I make them understand! Put away the *Why-Whip.* Talk to yourselves as you would to someone you love. Instead of self-condemnation, accept that you are not perfect and it's okay that you sometimes make mistakes. Can you cut yourself some slack?

***Just because you made a mistake***
***does not mean - you are a mistake.***

Your successes or failures are not who you are, they are just events you experienced. You are much more than your resume and bank statement. You can strive for perfection; only if you first know this goal is often unattainable. Have goals, desires, and dreams, but if you allow those to become your master, your *Why-Whip* comes out, then self-bashing begins again.

**Exercise**

Would you like to stop abusing yourself with your *Why-Whip*? If you want to get rid of self-flagellation, place your *Why-Whip* between this page and the next. Now say aloud, "I let my *Why-Whip* go." Warning – this will make Swampy very angry!

*Perfect is the enemy of good.*

Voltaire

If you again wish to self-trash yourself, you know exactly where to find your *Why-Whip.* You are in control; you can be hard on yourself or be gentle. Instead, learn from your mistakes – history is a great teacher. Did someone wish you a lot of pain?

Traveling over the Mississippi River Bridge on I-10, I was listening to the radio and not paying close attention. I missed the exit to Plaquemine, Louisiana. The next exit is in Port Allen 2.5 miles from the bridge. Having missed that exit, my normal behavior is to beat myself up for being such an idiot. *Why weren't you paying attention? Why are you so stupid?* I would judge myself, then convict myself, and then for the entire 5-mile detour, receive a much deserved *Why-Whip* lashing. Missing the exit is proof positive that I am no good, a failure, and deserve to be condemned for life in the fiery pits of hell. Can you hear my *Why-Whip* beating up my self-esteem? I now have another coping skill that works much better. This skill keeps my *Why-Whip* safely tucked away. Now when I make a mistake - which I am prone to do - instead of the self-whip of condemnation, I tell myself this: *Next time, I'll do it differently.*

Now on the next page, it is time to return and complete the Behavioral Cycle.

**Exercise**

Go back to your identified disagreement.

- Describe your behavior.
- Describe the results of your behavior.
- Describe your thoughts.
- Identify your feelings.
- Identify your core beliefs dictating your thoughts.

## Behavior Cycle – *revisited*

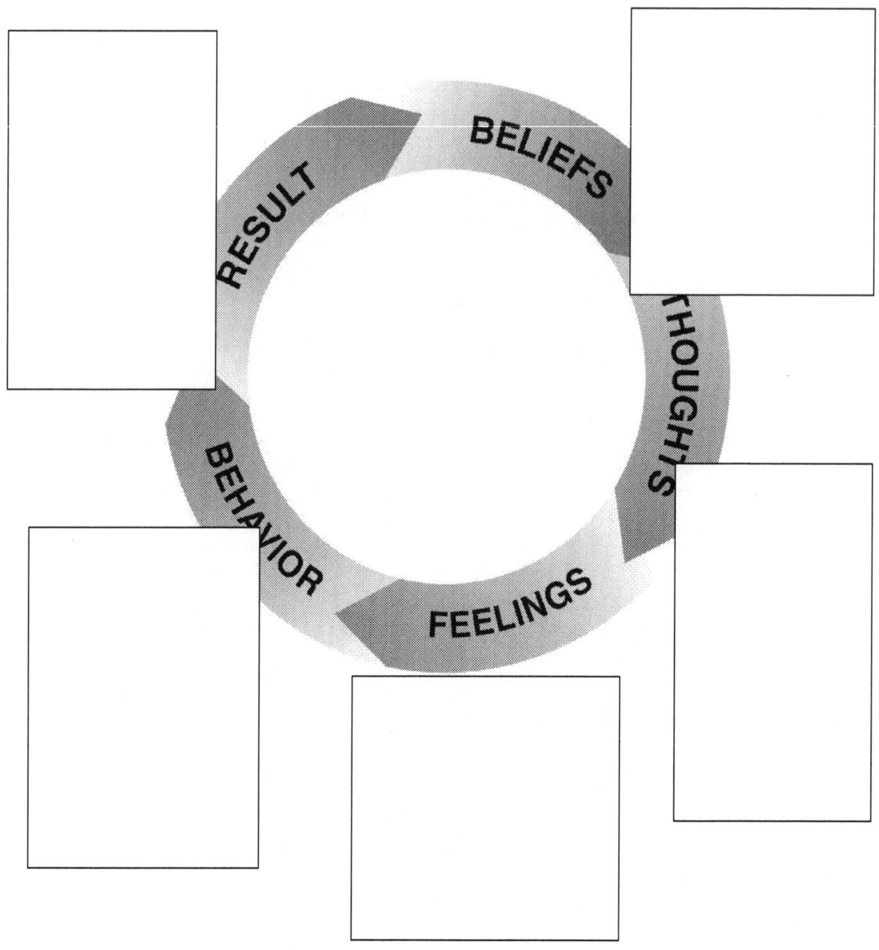


Once you are comfortable with knowing what was going on during that painful experience, use this model below to see how you would have had different results with improved awareness.

**Exercise**

Review your identified disagreement again. Using the Behavior Cycle, fill it in again but this time use changed *behavior*, *results*, *thoughts,* and *beliefs.* Think of yourself in the ***Force,*** but now with new and improved coping skills. Define the results you would like to have. Do not limit yourself. Be bold, be audacious, and define the best of all worlds.

After all, *you deserve it!*

- To experience release from your identified problem, what ***thoughts*** do you need to change?
- To experience release from this complaint, what ***feelings*** will you experience from these changed thoughts?
- With different thoughts, what ***behavior*** might you then experience?
- To experience release from this complaint, what basic ***core beliefs*** are you going to change?

Close your eyes
and you're 18.
Open your eyes
and you're 65.

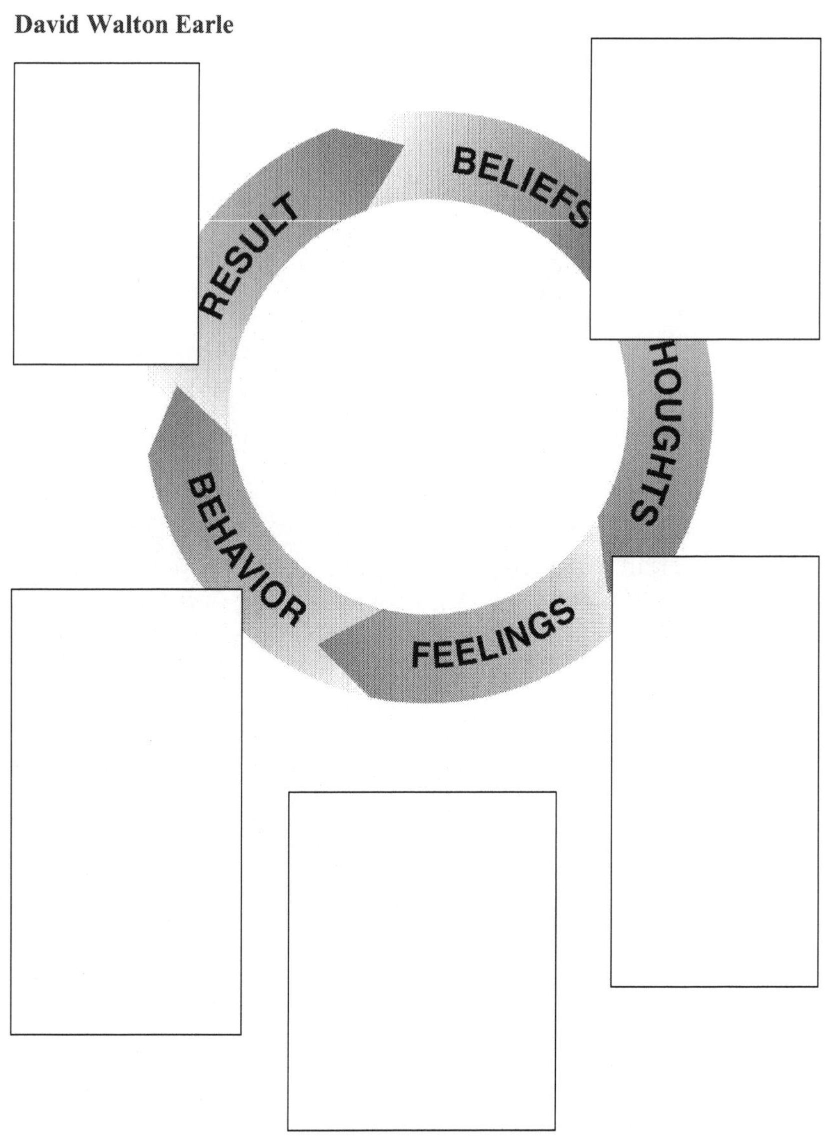


The **results** you acknowledge on the Behavioral Circle belong on the ***Can't*** side of the **Wisdom Line**. What different results might you hope for when changing your behavior, thoughts, core beliefs, and/or feelings?

# Chapter 11

## Amends

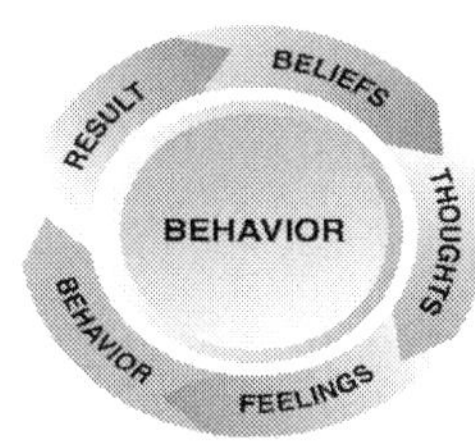


In a 12-Step program, the 9th step is: "Make direct amends to such people wherever possible, except when to do so would injure them or others." ***This is a powerful release from old Behavior*** that created many wounds and seriously affected many important relationships. Even when the offender recognizes their part of the problem, to protect their sagging self-esteem, many will still not admit what they did to cause the pain in others. They would rather focus on another person's shortcomings, transgressions, and how, "*you did me dirty*". Not admitting wrongs creates prideful posturing and provides little space for reconciliation. Having unresolved tension drives loved ones, business associates, and friends further away, increasing isolation in the dark hole of despair.

Life is much easier when you recognize a wrong you committed and make amends. Even when you played only a small part and the other person does not take responsibility for their action, by admitting your part, you are free to forgive, or let go, or forget. You are free. When not acknowledged, this wound can fester, grow, and like cancer metastasize and eat a person from the inside. One morning during my first week working at the PACE Center, one of my new colleagues was waiting for me. He jumped up, put his finger in my face, and shouted, "The door was left open last night, and you were the last one out. Don't you know we have valuable equipment here and when the door is left unlocked, anyone could have walked in here and stole them?"

Surprised and hurt, I told him to "go &^%$# himself". I stormed upstairs, poured a cup of coffee, and thought about our exchange. Ambushed, I reacted poorly. I calmed down, got emotionally sober, and then knocked on his door and said, "This morning I said something to you that I regret. I wish to make amends." He accepted my apology, but never express regret for his attack. Even though he did not acknowledge his transgression, admitting my part allow freed me of the burden of guilt and shame.

The funny part, his wife who was the office secretary overheard the entire exchange and whispered to me, "You know, he deserved that!" Maybe he did, but my reaction was not what I wanted nor valued, and correcting my bad behavior was my attempt to make it right.

Being willing to make amends is important but knowing how to make an apology is also very vital. A good atonement has three distinct elements.

> Definition of amend. transitive verb. 1: to put right especially: to make CHANGES in (something, such as a text) amended the manuscript. 2 a: to change or modify (something) for the better: improve amend the situation.
>
> Merriam Webster Dictionary

The first part is to express your regret, such as "I regret my behavior," or, "I know I hurt you with what I said," or "I wish I did not say that."

The second part and perhaps the most difficult is to be willing to listen to their response - how your behavior made the other person feel. Here, the person making the amends does not justify his/her behavior, rationalize it, or compare it to what the other person first did to them. Instead, a sincere effort to understand the hurt the other person experienced is what is needed.

The last part of this equation (often missing,) is to change one's behavior. Here you may attempt to repair the damage if possible.

The following are the three parts of successful amends:

- Express your regrets – apologize. ("I'm sorry" is often too shallow.)
- Be willing to listen to how your behavior affects the other person.
- Change your behavior.

***Making amends becomes very shallow***
***when the hurtful behavior continues.***

Once the three steps are completed, it is your turn to be quiet. Breaking uncomfortable silence can endanger the success of your healing attempt. You have done all that you can do on the ***Can*** Side, their response is on the ***Can't*** side of the Wisdom Line.

**Exercise**

How hard is it to admit *your* part of the problem? Does your pride get in the way of an apology? If you said, "I regret my behavior," what would this declaration cost you?

*How does one become a butterfly? You must want to fly so much you are willing to give up being a caterpillar.*
Trina Paulus

## Acceptance

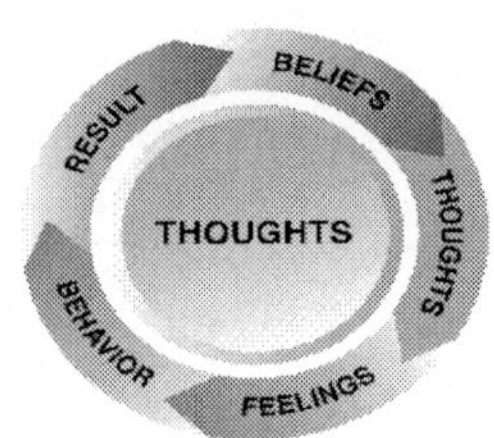


When I first started studying acceptance, I was rather judgmental. Back then, my thinking was either black or white. You were either for me or against me; good or bad, agreed with me, or were an idiot.

You either went to the right church or did not understand what was correct. You either agree with my political views or you must be vastly uninformed. And if you rooted for my team, you were okay, but if not, you were the enemy. Before acceptance, I was a closet racist, homophobic, and had the attitudes of a male chauvinist pig. Attitudes I find deplorable today but ones I must confess existed. I have made great strides in changing, but as my wife will emphatically tell you, I'm still a work in progress.

***Acceptance is the most beautiful word in any language.***

Black and white thinking is easy to see when viewing congress. The *work-with others* attitude has been replaced with the - *you are-wrong, and-I-am-right* posture - with very little wiggle room in between. It is easy to blame this dysfunctional attitude on *them*. If we were honest about our absolutism, doesn't today's congress reflect our own ever-hardening attitudes?

*Accept me as I am so I may*
*learn what I can become.*
Unknown

When I recognized my lack of acceptance, at the height of my arrogance and deepening dysfunction, someone must have wished me great pain. Feeling completely overwhelmed, I had to change. If I wanted to have peaceful grey in my life instead of the hard black or white of judgment's scorn, if acceptance was going to be mine, I had to do two drastic things. The first thing was to get off my judge's bench, take off my heavy black robe, lay down my authoritative judgment gavel, and step down from my judges' seat - three feet above contradiction. When my judge's gavel is in my hand, no *Thumb Work* is required, and I am free to *Finger Point.*

Choosing the more peaceful climate of acceptance, I can now view others on the same level, look them in the eye, and allow them to be who they are, thus releasing me to be me.

> I would not have to be a victim if everyone would quit doing me wrong.

The second item is knowing about boundaries. What was needed was a keen awareness of knowing and respecting where you stop, and where I begin. Once known, I must respect and defend other people's boundaries as strongly as I defend mine, with coping skills that do not complicate the problem.

**David Walton Earle**

How would you like to solve all your problems? *All your problems today*? In the *Big Book* entitled *Alcoholics Anonymous*, there is a wonderful paragraph on acceptance.

I marvel at its simple but powerful wisdom and relax in the quiet comfort this attitude has contributed to my life.

> "And acceptance is the answer to all my problems today. When I am disturbed, it is because
> I find some person, place, thing, or situation-some fact of my life unacceptable to me, and I can find no serenity until I accept that person, place, thing, or situation as being exactly the way it is supposed to be at this moment…unless I accept life completely on life's terms, I cannot be happy. I need to concentrate not so much on what needs to be changed in the world as on what needs to be changed in me and in my attitudes."

"And acceptance is the answer to all my problems..." Wow, does this mean, all I need to do, is to accept others as they are? Exactly! Too simple! Having acceptance will offer a solution to your feeling of discontentment, for when in acceptance, you face reality. In this *Big Book,* this attitude is called "*...living life on life's terms.*" In acceptance, you are not bemoaning your unhappiness and magically wishing it were different. You are no longer the victim exclaiming to anyone who will listen about how unfair life is. In acceptance, you decide to accept *life on life's terms*. You may not like the reality of the "...person, place, thing, or situation" you are faced with now, but that "person, place, or situation" is the *reality you must accept at this moment.*

Acceptance provides new glasses to see life as it really is and not how you think it should be. Remember John William's song, *"turn around and it might be you – making you sad, making you blue – Wickie-Woo*?

Can you change the reality of this moment? Can you accept the "...person, place, thing, or situation..." as being *exactly* the way it is supposed to be *at this moment*? If you want to be happy, that is the key. My friend John Williams wrote another song with this reframe "...when reality hits, it's not always what you want it to be." Reality may not be what you want, but it is the reality you must realize. Although it is human nature to try to hang on to what is already gone, you can deny that reality, try to wish it away, or you can accept it and not waste energy complaining.

*Acceptance of what has happened is the first step to overcoming the consequences of any misfortune.*
William James

Acceptance does not mean that you must like this current reality or that you cannot work for positive change, but it does mean that when you accept this reality, you regain the power you used to waste wishing it was different. Just because you now accept your current financial condition, the wolf howling at your corporate door does not mean you have to like it.

***Acceptance is a cornerstone of happiness.***

Everyone knows that a pessimist looks at the glass of water as half-empty and the optimistic view the same glass as half-full. In acceptance, no matter how that glass of water is viewed, half empty or half full, personal opinions do not change the liquid level!

***How we view the facts, drastically affects our thoughts.***

After my 20-year marriage ended, I needed lots of ***Thumb Work***. I was proud of my progress. Many months into my change process, I told my ex-wife that, "I was a recovering asshole". With all the righteous indignation an Ex can muster she said, "I doubt the recovering part!"

**Exercise**

Do you condemn your current reality and spend precious mental energy wishing it were different? Remember you are finite with limited resources of money, time, energy, and you.

***Other people's perception is the reality you must deal with.***

On a day trip to New Orleans with my two grandsons, Cody and Mitchell, we negotiated a rule for the day. I knew it was going to be New Orleans-blazing hot and I did not want any complaints.

We agreed to the following *if you say it once, it is a statement of a fact, if you say it more than once, it's complaining.* Once we understood this rule, we all agreed not to complain. This little realization allowed us to have a more enjoyable experience even when sweating rivulets of perspiration. It was okay to say, "I feel hot", a statement of fact and, if needed, we could find a cool place.

> I have a GPS system designed especially for seniors. It not only tells me where to go, it reminds me of why I am going.

## Lighting up the World

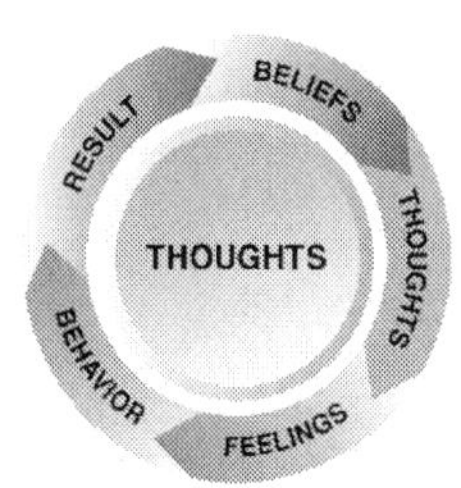


Acceptance was the topic of an internet video clip about a fashion photographer, Rick Guidotti. In this clip, Guidotti talks about his former photography subjects as being high-end fashion models sashaying down the runway. Now he takes images of people with physical abnormalities and medical conditions.

What is striking about his current photographs is that instead of the usual medical textbook images depicting people with deformities as being gross, abnormal, and ugly, he captures their beauty. Yes, he views them as beautiful, and his camera captures what he now sees. The change is striking!

Rick says he "…now interprets beauty differently." Medical textbooks capture their deformity but "misses their humanity…this is sad." Rick wants us to "…celebrate all differences" to see what is there "…their gorgeousness." One mother said about the photographs Rich did of her child with a medical condition, "I suddenly saw a picture of my child similar to the way I saw him…" not the "…way others view him." Rick wants the world to see not the diagnosis but a human being." Rick thinks the world has a "…set idea of beauty," and he wants us to see, "…beauty differently."

What Rick does through his photographic eye and records on cellulose is let go of what is not there and capture what is there. He lets go of his preconceived definitions and trains his eyes to see the image differently.

One Sunday, I looked at a large woman, not attractive by the world's standards, and mentally let go of all the usual definitions, such as, large, female, elderly, wrinkled, and started connecting with her on a different plane. I forced my eyes to see her beauty; I wanted the image to be one of Rick's photographs, one not distorted by other's definitions, and with this awareness I could now focus on pure acceptance. Doing this brief exercise, I felt my barriers to this woman melt and I then felt an overwhelming desire to send love to her. I did and it felt grand.

## Living in the Moment

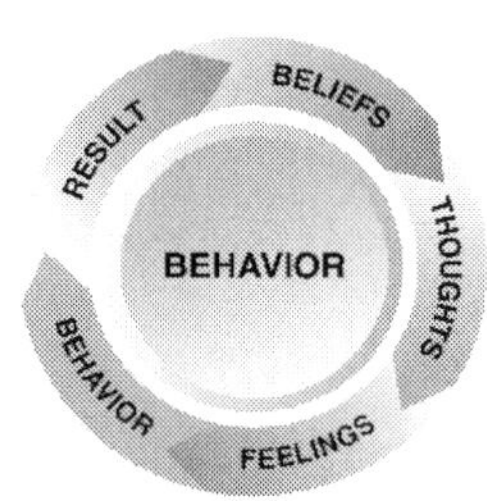


I am uncertain if the 12 Step fellowship created the slogan, *"One day at a time,"* or if, like many of the principles, they borrowed it. Most alcoholics can abstain from drinking for just one day. Picture walking into a bar and seeing a sign that says, *"Free Beer Tomorrow"*. If you enjoy beer, you'll rejoice, and vow to return. Again, on the next day, you read the same sign, *"Free Beer Tomorrow."*

*"One day at a time,"* is a powerful philosophy providing discipline for decreasing worry about the next day. In the comic strip Beetle Bailey, when Zero was asked how old he was, said, "8,667 days."

Beetle asked, "Why don't you count in years?" He replied, "I like to live my life one day at a time!"

From the Wisdom Chart, healthy living is the focus on what we ***Can*** control. Focusing on only one day at a time decreases tomorrow's uncertainties and allows today's joy.

*"One day at a time"*, works wonders. However, there is another level of serenity even more powerful, *Living in the Moment*. Once a person embraces this simple principle of living in this moment, peace becomes an authentic and beautiful reality.

Consider these questions:

- When you regret something, you did or did not do, where is your mind? Is it in the past, present, or future? **The past.**
- When you are worried about something, where is your mind? Is it in the past, present, or future? **The future**.
- When you are enjoying playing with your kids, making love to your spouse, or enjoying the sunset at the end of a beautiful day, where is your mind? Is it in the past, present, or future? **The present.**

***Today is the tomorrow you worried about yesterday.***

**Exercise**

Is there anything you need ***right now?*** Right now, is there anything keeping you from being happy, content, and peaceful. Right now, not in five minutes, not at the end of the day, not when your loan is approved, but *right now*. If you choose to have contentment, search within yourself. Is there anything you need, anything keeping you from the contentment you desire ***at this moment?***

Scan yourself and if your answer is "No," this means, *if I choose to be content, there is nothing I must have at this very moment to make me happy*. This peaceful mindset is called, ***Living in the moment.***

This harmony can be yours. All that is required of you is to claim it. ***Simple, not easy.*** Here are a couple of stories about living in the moment. The first is a Zen story and the others are mine.

A woman is running through the jungle and a huge lion is after her. She is running very fast, but since lions are faster than humans, she must do something quickly or be the lion's breakfast. She sees a cliff and jumps. Maybe she can catch a branch on the way down. If not, the fall will be an easier death than being eaten alive!

*My happiness grows in direct proportion to my acceptance, and in inverse proportion to my expectations.*
Michael J. Fox

Fortunately, she catches a branch, stopping her from a sure-death plunge. As she struggles for her breath from this temporary stay of doom, the lion reaches over the cliff and swats at her – *just missing*. She hears the Lion's roar and feels the hot breath as she recoils from this danger.

Then she looks down to see two more lions jumping up trying to grab her – *just missing*. There is one lion at the top, and two lions below, who are all trying to rip her body apart. Her peril increases when she notices two little rodents gnawing on the roots of the tree, the only thing keeping her from certain death. *A rather precarious place to be!*

The story continues and she notices a strawberry bush growing out of a crag of rock. This bush is in full bloom, covered with lush strawberries, now glistering in the early morning dew. The sunlight reflects off these luscious strawberries making them so inviting. One looks so lovely that, she hangs on with one arm, picks it, and takes a bite. Happily, she closes her eyes and exclaims, "Oh, how delicious!"

This woman knows how to live in the moment! She could not enjoy the taste of this luscious strawberry if she were regretting being in the jungle that morning or worrying what would happen if her branch failed. If not in the moment, the joy of the strawberry could not be hers.

I have been to the death house at the State of Louisiana's Angola prison. I have seen the holding cell and felt an icy chill when I saw the gurney for the condemned prisoners. I also have been in the large attic of the Baton Rouge City Court and witnessed the thirteen red steps leading to the hanging room, the marks on the rafter supporting the rope, and the trap door where the condemned prisoner would fall to instant death. These are spooky places with the aura of the condemned still lingering.

*If I can accept the truth of 'This is what I'm facing —*
*not what can I expect but what I am experiencing now' —*
*then I have all this freedom to do other things.*
Michael J. Fox

Picture the condemned man who has just eaten his last meal. The guards clear away his metal tray as he hears the footsteps of the warden and the chaplain walking to take him to the execution chamber. He hears the guards loudly announce the cry of the condemned, "Dead man walking." He knows he has only just a brief time to live.

Where is he to spend his last moments on this earth? In the past, regretting what he did to get there, or worrying if there will be a last-minute stay, or is he going to focus on this moment making the most of all the time he has left?

When facing a difficult situation and feeling condemned, how do you spend your limited mental and emotional energy? Do you beat yourself up for getting into this situation, worry about tomorrow, or do you choose to live in the moment and savor its peace?

*Don't spend time beating on a wall,*
*hoping to transform it into a door.*
Coco Chanel

At my 5-year-old daughter's T-ball game, I thought, *how boring. This is just a bunch of kids running around acting silly.* Instead of enjoying my daughter's game, I watched a little league game on an adjacent field.

> Although they never met, parallel lines have a lot in common.

Ten years later, after a lot of ***Thumb Work,*** I was with my girlfriend watching her 5-year-old play T-Ball. I was now excited to see how the kids were learning the game. I was delighted at their enthusiasm and chuckled at the umpire's futile attempt not to laugh at their childish mistakes. I enjoyed watching the excited parents and the joyful interaction of the kids with the crowd.

I was enjoying myself until I remembered that day of my daughter's game when I was not fully present and felt regret about what I'd missed. Tears of sadness ran down my cheeks as I realized how I had squandered a wonderful opportunity *to be there in the moment,* enjoying my daughter's game.

In the fresh vegetable department of a grocery store, I heard a woman talking on her cell phone. Every aisle I went down, there she was talking and throwing items in her grocery cart. At the checkout line, she was still talking and in the parking lot, she hadn't stopped. As she drove away in her large urban attack vehicle, I saw her still on her phone.

*Life is a test. It is only a test. If this were your actual life you would have been given better instructions.*
John and Ann Murphy

When I told Penny about this cell phone lady, she lamented, "How sad. She could have been enjoying planning her family's meals." Instead of extending love with her conscious thoughts, she was not in the moment. This woman, like me at the T-ball game, was not there.

The lesson is: *When at the T-ball game, be at the T-ball game. When you buy groceries, be with the groceries. When you eat a Hersey Bar, be with the candy.*

Not many people live in the moment. The prize for all of today's trauma would be worth it if you learned to live in the moment. My experience tells me it would be! You now have all the knowledge necessary. Where do you want to spend your time? You can spend it in chaos –with the ghosts of yesterday or you can burn your happiness in the furnace of tomorrows' worries, or you can be alive and be present in the moment. So, when you eat strawberries – eat the strawberries. When you do the dishes – focus on the dishes. When you eat the Hersey Bar – slowly enjoy every savored bite.

***Peace and serenity only exist in the moment.***

**Exercise**

- Look at your watch; what time is it?
- Where are you?

What is your answer to my question about what time is it? You probably said the time of day, right?

Consider another response.

- Say to yourself, the answer to, "What time is it? Answer...***NOW.***
- Say to yourself, the answer to "Where am I?" ***HERE.***

This is *collapsing time, a* simple method to return to the moment. In times you feel the chaos closing in, threatening to steal your hard-won serenity, ask these two questions, and then quietly remind yourself of the answers.

- What time is it? ***NOW***
- Where am I?" ...***HERE***

> If I harbored bitterness, my happiness docks elsewhere.

You can choose chaos, or you can collapse time by these simple questions. Your answers will return you to the moment, *the most comfortable place in the world.*

Practice being in the moment, scan yourself periodically during the day. If you get 5 minutes today, you can double it tomorrow. Keep up this awareness and living in the moment will become your default setting. Being in the moment is where you were created to be and here, you are peaceful, quiet, okay, *at this moment.*

*This moment right now*
*is the only time there is.*

## Gratitude Revisited

Hopefully, your gratitude list (from page 95) has expanded from your first entry. One Thanksgiving, I was looking forward to my family attending our traditional turkey feast. I pictured everyone sitting around the table holding hands and saying what they are grateful for. Then I wondered, if I just have a list of what I am grateful for, could there be another list hidden and unacknowledged, lying just beneath my consciousness *of what I do not have*? Perhaps it could even be what I am *NOT* grateful for? Consider a different point of view. What if you just were grateful. Omit the "grateful for" and substitute "***Just grateful.***"

- We got that wonderful contract. Be grateful.
- My best salesperson left for a competitor. Be grateful.
- My child got into the college she wanted. Be grateful.
- My banker is calling my loan. Be grateful.

*My life is a prayer.*
Mahatma Gandhi

Do you like the fact that your best salesperson has left your company, or the banker called the loan? No, of course not. Can you accept that reality? Acceptance is on the ***Can*** Side. Can you be grateful as in, "In all things be grateful". This scripture quote does not say, "For all things be thankful."

I could never understand Gandhi's message about his life being a prayer until practicing gratitude. Before sleeping, close your eyes and focus on just being grateful. When living ingratitude, just being grateful, isn't your life a prayer? When in gratitude, *you are in the moment.*

**Serenity is fleeting when gratitude is missing.**

*Gratitude unlocks the fullness of life. It turns what we have into enough, and more. It turns denial into acceptance, chaos to order, confusion to clarity. It can turn a meal into a feast, a house into a home, a stranger into a friend.*
Melody Beattie

What is the opposite of love? Many people say, "hate." Some might think, "apathy." Still others might believe, "indifference".

*The opposite of love is fear…*
A Course in Miracles

I was traveling to Baton Rouge from Houston, Texas and stopped at a rest stop. Out in front of the men's room was a 12-year -ld boy with a handwritten sign, "Dad's car broke down, need help." As I walked into the restroom, I wanted to help, then my mind went into overdrive. What if this is a scam? He's probably a drug addict and this is his con.

Is he taking advantage of my desire to help? Then I'd be a fool! Fear tried to limit my gift of love. Then I remembered, *The opposite of love is fear.* Armed with this wisdom, I overcame my resistance and gave him twenty dollars. Without my fear, I was free to express love to a stranger.

Then the next lesson hit! When extending a gift, my best love should be unconditional. When giving, what happens thereafter, I have no control over, and is *none of my business!*

## Strength of Humility

***The Force*** is a connection with the universe and the world. Being in the ***Force*** creates a bond with life and a higher sense of purpose. In this state of contentment, people feel more powerful, peaceful, and happy. The *Strength of Humility* defines the coping skills and attitudes necessary to live in ***The Force***.

It takes a strong person to be humble. Jesus, Gandhi, Mother Theresa, Nelson Mandela, and Martin Luther King are examples of humble people who were larger than life, stood up against injustice, accomplished much, and did so without violence or arrogance.

A truly humble person listens for understanding hues of grey in the vast wonderful world of acceptance. Through the strength of humility, this person has learned how to love without controlling others, does not fear death but knows it is a part of life, and boldly faces its finality with shoulders back, head high, ready for the next adventure.

Truly, humble people think for themselves and yet are very receptive to others' ideas. They are comfortable when they doubt, or when they strongly believe, and their thoughts are vetted through their journey of self-discovery, not just blindly accepting someone else's dogma. Humble people have a strong sense of limits, knowing other people's boundaries because they are keenly aware of their own. They can assertively and respectfully defend their boundaries and stand up for the rights of others. They live in the moment and practice gratitude. Through *Strength of Humility*, they stand up for injustice with the courage of their convictions. In this wonderful state, a humble person looks for areas of *Win-Win*, acknowledging the validity of others. When in a state of humility, they have immense strength.

*Would it not be heaven on earth*
*when all humans have self-love?*
Tom Lusk

The lack of self-love often breeds conflict and inflicts great distress on ourselves, and others – often the people we love the most. Although our intention is not to inflict pain but to express love, what our families often receive instead is *Nazi Nurturing.* Humble people are meek enough to love themselves, not with arrogance, but by appreciating their gifts and abilities all the while singing the praises of other people's splendor. Using the *Strength of Humility*, living in the moment is a natural state of contentment.

*Be the change you want*
*to see in the world.*
Mahatma Gandhi

Linking Gandhi's change in the world and Lusk's self-love wisdom together creates a great lesson for humanity. If we want heaven on earth, we must learn self-love and thus becomes the change we wish to see in the world.

Whitney Houston sang in song, *The Greatest Love* "...learning to love yourself ...is easy to achieve." Loving oneself is indeed the greatest love, but only can be achieved through the *Strength of Humility*. Self-love does not come easy and requires many guides, insights, and a tremendous amount of ***Thumb Work.***

## Final thoughts

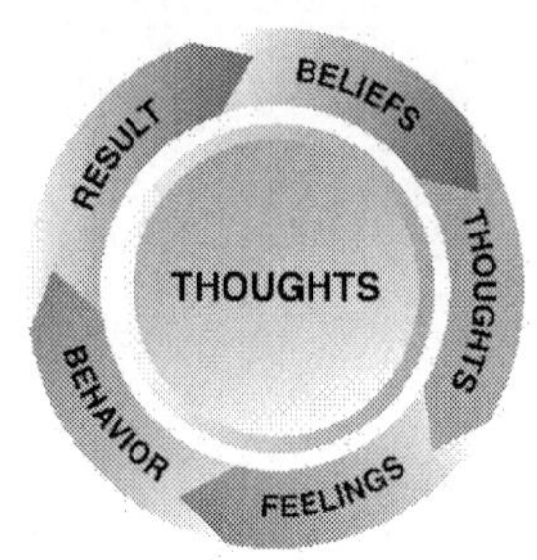


During a conversation about self-love with J. T. Bondi, he taught me a lesson. With his eyes as wide as a five-year-old could open, he said," I know what self-love is, Mr. David."

"You do?"

"Yes, when I was in my mommy's tummy, I loved myself. And when the egg broke (sic) and I came out, I loved my Mommy." I loved the part where the egg broke. J. T. for all his youth expressed this concept so beautifully. We are born with this love. Since we are a gift from our creator, it stands to reason, we entered this world with self-love.

Loving oneself is a concept that tends to bother a lot of us. This is especially true of someone just beginning to explore themselves in an emotional and/or spiritual journey. As J. T. taught me, *self-love is a birthright.*

So, *Outrun the Wolf* is dedicated to those who have a hollow feeling of disconnection deep within. People like me who attempted love and failed. We who wanted a happy life but knew not how to have one, and everyone who wanted the mind chatter to cease but could not turn it off. Your author looked down on *feet of clay*, knowing, like Michael Jordan, I've squandered many chances. His misses were in basketball, mine were chances to express love and did not.

To be successful, I try to focus on the progress made, not the shots I've already missed. The *Strength of Humility* is the tool that can help accomplish these goals. On the day I leave this life, on my graduation day, I want to leave it in a better condition than I found it. If this is my goal, I must learn to love better. Beginning with learning to love me ***again,*** and then learning to love others, and finally healing the wounds with dear mother earth.

*May the Force be with you…" is charming but it's not important. What's important is that you become the Force* **…** – Harrison Ford

## My Deepest Fear

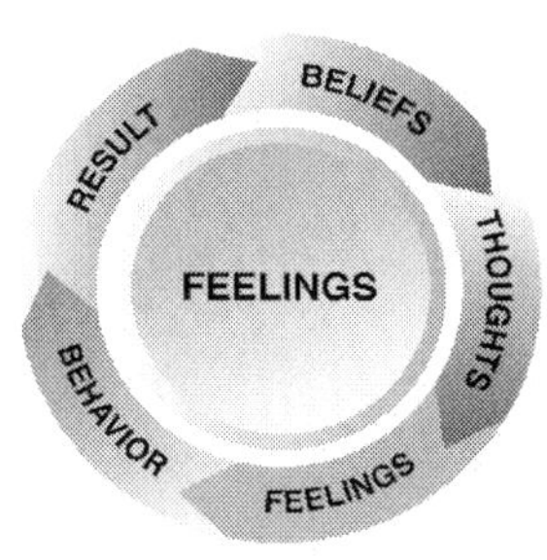


Nelson Mandela quoted this inspiration, but the source is unknown:

"I think my deepest fear is that I am inadequate. In reality, my deepest fear is that I am powerful beyond measure! It is my light rather than my darkness that frightens me. I ask myself, who am I to be brilliant, gorgeous, talented, and fabulous? Actually, who am I to be less than what God created me to be? I am a child of God, precious, worthy, and fallible … My playing small serves the world poorly. I limit my enlightenment if I believe shrinking so that other people will feel secure around me is an effective way to relate to others. By the same token, being overbearing is a manifestation of the human ego that is the flip side of the coin of believing that shrinking severs me best. I was born to manifest the glory of God that flows through me. God flows through more than just me. God flows through everyone. As I let my own light shine, I unconsciously give other people permission to do the same. As I liberate myself from my own fears, my presence automatically liberates others."

## Declaration Statement

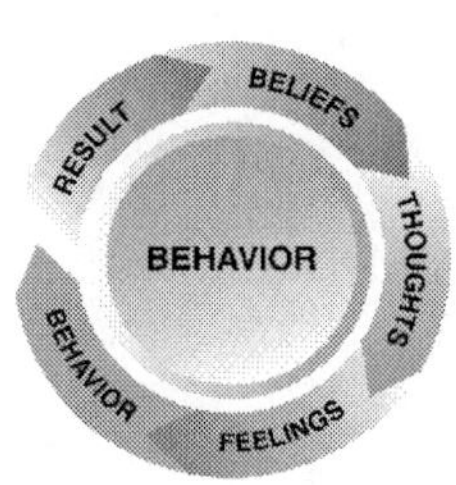


Write a declaration statement concerning the life you now plan to lead. Declare it, express it, own it, visualize it, and then live it! Do not be afraid of your limitations. Do not second-guess yourself or think that you may not achieve your dream. Be bold. Be bodacious. What the mind can hold, you and your creator can achieve. Shoot for your dream! Go for it!

P.S. Perfection is unreal and an abstraction.

## Declaration Statement

I ________________ (Your name) hereby **declare** that I will **re-gain my power over** ___________________________________ (The stated problem) **and will claim my strength** over fear and lack of trust.

**I am declaring that henceforth I will …**

**David Walton Earle**

# Community with Others

**Together we can turn your wolf into pot roast.**

# Chapter 12

## Trust

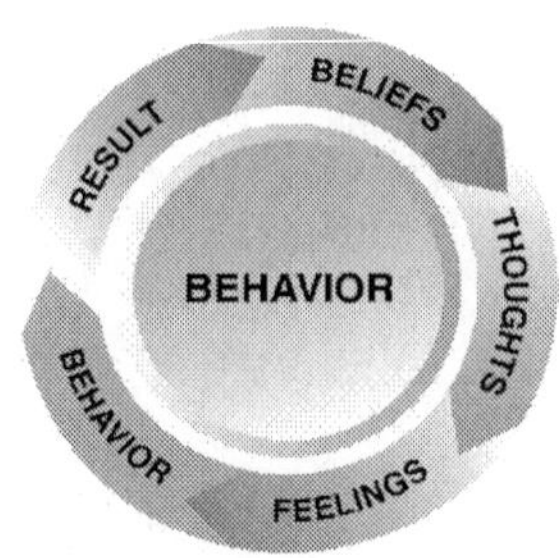


If the Corporate Fairy promised a 30% increase in production - just by sprinkling her magic dust, would you accept her offer? Are you eager to sign up? The price of her fairy dust is for a change in leadership style. Still interested?

Once her offer is accepted, she flips a mysterious tiny coin. ***TRUST*** appears on both sides. On one side of this magic coin, employees trust management, and on the other side – management trust employees. She hands you your corporate coin to contemplate.

When employees do not trust management, change becomes difficult. Because of the dire financial straits of American Airlines, their unions agreed to massive pay and benefit cuts. They were shocked when they discovered management gave themselves invested pension plans and hefty bonuses. For shattering the employee's trust, the Chief Executive, Donald Carty, lost his job.

***Many employee spirits die on the shop room floor.***

- Do your employees think management trusts them?
- Do your employees receive clear expectations?
- Do you provide them with the necessary training for success? Are they rewarded when they make achievements?
- Do they receive the credit when deserved?

- Do your employees perceive that they are an important part of the team?

Many employees' answers to these questions are sadly negative. "They don't trust us," is the message I often hear. If fairy dust is real, could employees produce 30% more without having to work any harder? According to two management studies, this is entirely possible. A University of Michigan study concluded that employees could perform the work assigned 60% of the time. A study by the American Management Association concluded employees, on average, could do 26% more work. Is mistrust a vital part of this lack of productivity?

*If you lead through fear, you will have little respect.*
*But if you lead through respect, you will have little to fear*
Anonymous.

Most supervisors will nod their heads in agreement with this quote. This is leadership primordial instinct. Even knowing this, negativity is true for most management. According to Mortimer Feinbery, author of *Effective Psychology for Managers*, dwelling upon shortcomings "will boomerang".

*You do not lead by hitting people over the head.*
*That's assault, not leadership.*
Dwight D. Eisenhower

The management style of *hitting people over the head* does not create the trusting environment to encourage this extra 30%. According to Ernst & Young, one of the best ways to motivate employees is to demonstrate how important their jobs are in making money for the company. A whopping 59% of employees rated this as a very effective method of involving them in their productivity. That may require showing employees sensitive accounting records relating to their jobs, involving them in decisions, asking for their input, and listening to their concerns. In short, building trust by respect.

*Sinking sailors bail faster.*
Lynn Tolleson

They bail faster because they have a common goal, clear direction, and know they are in the same boat with the admiral. It does not take magic wands and pixie dust to realize when people pull together the results dramatically increase. Productivity is directly related to trust and trust can only be achieved by respect.

The executive vice president of CertainTeed pointed his finger at the new plant manager, Frank Conrad, and me and demanded, "You two solve this problem by Christmas." This declaration was because most CertainTeed's employees in their Lake Charles, LA plant had contacted corporate HR complaining about the previous manager and the hostile work environment he created. He ran the plant with an iron hand – *my way or the highway* – with little employee empowerment. There was little mutual respect and trust.

One employee told me, "When I get to the gate, I keep my mind in the pickup truck." Having lived in Lake Charles, the Cajun people have wonderful ways of expressing themselves. I responded, "That is exactly what's happening. To be successful, we need your mind and spirit as well as your physical presence. Will you work with me to make this change?"

One of the first challenges Frank and I faced was the crew size on the autoclave. The old plant manager reduced the crew to 5, and the employees wanted 6. "What shall we do?" He asked.

"Put it back in their hands. Get the employees to calculate the amount they produced with 5 people, and how much more production is needed just to break even with the additional person." When the employees reported back, Frank asked them if this increase was a realistic possibility. They agreed that it was. This production was now theirs, not management.

They not only produced that amount, but one day Frank had a freshly shaved head. It did not improve his appearance. He said, "I bet the guys that if they could produce this additional amount, I would shave my head. And they did!"

During this turnaround, I asked the mind-in-the-pickup employee, "Have you been bringing your mind past the gate?" His eyes sparkled, "You know, I roll down the windows and brought it in. It tweren't so bad!"

The previous manager's style was *hitting people over the head.* Frank showed respect by trusting his employees, and they responded with record production. To solve the autoclave problem, Frank Conrad and I used **P.T.T.S.T.W.T.H.C.**

***People tend to support that which they help create.***

David Walton Earle

# Feedback

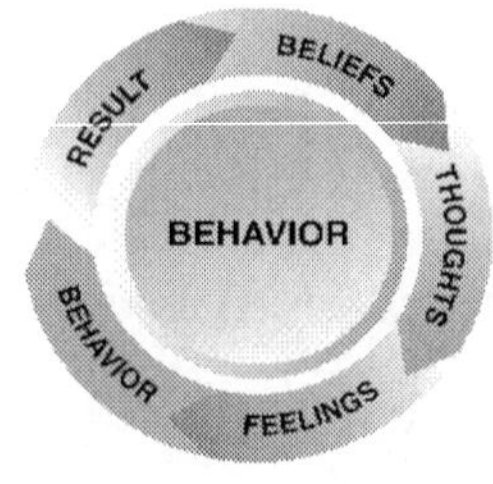


Wheaties has long been the cereal of champions, or so General Mills would like us to believe. Eat this breakfast and you will excel in athletic competition. The ultimate proof is the latest Olympic champion featured on the front of the box. Feedback should also be a prominent feature on any job site. Receiving correct and vital intelligence is to corporate success as what a good breakfast is to athletes. Management will not know unless they are told.

Responding is the critical feedstock for good decisions, proper quality assurance, a safe worksite, and effective customer service. When promptly received, feedback can be the difference between success and failure. This is true for positive feedback or critical analysis; one is delightful and the other can be uncomfortable, yet both are incredibly valuable.

It is sad to see human spirits when not appreciated. Valued employees are more enthusiastic, with higher productivity than their co-workers who do not share the same attitude.

A manager took over a New York City maintenance crew where the job of one of his employees was to paint fire hydrants. His normal productivity was one per day! A person must work hard at being that unproductive, and yet the previous manager could not force any more out of this long-term employee. The new manager asked him to report the number of fireplugs painted that day. He requested, "On this 3x5 card posted on the bulletin board, please let me know how many fireplugs you did today." After this system began, the manager would make daily comments about this worker's productivity. The first day a big number "1" was on the card, but the next day there was "2". The manager made a positive comment about the increase, and the following day the number was "4". He then received more positive reinforcement. After a short time, this formally non-productive employee was taking paint home so he would not have to go to the shop before work, but head directly to his fireplugs! This "non-productive" employee transformed himself when he found meaning in his work.

Many supervisors have a common reaction to this story. They would argue, "The employee's job was to paint fireplugs, and that is why he was paid." All employees need a sense of worth. They need to be appreciated for what they do. Without this meaning, spirits languish on the border between just enough and not enough.

In Viktor Frankl's equation: D = S - M, finding *meaning* is a critical key in managing suffering. Validating the meaning each employee has to the organization is an important motivational tool. The key question is why is this so difficult? What makes saying, "Thank you," or "Good job," or "This is why your job is so important to our success"? Maybe it's because so many supervisors are not getting this validation from their leaders, or maybe they think the "nice job' complement will cost them at raise time.

If it is important for Wheaties to provide athletes with proper nutrition, then helping others find meaning is equally important. ***This awareness doesn't cost a dime***.

Richard Szekelyi, CPA at Phoenix Management Services thinks a key component of communication is *productive tension:* "Each member of the team free to express their views and opinions within the team, even those views and opinions differ from those of other members." Many leaders deceive themselves thinking they already have good *productive tension.* These difficult times provide an opportunity to explore – just how healthy is the *productive tension* is in your organization? Celebrate employee feedback.

During a debriefing session with one of Valero's shifts, many operators expressed dissatisfaction about how the last turnaround was handled. "Whoever decided to contract the turnaround on a firm bid must have been nuts. Valero wasted a lot of money doing it that way!" The person who made that decision was Ralph Youngblood, the plant manager. Although this was painful to hear, to his credit he did not justify his decision or reject their passionate opinions but listened to the truths of their message. This was *productive tension* at its best.

### *Feedback is the Breakfast of Champions!*

Right now, you are working many hard hours. Physically you cannot work any harder. Since management is getting work through others, helping employees increase their importance is on the ***Can*** side of the Wisdom Line. Receiving feedback is so vital to success that management must constantly nurture, encourage, and value this perishable commodity. Humans want to do a good job. They want to take pride in their accomplishments and receive effective feedback. We all want and need to know that what we do has meaning and is important.

## Most Important Function

What is a supervisor's most important function? This is a key question in successful management. The most important function is not safety, making a profit, or satisfying the customer. *Blasphemy* you shout!

*A supervisor's most important function*
*is to develop his/her people.*
Gene Clouatre

Fully developed employees are safer, make money for the company, and treat customers like their own. Inappropriate *SHOULDS* does little toward developing the employees your company needs.

*It's not easy to pull yourself up by the bootstraps*
*when your boss has his hand on your leg.*
Naomi Wolf

Often control statements are counter to employee development. Company success depends on employees who are free to think through problems and do not need the hot breath of a *SHOULD*. David Abbott advocates considering all your employees as managers. Don't they manage what is in their control including their time, attitude, and resources? All of which can readily be converted into dollars. There is a direct financial relationship between an employee who **owns** his/her job, sees himself/herself as a manager, and the bottom line.

I had a two-day contract with Trader Joe's in Metairie, Louisiana. Upon entering, I felt an immediate awareness of the employees. They were different. They seem happy, joyful, laughing, and working together. I have been in many different companies, stores, plants, hospitals, etc. but never experienced employees like this before. During the two days I was there, I met probably 100 of the 157 employees at this store. Everyone had a deep sense of ownership with an obvious sense of *joy of job*.

***It is much easier to lead employees who see themselves as managers!***

Since I am a student of leadership, I quizzed many employees and their management as to this store's environment. What I discovered is management sets clear expectations of their staff, supports them in achieving goals, asks for what they may need, and praises them when success is achieved. All employees share all duties, whether it is stocking shelves, checking out customers, or bagging groceries, they did their assignments with an obvious sparkle. When it was their turn for a buggy roundup or clean the toilets, no one, including the management, was too proud to do whatever was necessary.

The corporation authorizes each employee to spend up to $5.00 to make a customer happy. I watched an employee observing a woman admiring a shopping bag, then she looked at the price and sadly returned it to the rack.

The employee asked, "Do you like this bag?

"Yes, very much," answered the customer.

With a wide grin, the employee said, "Take it with our compliments."

When I was leaving, I picked some Columbine flowers for my wife. Standing at the register to pay, a manager gave me a wide grin, "I want you to have this." It was a great feeling.

These employees knew what was expected, what they *should* do. They did not have to be told. I said to the store manager, Randell Stevens, "you treat your employees as managers."

He thought for a minute and smiled, "Yes, that's true."

For anyone who doubts treating your employees as managers do not pay, Trader Joe's has customers waiting in line – a snake line around the outside of the store of eager people waiting for it to open. Then for most of the day the line of customers waiting patiently for their turn to shop continued!

Other good examples are Kimberly Clark's "No Questions Asked" money-back guarantee, Southwest Airlines fun at work attitude plus, and the correct The Ritz response to a customer request is, "My Pleasure," which sure beats, "No Problem."

## Ethics

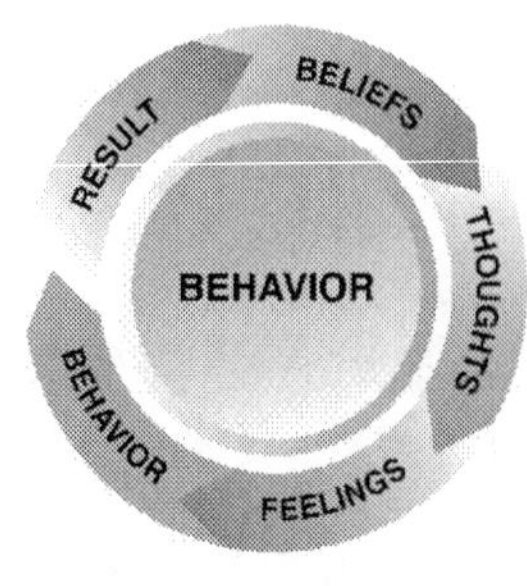


The ethics of your company are about you. If you have not yet been tempted, you may be soon seduced to violate your ethics and perhaps even the law. An insightful way of viewing your temptation is to consider your actions described in vivid detail on the front page of the newspaper the next morning. How are you going to feel when you read this article – about you? What will your loved ones think? How will your employees, and stakeholders view your transgression?

A man described his retiring coworker, "You could always count on his word." What will they say about you at the end of your career? When thinking about making a questionable decision consider this: ***What is it I might get…what is it I might get – but do not want - because of this decision?***

*Many men lose their inner hold on their moral and spiritual selves, these people eventually fell victim to the camp's degenerating influences.*
Viktor Frankl

## Most Valuable Resource

According to the CDC, in the second quarter of 2020, the national anxiety rate tripled, and depression quadrupled. The uncertainty about your company's future has added to these unsettling times. All this pressure grinds down wellbeing. Is it no wonder employee performance has suffered as their behavioral health erodes? Although you feel much the same, *you are the message*. Start company *fireside chats,* be the calm and reassurance they need, and inspire them to great heights. As valuable as your employees are to corporate success, right now you are the *most valuable resource.* Pull your shoulders back, take a deep breath, and explore the territory of confidence and competency this crisis has provided. Be the change your company needs.

# Chapter 13

## Conflict

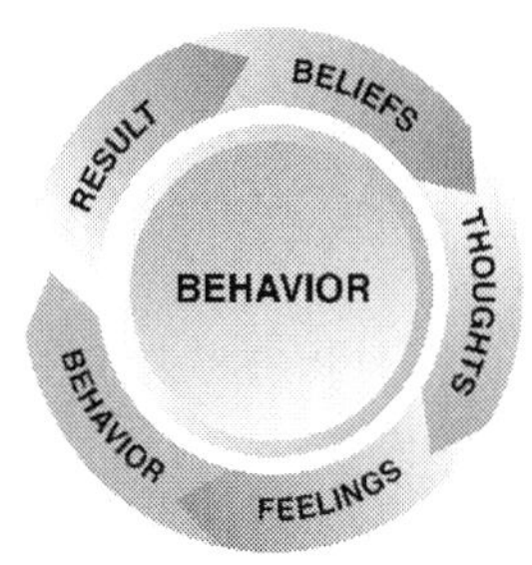


Conflict is natural. It is a part of life and is neither good nor bad. It's just what it is. Water against rock created the Grand Canyon. When water hits rocks, water always wins - eventually. When people live in close connection to one another, there are going to be rub-points of divergent opinions, needs, and points of view.

*... there is always going to be conflict.*
Thomas F. Crum

The goal of competitive sports is winning. Successful conflict resolution is not about winning or losing but what makes the difference is how it is viewed and handled. Crum thinks conflict resolution is "...rarely about being right..." but it is about

"…acknowledging and appreciating differences." The sad truth is that not all conflicts can be resolved, but if our goals are "… to learn, grow, and cooperate…conflicts can be managed."

All behavior has positive intentions, regardless of the result. That is rather a profound statement when considering all the damage inconsiderate or selfish people do and how others are treated.

***Conflict means there is caring.*** Take this startling statement as a working hypothesis, understanding there may be exceptions. If a person did not care about the situation, why waste energy and time? In conflict, look for what the other person cares about.

***It is easier to destroy***
***then to build.***

Webster's 9th New Collegiate Dictionary defines conflict as "…an antagonistic action, struggle resulting from opposing needs, drives, and/or wishes.

*Boldness becomes rarer,*
*the higher the rank.*
Carl von Clausewitz

In Webster's definition, conflict is about different opinions or needs. Instead of focusing on the ensuing battle, look deep for the underlining cause of the issue. Most disputants focus on what is not there, a perception of *lack.* Aren't most conflicts really about what is lacking - the perception of scarcity? Disputants battle over money, power, control, respect, understanding, etc.; you name it. How about love, do people fight over love?

***All behaviour makes sense to someone.***

## Win-Win Questionnaire

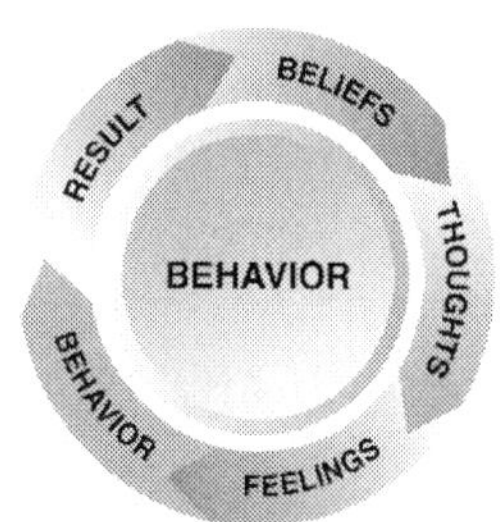


Scoring: record your responses to the questionnaire in appropriate boxes. Be careful because the sequence of the boxes is not always the same as in the questionnaire.

Directions: Here are 12-paired items (*even-odd*), read each pair of statements and put a checkmark next to the statement more closely applying to you. If both statements in the pair apply, mark the one most applicable to you, however marginal the difference.

Record your answers on the form found on the next page.

| | | | |
|---|---|---|---|
| | 1. When negotiating, I prefer to keep my "bottom line" to myself. | | 2. When negotiating, I prefer to avoid having a predetermined "bottom line." |
| | 3. I prefer to go into discussions with a general goal and be flexible about my specific objective. | | 4. I prefer to go into discussions with a fixed objective in mind. |
| | 5. I rarely ask other people about their objectives. | | 6. I frequently ask other people about their objectives. |
| | 7. I often feel determined to get my own way. | | 8. I often feel determined to find a better way, even if it means compromising. |
| | 9. When negotiating, I prefer to reach an agreement however difficult it might be. | | 10. When negotiating, if I can't find an acceptable outcome, I prefer to agree to disagree. |
| | 11. I prefer to explore people's objectives and search for common ground. | | 12. I prefer to push ahead and do my best to achieve my objective. |

| | | | |
|---|---|---|---|
| | 13. At the start of discussions, I tend to be open about what I hope to achieve. | | 14. At the start of discussions, I tend to keep what I hope to achieve to myself. |
| | 15. In negotiations, my primary aim is to reach an amicable agreement. | | 16. In negotiations, my primary aim is to reach an effective outcome. |
| | 17. Whenever my opinions differ from others, I like to explore the reasons for the difference. | | 18. Whenever my opinions differ from others, I try harder to persuade them to accept my point of view. |
| | 19. I often feel compelled to win concessions from other people. | | 20. I think the best solutions do not require concessions from anyone. |
| | 21. I often find people take up entrenched positions and refuse to budge. | | 22. I find people are prepared to divulge why they have taken up a position. |
| | 23. When negotiating, I confront the problem, not the person. | | 24. When negotiating, I am confrontational or conciliatory with people. |

| **Column *One*** | | | **Column *Two*** | |
|---|---|---|---|---|
| **Confrontational Tendencies** | | | **Win-Win Tendencies** | |
| 1 | | | 2 | |
| 4 | | | 3 | |
| 5 | | | 6 | |
| 7 | | | 8 | |
| 9 | | | 10 | |
| 12 | | | 11 | |
| 14 | | | 13 | |
| 15 | | | 16 | |
| 18 | | | 17 | |
| 19 | | | 20 | |
| 21 | | | 22 | |
| 24 | | | 23 | |
| **Total** | | **Total** | | |

Your total for a win-win approach should exceed your total for a confrontational approach. Check your results against the following norms based on the scores obtained by 150 North American and British managers drawn from a cross-section of different organizations and functions.

| | | Interpretation |
|---|---|---|
| **12** | | A very high score was only obtained by 10% of the managers in the sample |
| **10-11** | | A high score was only obtained by the next 20% of the managers in the sample |
| **8-9** | | Moderate – achieved by the middle 40% of the sample |
| **6-7** | | Low – indicating a tendency to be more confrontational than win-win |
| **0-5** | | Very low – the bottom 10% of the sample was this confrontational |

Win-Win Questionnaire - Unknown author

In 1776, the Continental Congress met to decide what form of government America would have. There was a heated debate about how to configure the new representative government. The larger states wanted to be represented by population. The smaller states knew their influence would be watered down by this and feared their voice would be lost. This debate raged over many days until our nation's fathers devised something else. We now have a bicameral form of government dividing congress into two distinct groups. The House of Representatives is based on population and the Senate has only two senators from each state - regardless of size.

I hope you are taking notes on this for it will be in your 6-weeks civics exam next week.

People call the 1776 agreement a compromise, but it was not. The correct label is a *win-win.* Our founding fathers created a *win-win* when both conflicting positions obtained what they wanted.

Employees argue over what they think is best for their organization. They both want success but sometimes have diverse opinions. In this case, the argument is a good sign because it means they are both committed to the problem and have ownership of their job. Both opinions may be valid and need exploring. In the absence of a *win-win* attitude, however, this becomes a battleground *to be right.* Battleground arguments cause the hardening of attitudes and the loss of possibilities. To determine what is best, diverse opinions are often essential for the best solution.

With conflicting opinions, try not to put those with who you disagree into categories as labels tend to increase polarization and decrease the chances of resolution. Instead try to get behind their eyeballs and see the issue as they might view it, putting you in their shoes where understanding is greatly increased.

***Arguing to win is counterproductive***
***to a successful relationship.***

In my twenty-year marriage, we both fought to win, and constant tension was our reward. I argued to be right - my righteousness compared to her incorrectness, my magnificence to her obvious failings. When successful, then I could win and feel good. My shallow self-esteem left me no place for understanding.

Somehow, if I could put her down and climb on her shoulders, I could raise my head out of the miserable morass of unhappiness. On the rare occasions when I won, I lost. The joy of the victory was greatly overshadowed by the bitterness the triumph created. We both were not bad or vicious people but ignorant.

Learning this painful lesson, Penny (my second wife of over thirty years) and I adopted a sentence that works so much better. Instead of fighting to be right, we now have a much different attitude:

***Would you rather be right***
***or***
***would you rather be happy?***

Now during arguments, that wonderful sentence creates a shift from being right towards *win-win.* Animosities decrease with this attitude adjustment. From my past twenty-year battle, fighting to be right is a painful way of living.

***I think I would rather be happy.***

**Exercise**

In your **difficult event,** how much of it was about your being right? What if your part of the argument did not include this obsessive demand? Observe your company meetings. Who is trying to win and who is working towards getting to the best solution?

*Try not to become a man of success.*
*Rather become a man of value.*
Albert Einstein

In mediation, the mediator's job is to facilitate an agreement...*yet unborn*. The mediator supplies the necessary energy and does not care about the outcome other than assisting the parties to come to ***their resolution***. The mediator has no dog in the hunt.

One mediation tool is to increase the size of the pie. When the perception of what is lacking is paramount, the intensity of the polarization is increased. If the mediator can find areas to increase the pie size, this posturing dampens, and the possibility of agreement increases.

When disputants feel very strongly, it is difficult to find a solution. What would happen if you said, "We both are very committed to our different points of view, will you work with me to obtain a resolution that meets your needs as well as mine?" How strange this might be in the middle of an argument. Negotiating for a *win-win* is much harder, but the attempt just may prove successful. Once achieved, all feel satisfied and more willing to try again in the future.

There is an excellent example in Roger Fisher and William Ury book, *Getting to Ye*s. Two men are arguing with raised voices in the library, an absolute no-no. Picture a little librarian, with her grey hair tied up in a bun, bespectacled, and stern but helpful expression.

***Conflict is the attempt to satisfy a lack.***

"Gentlemen, this is a public library; you'll have to keep your voices low. Now, what seems to be the problem?"

One man says, "I want the window opened."

The other man demands. "Well, I want it closed."

"Open!" "No, Closed!"

Trying to understand, she asks, "So you want the window open?"

"Yeah," he answers.

"Well, I don't!" the other man demands not keeping his voice within the library's limited decibels.

"So, you want the window closed?"

"You got it."

This is a case of absolute *positions*; the window cannot be open and closed at the same time. What is this librarian going to do? The open-close debate continued. It got louder and more polarized.

She continued, "Why do you want the window open?"

"Well, it's stuffy in here and I need some fresh air."

"Sir," she asks, "why is the window being open a problem for you?"

"I just got over a cold, and don't want a draft."

The librarian very skillfully identified the two diametrically opposite positions - *open vs. closed.* Then with skilled questioning, she discovered the disputants' *interest* as well as their *positions*. Until she learned their underlining *interest*, what each needed, no satisfactory solution was available. She achieved a *win-win* conclusion when she closed the offending window and then opened another in an adjacent room.

"Gentlemen, I closed the window in this room but opened another window in the adjacent room. I believe there will be sufficient fresh air, and the draft is eliminated."

She understood these two men's argument. She learned their *positions:* open vs. closed, the easy part. Digging deeper she discovered their *interest,* the reason behind their two diverse *positions*. No *win-win* solution was possible until she discovered the *interest* driving these two diametrically opposite positions.

## Negotiations

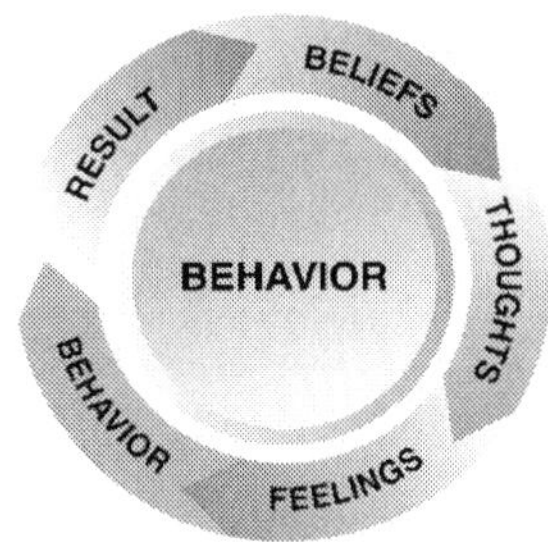


Other than **Win-Win**, there are various types of conflict postures of **Win-Lose:** Distributing Bargaining, Gamesmanship, and Brinkmanship.

**Distributing bargaining** - If an ongoing relationship is not important and further dealings are not the goal, then it may be appropriate to attempt to increase your part of the pie at the expense of others.

**Gamesmanship** – this posture pushes the limits to gain an advantage. There is a line in this type of negotiation that once crossed becomes **Brinkmanship** – first to blink loses.

If an ongoing productive relationship is a future goal, distributing bargaining, gamesmanship, and brinkmanship all have a large downside drawback. Playing hardball is an attempt to put the other at a distinct disadvantage. Being underhanded, deceitful, and/or manipulative undermines trust. When the trust is violated, opponents become uncooperative, decreasing the potential for resolutions.

## *Kitchen Sink*

Have you ever had a Kitchen Sink fight? "No, but I once threw the bathroom plunger!"

When you hear or use such statements as, "oh, and another thing," or "well, last week you did…" or, "…your problem is…".

Picture just one dirty dish in the sink, that is not much to clean up, right? But if the sink is full of dirty dishes and stinky pots and pans, who would want to clean up that mess?

Using the dirty dish analogy, when there is an issue to discuss; one dish represents one problem. What compounds the problem is putting other dirty dishes in the sink. Additional dishes represent something else added before the original difficulty is resolved.

Work on one topic at a time and if someone throws another dish in the sink, just say, "Let's just focus on this problem before we discuss any other." If that first dish is not scrubbed, all the other dishes will also stay dirty.

## *Person / Problem*

Wounded people tend to lash out and attack the person. "Well, your family is all crazy," or "you never can do anything right," or "if you would only make more money…" All these are examples of attacking the person *not the problem.*

> My motto is to love things and use people.

When feeling tension, *separate the person from the behavior.* Every person, regardless of what they did, deserves respect, just like you. Attacking the problem through the person creates additional pain and requires further healing. When the problem is attacked through the person, the other person now has hurt feelings and a large resentment, probably not what was intended. When confronting problems, separate the person from their behavior.

**Exercise**

Think about your **difficult event.** Did you attack someone you love while trying to solve the problem? Would it be different if you had separated the person from the behavior?

***Be hard on the problem***
***and gentle on the person.***

## *Responsibility*

One New Year's Day, Penny and I argued. Now our arguments are much different than with my first wife where there was much animosity, hurt, and resentment with rare positive outcomes. The winner always out blasted the other. Afterward, both the victim and victor felt wounded.

Penny and I might raise our voices but because we do not attack, there is seldom a reason for an apology. This New Year's Day when I presented my concerns, I knew I was right, but she told me she felt attacked. After exhausting our different points of view, we both fell silent, both struggling to find a solution. Then it hit me! I knew how to solve this problem…but…*I really, really did not want to.* But because I knew someday, I had to live up to my advice, I said, "Alright, damn it, what do I have to do to solve this problem?"

She thought for a moment, and said, "Just ask me." Her response hit me between the eyes. I was acting like a victim, blaming her instead of taking the assertive high road and asking for my needs. I immediately saw the wisdom in her statement and asked her what I wanted. Victim no more!

**Exercise**

Think back to your **difficult event** argument. This will be hard to hear, but were you acting like a victim? Would the argument be different if you focused on your part of the problem?

## *Honesty*

Comedy becomes humorous by exaggerating and magnifying human behavior. In these sketches, the actors manipulate, control, and are never direct in their dealings. We can laugh at their dysfunction knowing - we may have the same traits.

***Successful relationships have a high degree of honesty.***

Without this core component, life becomes a real version of situational comedy, but without humor. Honesty is perhaps the most difficult characteristic to develop, and it is key in dealing with others.

***The cornerstone of good relationships is honesty.***

**Exercise**

In your **difficult event**, what did you want the other person to understand but were afraid to say? How did your lack of honesty affect the outcome?

*If you get up one more time than you fall,*
*you will make it through.*
-- Chinese proverb

## Avoidance

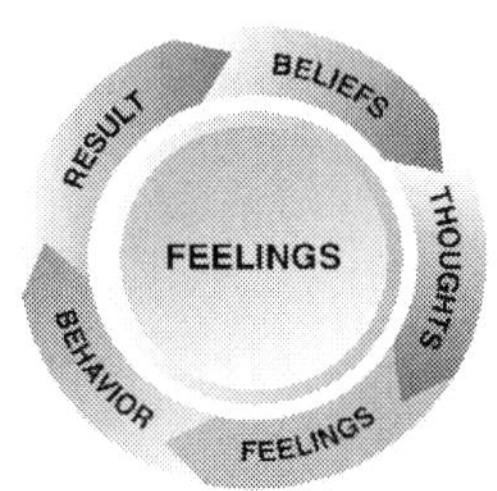


Some patterns of thought are constructive, and some are not. A great deal of energy is expended by not choosing which battle is worth fighting. You are now engaged in a great struggle of survival. You have finite resources of time, money, and your physical and psychic energy.

***If everything is important,***
***then nothing is important.***

Wonder why you feel overwhelmed and in need of a superhero with a flowing cape? During this crunch, there are some things that you would normally have the time and energy for, but not now. Discernment is a useful tool to practice and now is an absolute necessity. General, ***pick your battles***.

Maybe a useful insight might be helpful. ***How important is it?*** One manager who was faced with this same dilemma asked herself: ***Is there going to be blood on the floor?*** If yes, then it was important. If not, she added it on the to-do list with an appropriate weighted value.

**Exercise**

In your current crisis, when the revised financials must be at the bank by 2:00, a customer's late shipment needs to be sent, and your banker is on the line, this awareness may not be on the horizon. On other days, this perception helps with picking battles.

# Uproar

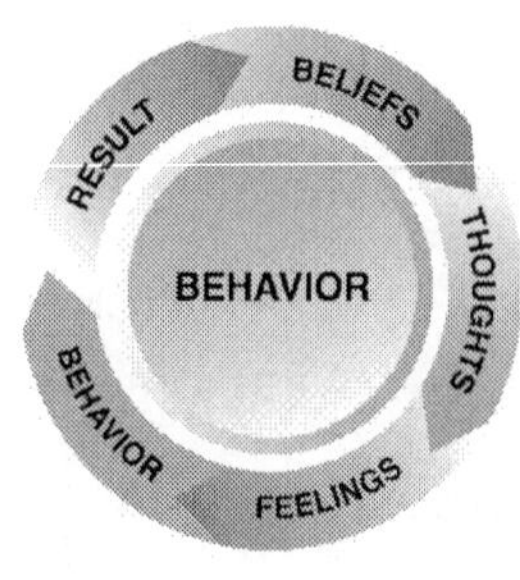


All companies have a certain culture of behavior. In some, it is a blueprint of dysfunction. No one acknowledges this pattern, nor talks about it at the breakfast table. It is seldom addressed at the morning meeting, and it is never posted on the company bulletin board. In a chaotic drama, members become experts at playing ***Uproar.*** As painful as it is, ***Uproar*** is what the group knows. Most hate it but do not have the awareness or the skills to change it.

What are the destructive patterns plaguing your company? As Dr. Phil says, "Are they working for ya?" Once you identified the pattern, carefully acknowledge your part of the problem. "MY PART? No, no, it's all their fault!" What part of the tension belongs to others and what part is yours? When acknowledging your part, you are halfway home when you identify your monkeys.

A client company's employees were in a smoldering revolt. Management expected me to quell the rebellion. I heard many tales of promises made but not kept, disrespectful statements, and not listening to employees' suggestions. Many of these employees were college graduates. At an employee appreciation dinner, they were told they were glorified farmhands, and if they did not like it here, they would be easily replaced! This company had a severe *us* - and - *them* divide. Employees are keenly aware of this dichotomy, and know they are not all of the problem.

Often there is a designated member or group whose job is to start the ***UPROAR*** game. They may say something, act a certain way, or omit what may be required, just to *get your goat*. Little Billy leaves his Big Wheel on the driveway knowing this will make you angry. A supervisor fails to finish the financials you need for your bank presentation. Once this game is triggered, you have just received your engraved invitation to play, ***UPROAR***.

### *Determine your part of the problem.*

Recall the comic strip, "Blondie" where Dagwood was Mr. Dithers' designated ***UPROAR*** employee. When Dagwood puts his feet on his desk, loiters at the water fountain, or mishandles a contract, these are their well-worn signals to start their game of ***UPROAR***.

Think of this as bait. An employee drops a line into corporate waters with a baited hook, knowing great fishing is here. Once you bite, the ***UPROAR*** game begins. These patterns are not consciously realized, but everyone knows the rules.

### *The question is not WHY we started this painful game, but what can "I" do to change it?*

When someone attacks, remember the bait. You can bite the bait and continue the chaos game, or you can now choose not to bite the bait. You may not remember this option until after taking a huge bite, and now are fully engaged in this painful battle – a fight no one wins. As your awareness increases, so does the skill to recognize patterns and decide to bite or not.

**David Walton Earle**

Many times, I have been the tip of the corporate change arrow. One intervention I use is to invite just the employees of a department, shift, or team to vent their frustrations and concerns on a flipchart. Besides the BS, there is a lot to be learned. Later I will invite the same team along with their management (including the top executive), to review the flipchart together. Great discussion, although sometimes contentious, flows from this exchange, where the ***Uproar*** game changes from negative to positive.

Think about a time you bit the bait and played ***UPROAR***. Acknowledgment increases your ability to resist the bait's temptation. Even when you've swallowed the bait, you can spit it out as soon as you realize it. By the way, how does the bait taste?

***A problem fully identified***
***is half solved.***

**Exercise**

From your results of the *Win-Win* exercise, do you try to increase the *size of the pie* instead of looking for what was lacking? Knowing the interest of the other person helps to overcome rigid positions. In the example of your **difficult event**, what was his/her position? Now try to discover their interest. How much of the argument was about the topic and how much was it about your being right?

*Be right ... be alone*
Amy R.

During the 2012 presidential primary, the moderator asked all candidates, the same question: "If you were negotiating with the president and you could get 90% of what you wanted, would you settle?" Everyone answered, "No". These were intelligent men and presumably knowledgeable about negotiations. Was this absolute statement made to demonstrate their complete lack of negotiation abilities, naivety to the extreme, or was it political posturing? It was clearly not a *win-win.*

*We are caught in an inescapable network of*
*mutuality; tied in a single garment of destiny.*
Martin L. King

**Exercise**

After taking the Win-Win questionnaire, did you discover areas needing improvement? Where do you need to improve? If your team took this quiz, would team cooperation improve? Win-Win is hard work but is so satisfying.

*Wherever you go, no matter what the weather ....*
*bring your own sunshine.*
Anthony D'Angelo

If conflicts are about caring, disputants must care enough about the problem to fight. Conflicts can be constructive or destructive, all depending upon how they are handled. If what is fought over is perceived to be limited, not enough for one, the struggle becomes a win-lose fight to the bitter end.

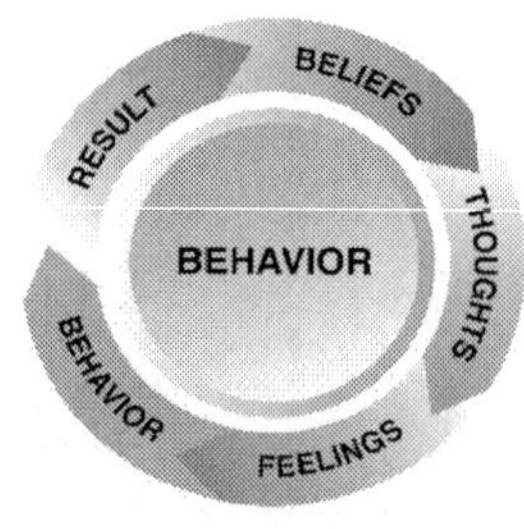


Without the proper defense, one person becomes the doormat to the other. Who wants to have someone wipe their feet upon them? This is true at home as well as in business. When in conflict, here are some ways that can produce more positive results.

**Exercise**

Hold your hand straight out - palm up. A beautiful bird just flew on your hand. It sings so pretty; it's a beautiful bird; you want it always. Now when I say three, grab it.

"One, two, three!" Grab the bird. Got it?

One of two things will happen to this bird. As strong as you are, your hand will get tired and it will escape. Once imprisoned, will it return? The other possibility is that you will crush the life out of this splendid bird.

> When she accused me of not being romantic, I bought her a padded commode seat.

You lost the first bird, but now comes another. It is even prettier than the first. Its song is so magnificent that you know - this is the one. Since you have the experience of the first bird, what are you going to do differently? You can grab it and repeat your mistake or keep your hand open - freeing it to come and go. With this freedom, this bird knows your hand is a safe place where it will not be crushed.

Relationships are like this. We can grab and hold on for dear life, not wanting what we prize the most to get away, or we can love with an open hand.

Loving with an open hand means, you assist your employees with their dreams even if this means they may someday leave you. When letting them go to seek their fortune, they may decide you are the best place to have their dream come true. Can you love your significant other enough to love them with an open hand?

***Giving a person the freedom to say no, they just may say yes.***

**Exercise**

> I bought the latest in GPS designed for seniors. It reminds me of why I went into the next room.

A healthy relationship allows each to be who they are, not demanding conformity to another's expectations. Think about your **difficult event**. Were you holding on too tightly? What would be the cost to let go?

## Seagull –

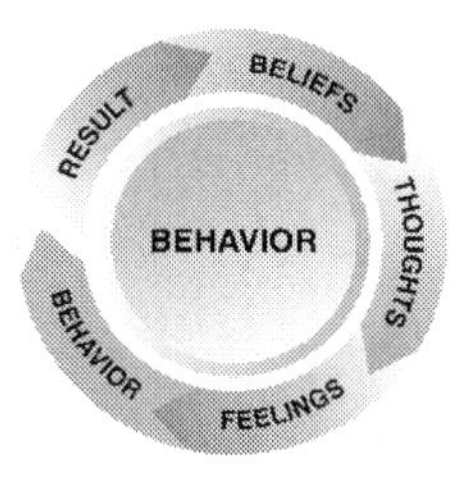


The seagull flies over the beach drops its business on your shoulders and then flies away. You feel disgusted and enraged; you have been "pooped upon". In a Sea Gull attack, someone dumps their load, then leaves without the opportunity of response or allows for problem resolution.

Richard, a former friend, accused me of three things, one of which was, "You insulted my wife." Then he stood up and said, "I can't be your friend anymore," and immediately left with no discussion, no chance for me to understand, and no chance to correct any wrongs. He then threatened me in a text that if I tried to make amends to his wife he was going to "beat me up."

Three different times I attempted to discuss these transgressions. Three times he either flatly refused or would not respond. To this day, I am not sure how or even if I insulted his wife. The other allegations were also very confusing.

This was a Seagull Attack. Richard flies in, sucker punches me with three problems, then after dropping his load, flies away, and refuses to talk. If I owed him or his wife an apology, I wanted to express my amends. Because of his seagull behavior, *I felt pooped upon!*

**Golden Rule** (revised)

*If you poop on others, thou shalt remain to cleanse*
*others of your poop, as you would wish them –*
*to cleanse you - from their poop.*

**Exercise**

Has a seagull, disguised as a person, ever dumped upon you? Have you ever been a seagull? Seagull Attacks are disgusting when they fly over, dump their load, and then flies away.

## Electronic Emotions

Email, texting, or Facebook arguments are ***not*** communication but an *illusion.* People engaging in electronic warfare think they are communicating, but really are hiding behind electronic impulses - preventing real dialogue. Texting is great to convey facts. "What time are we going? or "What's for dinner?".

When emotions are involved, text-type communications are fraught with misunderstanding. In a heated debate via text, what the recipient receives is your unfiltered thoughts spitting out as fast as your thumbs can type. What is said in the red-hot moment of verbal combat often inflicts pain. Thoughts expressed in the calmness of time, reflection, and emotional sobriety become much more conciliatory. When in a cell-tower argument, ask to meet the person to discuss the matter. They may ignore your logical appeal and continue to fill the airwaves with negativity. Continuing to engage in opposing broadsides will not solve the problem.

People often show me: "Look what she/he said!" There it is in black and white, hurtful words to be remembered with ever painful reading. Now the recipient can prove the injustice and have the moral high ground to continue the argument. When emotions are involved, do not text but wait until you are together and emotionally sober.

**Exercise**

Look back over your text messages. Explore for any emotions in those messages. Could these exchanges be improved if the emotions were not expressed or implied?

*The task of the leader is to get people from were they are to where they have not been.*
Henry Kissinger

## Empathic Response

Are you a mind reader? Probably not! Assuming what the other person is feeling, or thinking is fraught with misunderstanding. Breaking down the word "assume" into three parts: making an ***ass*** out of ***you*** and ***me.*** Since you do not have long pointed ears, fur at the end of your tails, and four legs, I assume you are not an ass, so maybe assuming is counterproductive. When we project words, behaviors, or feelings of another person, we tend to assume our conclusions. Assuming adds another layer keeping resolution at bay.

You probably do not know anybody's exact feelings but often have a good idea of what is emotionally brewing. An empathic response might be: "That must have been a humiliating experience," or "I bet you are mad," or "Does this scare you?" Even when you misunderstand their feelings, your attempt conveys you care.

My first wife, called full of anger and bitterness as only an ex can express. Before I learned to listen, whenever she lit the anger flame, I was the kindling. Our fighting sucked the love out of our relationship.

Back then my old behavior was to bite the bait, inflicting my rage back. I always thought she was an angry woman. My term of endearment was then *War Horse*. (Have you any idea why she left me?) Since we taught my daughter the same violent temper, I called her, *War Pony*.

But this time, instead of my old attack retort, I heard something I missed for 20 years. Under her rage, I heard fear. I was not married to an angry woman; I was married to a fearful person. I heard the anger, but when now listening, I heard the emotions beneath, fear. Instead of my usual broadside of wrath, I quietly said, "Does this scare you?"

"You're damn right it does," and then strangely, we discussed the fear.

*If you want to learn to love better, you*
*should start with a friend who you hate.*
Nikka - age 6

> I am so dedicated to change that I gave my wife self-improvement goals.

Making an empathic response is another emotional sobriety tool. Don't bite the bait, listen well, and respond empathically.

**Exercise**

During your identified **difficult event,** your bad day at Black-Rock conflict, what is your best guess of what the other person was feeling? Had you responded empathically, would the conversation be different?

***You can out-listen most people's anger!***

## The Four Questions–(4-Qs)

There are four wonderful questions (4-Qs) to ask yourself before responding. This is hard to do when emotionally drunk. Just like alcohol, unmanaged emotions lubricate inhibitions, so the first thing said when emotionally drunk comes with unintentional consequences.

**Question I -***Does it have to be said?*

We all experienced saying something we were ashamed of, and then wished we could take it back. Communication like this is a sticky black cloud of regret and hurt. Before offering a comment, ask yourself this question, *does this have to be said?*

**Question II** – *Does it have to be said,* ***by me****?*

Some things need to be addressed but in quiet reflection, ask yourself, "am I the best person to say this?" This momentary reflection provides a frame of reference, enabling the necessary consideration to determine what is best. *Am I the best person to say this? Is this my monkey?*

**Question III** - *Does it have to be said, by me* ***-now?***

When contemplating the first two questions and then concluding in sober reflection, does "it" need to be said? Yes. Are you the correct person to say it? Yes. Then ask, is this the right time? Maybe tomorrow is better. When criticizing an employee in front of other employees, the reaction is much different than if you had waited to talk to her alone. In front of other employees, they may try to protect their perceived *position* in the co-worker structure and strike a position they would not have if alone. Is now the right time?

**Question IV** – *How best can it be said?*

After obtaining a YES with the first three questions, the *See/Feel/Need* Formula is an effective method of presenting your concern.

For example, if I sincerely wanted to resolve our conflict, but hit you over the head with an attacking statement. *Boom! There goes-the dynamite.* The attack then becomes the focus instead of the topic, and we argue over *how it was said,* instead of the problem. This is not what you want, but your attack just increased the magnitude of the problem.

When confronting another, often it is an accusatory tone, "You didn't," or" You always," or "You promised me." When starting with the word, "*you*", the word "*you*" itself becomes a form of personalized assault. When feeling attacked, most people will defend, withdraw, or attack back. If the intent is to use a neutral method to resolve the conflict, attacking makes it worse.

Let's pretend you and I are great friends, (If we met, I am sure we would be). We do things together and we enjoy each other's company. In this illustration, I do something that irritates you, locks your jaws, gives you the red butt and pisses you off - to the highest degree of *pissitivity!* Get the picture. Whose problem, is it? Is it your problem or is it mine?

The truth is - this is *your problem*. It is my behavior, but it is your anger. Instead of attacking me with a "***you***" statement, say instead, "I got a problem." This would be a true but by preference your concern with, “I have a problem,” you are taking responsibility for your part. You cannot control my behavior; however you do have control over how you address the problem.

Note: it is important to read the period at the end of “I have a problem”, otherwise, it comes out as “I have a problem with…” which would negate the neutral tone intended. When missing the pause, the other person may feel attacked, magnifying the problem. Presenting the message in a calm tone decreases the possibility of unintended offenses. Say it peacefully as in, “It’s raining outside.”

*…we all live our lives in chains, and*
*we never even know we have the key.*
The Eagles

**Exercise**

For the next part of this model, think of someone you need to confront, someone whose behavior is causing you problems.

- Who is this person?
- What is the behavior that irritates you?

After presenting your concern with, “I have a problem”, then use the ***See/Feel/Need*** method.

## See /Feel /Need

**SEE** –Here you describe the problem. In this section, for the sake of clarity, it is often necessary to use the word *you,* but when preceded with “I have a problem,” it comes out differently.

**FEEL** – Let the other person know how you feel (Mood Chart…Mood Chart…Mood Chart). Be *REAL.* This is a very important but overlooked part of this model. Most people live in their heads, short-circuiting their emotional navigation tool. With feelings known, you decrease the possibilities of miscommunication.

We experience feeling words more profoundly and on a different level than other words. I will prove this to you. Think about someone you respect and trust. Do not read on until this person is firmly in your mind.

Now if this respected person said to you, "You disappointed me." Did you feel it? This is just an exercise, but you felt the power of disappointing someone you respect.

***Emotional words are heard differently.***

My heart pumps well in chaos.

Emotional honesty–*REAL* – provides the best chance of being heard. Although alien to our culture, when this honesty is lacking, the understanding we so desire suffers.

Have you ever had an argument that seems to run in circles, going nowhere? Emotions run high in these types of disagreements. Some part of us knows this is a silly argument but both parties have bitten into the conflict with the clenched jaws of a bulldog – unwilling to let go. No one acknowledges the emotions driving their energy. Until this happens, a resolution is a long way off. It is hard to understand how to solve the problem until we know our emotions.

- **NEED** – After stating the problem, acknowledging the emotions derived from this concern, the problem is much easier to identify. So, now express what you need. Sometimes it is just for another person to understand you.

**Exercise**

Consider your **difficult event** conflict. Describe the behavior you wish to confront. When you think about this behavior, what are your feelings? Pick out the most descriptive feelings, the ones with the most energy. Be sure to consider other feelings in the Sad, Hurt, and/or Fear columns not just the Mad column.

*... it did not really matter what we expected from life,*
*but rather what life expected from us.*
Viktor Frankl

Now that you have identified the problem and listed your feelings associated with that behavior, what do you need to solve the problem?

Here are some examples of the model at work.

- "I have a problem." (Remember to pause after the period.) "When you are late and do not call, I feel scared and worried. I need you to phone when you are late."
- "I have a problem. When you don't put away your tools after work like you are required, I feel disappointed. I need you to put them back at the end of the day."
- "I have a problem. When I see you smoking, I feel scared; I need you to know that."
- "I have a problem. When you are late for staff meetings, I feel irritated, I need you to respect this group and be on time."

**Exercise**

Now it is your turn. Using your **difficult event** example, say "I have a problem." Describe the problem using the fewest words possible but adequately explain the concern. Remember, people, ***especially men***, hear fewer words better than many. *Do not explain yourself, beat around the bush, or justify how you see the situation.*

- Then list your feelings:
- What do you need to solve this problem?

> Of course, I am talking to myself, who else would I trust.

The *See/Feel/Need* model is simple, but powerful. When you consider using this model, first write it out to make sure it as simple and accurate as possible. Guarantee: You need this model. Practice it so you will have it when you do. Now, here are a couple of whistles and bells to increase its effectiveness:

## Consequences

In this part of the model, you can express the consequences for non-compliance – either positive or negative. For example, "If we can get this problem behind us, I think our relationship would drastically improve," or "This is such an important problem, if you do not improve, you cannot continue to work in this position."

When explaining the consequence, the person learns the seriousness of the problem. Using positive consequences is more in the coaching mindset. With negative consequences, you are drawing a line in the sand. When declaring outcomes (positive or negative) think about which best suits the situation. *Do not make threats you do not intend to carry out.*

**Exercise**

What are the consequences of your **difficult event**? Practice with a positive consequence, and then with a negative one.

## Request Statement

The cherry on the top of the *See/Feel/Need* model is to ask the other person to work with you. A great sentence is a simple request, "Will you work with me to find a solution to this problem?" When words are gently said, most people will hear our sincerity and be more inclined to react positively.

Here is a word of caution. I love to play tennis and Moe is my teammate. We enjoy playing against each other, trying to score points but in a friendly competition. It does not matter who wins the game so much, just that we play well, and we both take great pleasure in scoring points against each other.

After the coach hits a basket of tennis balls, we pick them up to repeat the process. During one practice, Moe was distracted and repeatedly did not do his share. I heard the other players mumbling about Moe's nonparticipation. At the end of practice, most of us were a little irritated.

I elected myself to confront my friend Moe about his behavior. I said, "I have a problem. You did not pick up the balls today. I felt irritated and I need you to participate. He did not respond, but the next practice he was not talking to me. He would not say, "Hello," or "Good shot;" none of his usual friendly remarks. This went on for weeks. The other students and the coach recognized Moe was not talking to me (*Aloof/Distant*).

The coach even put us playing doubles together hoping our communication would improve. It did not. In doubles, communication is important, and his silence was contributing to our lack of success. I could have berated Moe, accusing him in front of others of how juvenile he was acting, but I did not want to make the fracture worse, so I held my comments to myself. Restraint was difficult for I wanted our friendship to return. It seemed it never would.

After about six weeks he said "Hello", and soon our relationship was normal. I was glad, but I knew there was an "it', a crucial conversation needing resolution. After one practice, we sat on the bench cooling down, and I thought it was time to confront the unexpressed "**it**".

I said, "Moe, can we talk about what happened that caused us to be upset with each other?" He said, "Sure." I then asked him, "Tell me what happened when I asked you to pick up the balls."

"Well, what business was it of yours if I picked up the balls or not? And when you told me about it, you were angry."

"So, my anger magnified the problem?"

"Yeah"

"I guess I need to work on my anger. Moe, I value our friendship."

"I value yours." After the long drought, this acknowledgment felt good.

"Knowing me," I continued, "I will probably piss you off again some other time. Can we have an agreement that when that happens, you will come directly to me? I don't want to go through these last few weeks being mad at each other?"

"Yeah, sure. Good idea."

I learned a valuable lesson. Moe heard the anger, and I was not the neutral carrier of the message. I was *emotionally drunk* with irritation. For this model to work, emotional sobriety is an absolute necessity. And did it have to be said, **by me**?

*I hadn't conquered fear. I'd let it speak*
*but had not allowed it to govern.*
Kenneth Sutton

To improve leadership success, have more friends, and build closer connections with the people you love, more effective methods of confrontation are necessary. If not, resentments fester under the surface collecting more energy and often later exploding.

People will sometimes build an *Aloof/Distant* wall when upset. You might be the cause of the wall, but the wall belongs to them. When experiencing this barrier, all you can do is throw flowers over the wall. Their reaction is on the ***Can't*** side. If the relationship is important, keep the flowers flowing.

**Exercise**

You don't know, but it may be your entire earthly mission to listen to one person at one given moment, making all the difference in their life. To obtain a high level of awareness, read over these Rules of Effective Listening outlined in the Appendix each day. Scan yourself to know when you are listening and when you are not.

When I started my ***Thumb Work***, I read these rules every night before I went to bed, thereby indelibly embedding this new behavior into my conscience. *I am so thankful I did.*

Think of a person who is difficult to listen to; get them firmly in mind. Consider changing your label of a *person that is difficult to listen to,* into your *teacher.* If you can listen to this person (now your teacher), you can listen to *anyone*. When you receive your degree of Excellent Listener from the difficult person (your teacher), you may just discover a friend.

***Effective listening is unconditional love.***

When most people think about conflict, they automatically think about conflict with others. This is a prevalent form of conflict and is very apparent when viewing the headlines screaming of wars, murders, and injustice. Sadly, we also experience it with our coworkers, spouses, and especially with family members, (hopefully, not the murders and wars).

***The heart of most conflict is caring.***

Have I lost it? Stop to consider, if the disputants didn't care, why would they disagree? Discovering what the other person cares about is a long way down the road toward resolution.

> Many people are on their phones all the time. I guess that is why they are called cell phones!

Discord with others is difficult. However, the most challenging one causing many other problems is the struggle we have with ourselves. This inner conflict is greatly dependent upon how we view ourselves. With better-coping skills, our inner conflict is milder and easily resolved. When embattled in self-hate, self-conflict is a constant companion, and it compounds our problems with others. When hurting from the pressures of life, if not careful, we can inflict this pain on others and sadly, on those we love.

**Exercise**

When you feel hurt, do you unintentionally inflict your pain on others, your employees, or your loved ones? Perhaps your way may not be working.

*Hurt people tend to hurt other people.*
A San Quentin prisoner

## Co-worker Conflict

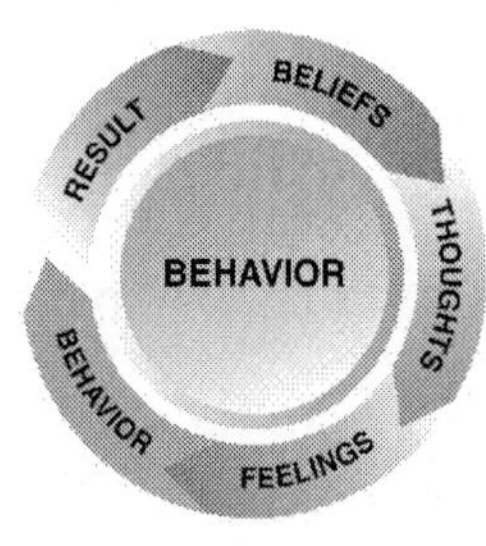


Co-workers often seek conflict resolution from their chain of command. As a leader, be aware, these situations can be likened to making love to a porcupine. It must be done *very* carefully. Co-worker conflicts are a toxic source of disruption. When not resolved, they ultimately become the leaders to handle.

When helping the disputants settle the agreement, be aware of whose monkey is whose.

A good parent had two boys who were constantly fighting. I was sitting next to the dad when these two complained about the other. He said, "Boys, I know how to solve this problem, but you are not going to like it." They left, and I assumed handled their disagreement.

The engineering and purchasing departments had consistent and expensive disagreements with each pointing their fingers at one another. David Abbott required the head of engineering and the head of purchasing to swap jobs for two weeks. In addition, they were to share lunch every day and, "You are to talk bad about me like you would to a dog." After two weeks of job swamping, these two departments started working together. Abbott used the PTSTWTHC method of problem-solving – *People tend to support that which they help create.*

As a leader or as a parent, you will have to mediate between two people whose conflict is affecting productivity and morale. When this happens, setting the stage is an absolute necessity. When the meeting begins, the disputants will stare at one another, jam-packed with strong emotions, and justifiable positions of being right. They will attempt to inflict their perceptions upon you to win the argument. Consider preparing for this meeting this way:

- Give each disputant the Rules of Engagement.
- Provide each with the Mood Chart and have one at the meeting

- Before the meeting, ask each to submit a confidential note to you:

  Description of their position.

  Description of what they think is the other person's position.

  Define their definition of success.

- Set the meeting time/date in a secure location.
- Sharpen your listening skills – review the rules.

**At the meeting**

- Read the Rules of Engagement to everyone present.
- Ask if they are willing to abide by these rules.
- Have each identify his/her current feelings, yours first.
- When a person violates the Rules of Engagement, remind them of their pledge.
- Ask them, "Will you work on getting your needs met and try to help the other person also get what they need?" Win-Win
- You may set your expectations: say, "You may never be friends, but I expect cooperation," or "I expect you two will find a way to work together so I do not have to make any drastic decisions that you may or may not like," or "This dispute is yours, and I expect you to solve it," or "I believe you will solve your differences," or "I know we did not resolve this problem today, but I think we cleared the air. Go to lunch and come back with possible solutions."
- Once you learn each person's position, try to discover their underlining interest.

- Be aware of your monkeys and know which monkeys do not belong to you.
- If it feels right to you, have disputants recognize the good qualities of the other employee.

## Rules of Engagement.

I will express my emotions from the Mood Chart.

I will treat others with respect.

I will express myself honestly and tactfully.

I will listen, seeking first to understand before being understood.

When confronted, I will not be defending or attack.

One person shall talk at a time.

I will not interrupt, either verbally, admitting sighs (etc.), or by negative body language.

I will exhibit patience.

I will not monopolize the discussion.

I will check my corporate title at the meeting door.

When wrong, I will promptly admit it.

I will not be defensive, negative, condescending, or sarcastic.

I will work to get my needs met as well help others.

If in *the opinion of others*, I am violating this agreement, I agree to be reminded of my consent to abide by these rules.

Note: In most mediation, 90% of the results happen in the last 10% of the time. Number one rule in mediation: **Be patient and never give up.**

*Success is not final; failure is not fatal:*
*it is the courage to continue that counts.*
Winston Churchill

# Chapter 14

## Teams

Review the Counter-Productive vs. Productive chart at the end of this section. Where are your teams? Some departments may have a better score than others. Share this chart with your various teams and ask them to assess themselves. This also works well with your family. What problems do they recognize and what do they want to work on? Always start with the management team. Without the management team acknowledging their part of the problem and making improvements, employees will see this exercise as further proof of the *us vs. them* attitude, which is so destructive to morale. ...Provide your assessment of your team's effectiveness and consider what you expect. Ask each team to report on how they plan on improvement and what they need from you to be successful.

*if you look at the people in your circle and don't*
*get inspired to grow beyond yourself,*
*you don't have a circle; you have a cage.*
Warren Buffett

SMART GOALS provide a target with direction, motivation, checkpoints, and clarify importance.

SMART is an acronym:

- Specific
- Measurable
- Achievable
- Realistic
- Timely

When managing a team, Bob Hambright focuses on ***value-driven behavior.***

- Are our values clear and understandable?
- Do we really buy into them?
- How do they drive behavior especially during times of stress?
- Do they make us better?
- Do we have a culture that allows us to find the collective wisdom of our teams?

I had my patience tested.

*I tested negative!*

# Team Assessment

| ***Counter-Productive*** | ***Productive*** |
|---|---|
| We lived in separate departmental silos working at cross purposes. | *We are ALLIES.* We are responsible for our work with good coworker cooperation. |
| We often tried to control others. | We work together and collectively we will be successful. |
| We blame others and then cover our asses. | We seek to settle conflicts in non-destructive manner. |
| We tear down and gossip about coworkers. | We valued our coworkers with respect. |
| We must have the last word and do not listen. | We listen to understand intently. |
| We blame coworkers or circumstances responsible. | We accept responsibility and work toward solutions, not blame. |
| We exhibit high arrogance or played the victim. | We are stronger together and learned how to compromise. |
| We argued to be right. | We sometimes agree to disagree but work toward solutions. |
| We do not give coworkers the benefit of the doubt. | We learned to be patient and to trust our fellow coworkers. |
| We exhibit anger about past problems. | We are committed to being successful. |
| We often communicate in negative ways. | We communicate openly and honestly. |
| We lost our joy of job and exist in despair. | We value humor and enjoy our coworkers. |
| We often complain. | Our complaints are directed through the chain of command. |
| We made rules instead of solving problems. | Rules are only implemented if no other solution is available. |
| We stole others' suggestions/ideas. | We praised coworkers for their suggestions/ideas. |
| Problem employees are seldom corrected. | Problem employees are coached and disciplined appropriately. |
| Managers focus on faults. | Managers focus on fixing problems. |
| Management has the attitude of always being right. | Management validates employee's positions. |

## Culture

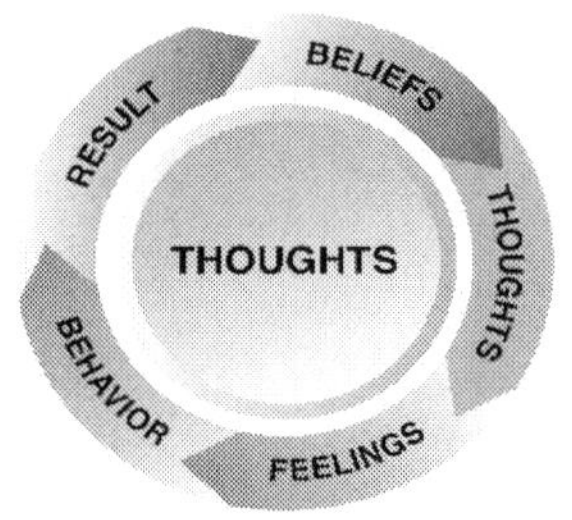


*Organizational culture encompasses values and behaviors that "contribute to the unique social and psychological environment of an organization."*
Wikipedia

There are two powerful forces driving organizations - two different and distinct cultures. One is a culture of *excellence* such as "*We're going to be a first-class plant.*" The other culture is rooted in a corporate *comfort zone* where excellence is nearly impossible. When comfort zone is in the driver's seat, Michael Manes with Square One Consulting warns, your fate and that of your organization is out of your control - *the inmates are running your institution.*

Understanding culture, Manes explains the difference:

- Marketing - What people say.
- Operations - What they say they do.
- Culture - What people do!

Manes wonders if your culture is sustaining excellence, or trending toward mediocrity, or perhaps already heavily committed to defending turfs, or worse, sabotage.

*What people say, what people do, and what they say they do are entirely different things.*
Margaret Mead

Your organization is under enormous pressure and everyone (from the janitor to the senior executive) feels this anxiety. Although this is a tumultuous time, it does present a wonderful opportunity for change – a radical reinvention so necessary for continued survival.

In the competitive wars of the marketplace, Manes wonders if you will:

- fight or run,
- be missing in action,
- become a combat casualty,
- or prevail?

My motto is to love things and use people.

Sometimes, what is needed is an outside force such as a business coach who provides comfort when stress becomes overwhelming. A coach is also a disquieting awakening when the organization is stuck in its comfort zone. When management is willing to make changes only if it does not affect the status quo, the coach provides a desperately needed *kick in the butt.* A good business coach like Bob Hambright, David Abbott, Michael Manes, Jack Chapman, or yours truly, may be a key ingredient needed in the change process. We ask the hard questions, shake up the status quo, and bring unsettling realization to the surface with Socratic questioning.

*Business owners often need help and want to talk about their family, fears, and dreams and need someone who is willing, so be vulnerable to talk to and feel safe.*
Clarity Management

One business coaching technique is the *anvil and the velvet.* Top management provides the anvil by demanding change and backing the coach in the change process. The coach provides the velvet – a safe place for supervisors to improve their people skills.

The coach's presence is like the bit of sand in the oyster creating an agitation. Working together we can produce a pearl.

***Culture is what happens***
***in the absence of observation.***

## Respect

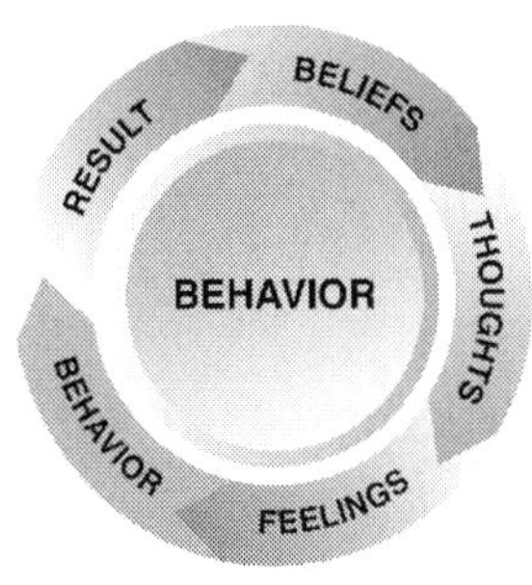


An investigator reporter wanted to know why a local school stood out so positively when compared to others in the system. As the principal walked her around his school, they came across the janitor mopping the hallway. The reporter got her answer when the principal stopped the tour and introduced her to the janitor. "This is Mr. Johnson; he sets the atmosphere for learning." How many jobs in your company are like this janitor's; one that only gets acknowledgment when there is a problem? When the only notice an employee received is negative, how difficult would it be to maintain the joy of job?

The principal valued what this person did. By acknowledging his excellence, the janitor felt pride because a powerful person bragged about his work. Ever since learning of this incident, I try to recognize those who are often not valued and sometimes invisible. This is respect.

*A boo is louder*
*than a cheer.*
Lance Armstrong

**David Walton Earle**

Employees respond to sincere and timely praise. The theory is- *what is acknowledged is often repeated.* I had a contract with Connelly Press and Copy and often put my training projects together at this shop. I was using Peter Connelly's stapler and hit it with a great deal of force. "You are hitting my stapler awful hard." The next time I used the stapler I was used the correct amount of force. Peter gently put his hand on mine and said, "I like the way you are doing that." That happened 20 years ago, and every time I use his stapler, I still feel his hand on mine and hear his kind words.

Praising in public is respect. Just thanking a person for being on the team is respect. Acknowledgment does not cost and is sadly lacking in the rush for profits.

*The only person who likes*
*change is a wet baby***.**
Roy Z-M Blitzer

Compulsive gambling is so addictive because the rewards are unknown, intermittent, and a happy surprise when successful. Praise is like that. When praised too much, the reward decreases with redundancy. Praise, when used with disparity and at the right time is what we all seek.

**Exercise**

How many of your employees only get acknowledged when there is a problem. If you think you need to practice more effective acknowledgment, give yourself an assignment.

*Enjoy life now –*
*it has an expiration date.*
Michael Gartner

# Appendix

## Out thinking the wolf.

**David Walton Earle**

## Manager's Stress Relief

**Mount on your wall**

**and …**

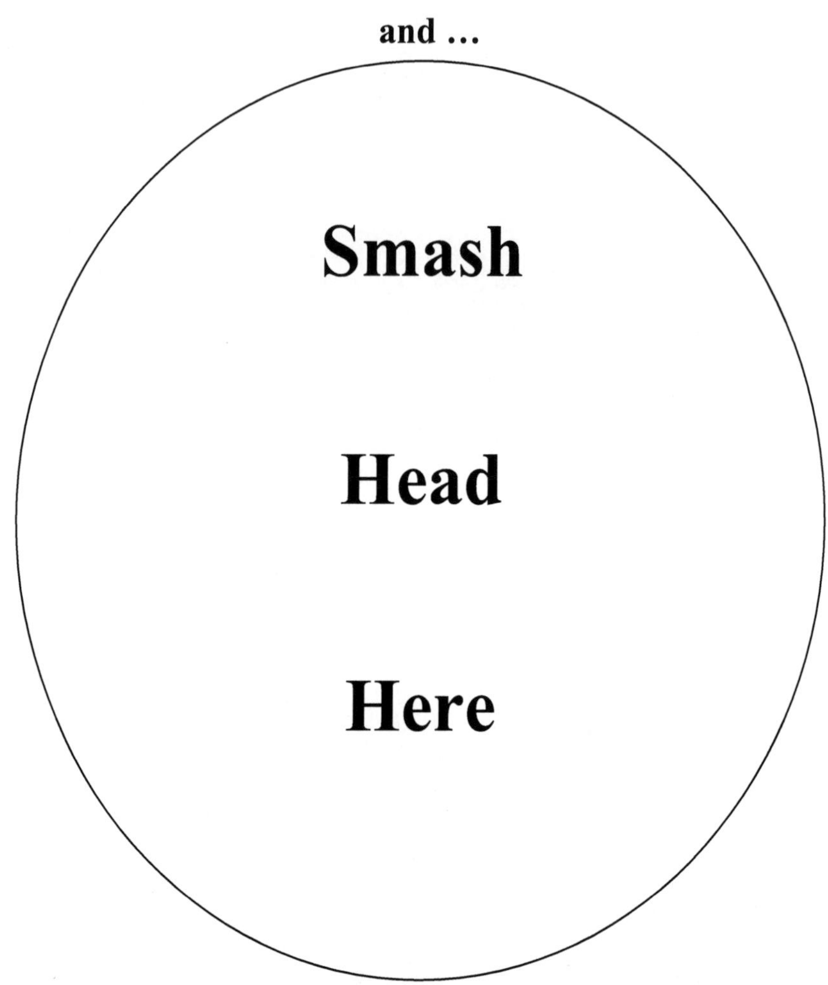


You will become increasingly less aware of your current problems in direct proportion to the number of head blows and their intensity.

## Taking Care of Your Health

Review the various events you experience this past year to have a rough estimate of how stress may be affecting your health.

| Life event | | Life event | |
|---|---|---|---|
| Death of a spouse | 100 | Child leaving home | 29 |
| Divorce | 73 | Trouble with in-laws | 29 |
| Marital separation | 65 | Outstanding achievement | 28 |
| Family death | 63 | Beginning or end of school | 26 |
| Marriage | 50 | Revision of personal habits | 24 |
| Dismissal from work | 47 | Trouble with boss | 23 |
| Marital reconciliation | 45 | Working conditions change | 20 |
| Retirement | 45 | Change in residence | 20 |
| Change in health of loved one | 44 | Change in schools | 20 |
| Pregnancy | 40 | Change in recreation | 19 |
| Sexual difficulties | 39 | Change in church activities | 19 |
| Gain a new family member | 39 | Change in social activities | 18 |
| Business readjustment | 39 | Minor mortgage or loan | 17 |
| Change in financial state | 38 | Change in sleeping habits | 16 |
| Death of a close friend | 37 | Decrease family reunions | 15 |
| Change jobs | 36 | Change in eating habits | 15 |
| Increase arguments | 35 | Vacation | 13 |
| Foreclosure of loan | 30 | Minor violation of law | 11 |
| Responsibilities at work | 29 | ***Being chased by a wolf*** | 100 |

Based upon the work of Carole B. Dahlem, and others

- **Score of 300+**: Risk of illness is high.
- **Score of 150-299**: Risk of illness is moderate.
- **Score <150**: Only has a slight risk of illness.

An executive dealing with a company's financial crisis may have a score like the one shown on the next page. This sample score does not consider the effects the crisis has on any personal and/or family life events.

| | |
|---|---|
| Business readjustment | 39 |
| Change in financial state | 38 |
| Major mortgage | 32 |
| Foreclosure of mortgage or loan | 30 |
| Change in working conditions | 20 |
| Possible TOTAL | 159 |

## Depression Questionnaire

On the next page is a Depression Questionnaire. Your score on the Depression Scale may indicate a need for self-intervention. Call a professional counselor if the score is elevated and/or if these problems persist. If you are thinking of hurting yourself or someone else, please take yourself seriously and find someone who will help you or call the appropriate crisis hotline number or call 911.

Over the last week or two, how often have you experienced any of the symptoms below?

1 = not at all 2= some 3=more than half the time
4 =most of the time… 5 = almost everyday

| | | 1 | 2 | 3 | 4 | 5 |
|---|---|---|---|---|---|---|
| 1 | Lost interest in pleasurable things | | | | | |
| 2 | Sleep problems: too little or too much | | | | | |
| 3 | Thoughts of being dead | | | | | |
| 4 | Thoughts of hurting yourself | | | | | |
| 5 | Thoughts of hurting someone else | | | | | |
| 6 | Thinking you would be better off dead | | | | | |
| 7 | Motion exaggerated or speaking slower | | | | | |
| 8 | Restless, fidgety, anxious | | | | | |
| 9 | Tired with little energy | | | | | |
| 10 | Think you are a failure, no good, loser | | | | | |
| 11 | Appetite: over or under | | | | | |
| 12 | Feeling depressed, melancholy, or down | | | | | |
| 13 | Feeling hopeless | | | | | |
| 14 | Has any of these affected your work? | | | | | |
| 15 | Has any of these affected you physically? | | | | | |
| 16 | Affected relations with others. | | | | | |

***You are valuable!***

This scale only represents an order of magnitude and is only an indication of problems. It is not suitable to make a clinical diagnosis of depression. ***Scores of 3, 4, or 5's are not to be taken lightly and must be taken very seriously immediately***. Are there any guns in the house? Do you consume alcohol? ***Depression, stress, guns, and alcohol often make a deadly combination.***

This is worth repeating, please do not compound the problems you are facing by ignoring elevated scores. If needed, please contact a mental health professional, mental health hospital or clinic, or call 911

Take care of yourself. Your loved ones need you. Your company needs you. You are much more than your balance sheet, or the total of your successes and failures.

## Capstone Exercises

***We can't solve problems by using the same kind of thinking, we used when we created them.***
Albert Einstein

The best quarterback in the NFL must practice his skills to maintain effectiveness. You may be the best communicator in the world, but everyone needs to practice throwing for touchdowns if they want to win. To sharpen your listening skills, reread the Effective Listening rules for a few days.

## Effective Listening- outline

**Decide to become a good listener**

To begin any journey starts with the first step.

**Decrease talking**

Let the other say more.

**Seek first to understand**

"Seek first to understand then to be understood."

**Decrease response preparation**

Decrease thinking about your response. Instead, focus on what is being said.

**Increase patience**

Good listeners need patience.

**Listening environment**

Create an environment conducive to listening.

**Decrease criticism**

Focus on the message not how it is said.

**Increase maturity**

Decrease your needing to talk

**Body language**

Listen with your eyes, have good listening posture:

| | |
|---|---|
| Face the person | Open posture |
| Good eye contact | Inviting smile |
| Forward body lean | Nodding the head |

**Overcome fatigue**

Get physically ready to listen

**Non-judgmental listening**

Be careful when judging others

**Absolute statements**

Be aware of *always* and *never* statements

**Fixing it**

Be careful when giving unsolicited advice

Consider any *Should* statements

**Emotional communication**

Effective communication decreases when emotionally drunk

Use feeling words – Mood Chart

**Interest vs interesting**

Increase being interested instead of being interesting

**Value people**

"Make people feel valuable."

**Exhaling**

"Help people exhale mentally and emotionally."

**Anger and listening**

Manage your emotions.

**One issue at a time**

Beware of Kitchen sink communications.

**Separate the person from the problem**

Be hard on the problem and gentle on the person.

**Honesty**

Deal directly instead of manipulation or control.

**Win-win**

Look for win-win solutions.

**Seagulls**

Do not dump and then fly away.

**Electronic communication**

No emotional email or text messages

**Assuming**

Ask, do not assume

**Empathic' response**

Respond with what you think the other person could be feeling.

**Mood Chart**

Identify your feelings from the Mood Chart.

**Decision questions**

"Get furious or curious."

**Triangulation**

Communicate directly with the person you have the problem with

**4-Qs**

Q1- Does it have to be said?

Q2 - Does it have to be said **by me?**

Q3- Does it have to be said **by me now?**

Q4 - How **best** can it be said?

- I got a problem.
- See/Feel/Need
- Consequence (chose positive or negative)

- Use the "*will you work with me*" statement

**Ask questions**

Indicate interest with questions

*Make your mind not merely to overcome a thousand obstacles, but to win despite of a thousand defeats.*
Jack Chapman

## Monsters under the Bed – *outlined*

When thinking about change, remember Bob Pries 10 Premises:

- Premise # 1 – Change is Messy
- Premise # 2 – Change in the absence of context is chaos.
- Premise # 3 –No such thing as too much communication.
- Premise # 4 - Nothing substitutes for face-to-face dialogue.
- Premise # 6 - You are the message.
- Premise # 7 - Do not expect of others that which you do not expect of yourself.
- Premise # 8 - Lead the change
- Premise # 9 - Simple Model
- Premise # 10 If it looks screwy, *it probably is.*

## Affirmations

Here are some additional affirmations. Which ones would you like to believe about yourself? Not all these fit exactly with what you may want to believe. Pick out the ones that work for you and add your own you deem important. Write them in your handwriting, always positive and written as they have already occurred (in the here and now). This exercise will begin to change your self-definition and your beliefs. Tape them to your mirror at home and repeat them every night and morning. This will help to reprogram your subconscious mind.

- Every day in every way, I am getting better and better.
- I set my boundaries, and that is okay.
- It is okay for me to ask for my needs.
- I am worthy of respect.
- I am worthy of love.
- I am a valuable person.
- I am good enough.
- I love (fill in your name)
- I forgive others who have hurt me.
- I can feel past pain and still be okay.
- When I wrong someone, I make prompt amends.
- I feel worthwhile to others and myself.
- I accept compliments well.
- I can say "No".
- I do what is important.
- I accomplish goals promptly.
- I plan and finish what I start.
- I set my priorities and do what is important.
- It is okay to take time for myself.
- It is okay for me to relax.
- My word is impeccable.
- My employees respect me.
- I am a successful manager.
- I am good at handling crises.
- I am successful.
- Today, I have everything I need
- "And doggone it, people like me."

Al Frankland - SNL

## Circle or Cage

Warren Buffett thinks, "Someone once said if you look at the people in your circle and don't get inspired to grow beyond yourself, you don't have a circle; you have a cage. Look around you and count the number of people close to you. Do they genuinely inspire you to be a better version of yourself? You don't need multi-millionaires, celebrities, or national athletes to inspire you. The people you surround yourself with daily have a considerable influence over your mindset and, in turn, your actions.

*Fear is a reaction.*
*Courage is a decision.*
Winston Churchill

Keep away from people who try to belittle your ambitions, especially during these unprecedented times. According to Mark Twain, small people always do that, but the greats make you feel that you too can become great.

*If you have always done it that way,*
*it is probably wrong.*
Charles Kettering

Be careful about those limiting mindsets, and as Jim Rohn said: "You are the average of the five people you spend the most time with." If you want to make a difference in this world, if you're going to realize your potential, you must be around people who push you to become the very best version of yourself."

## How You Living?

**Uncover:** Make a list of three hidden issues of your thinking, your attitudes, your beliefs, and/or behaviors. What cause you for so long to ignore them? Was it ignorance, dysfunction, or denial?

**Discover:** What kind and how much damage has this dysfunction caused you and those around you. How long have you had this problem? What do you want to change?

**Tools:** What did you learn in *Outrun the Wolf* that will help change these problems?

**Recover:** This exercise is an ongoing review for you to evaluate how you are living your life. By doing this work, the **symptoms will** begin to lessen and, in some cases, even disappear. Then "Lather, Rinse and Repeat" to keep your change process alive.

> People who put on airs bother me when they talk about Mozart. I bet they cannot name one painting he his

## *Do* and *Be*

Mike Manes added to the Be-Have-Do discussion by posing the question, what do the words DO and BE mean? He explained, "BE is who we are – this is our core being – our mind, heart, and soul. DO are the roads we take as we travel through life – our actions – our thinking - the choices we make, our job, our behavior, etc.

He echoed the ***Be-Have-Do*** when he elaborated, "Ideally our ***DO*** and ***BE*** should be aligned; all too often these are not. An analysis of our life would probably indicate that we start to ***DO*** before we fully understand our ***BE*** (It's not good grammar. It's much more important than that). The difference between our ***DO*** and ***BE*** is often the stress and the dysfunction in our lives."

He pointed out the fly in the ointment, "We don't want to move from our comfort zone." The world demands that we leave what we know best and "accept and adapt to change."

"In business tomorrow," he continued, "the consumer (marketplace) will define/dictate what the successful manufacturer distributor/provider must ***BE***. A business can ***DO*** whatever it wants. Unfortunately, such independent actions might be performed with at least great stress and dysfunction and at most grave peril – including failure/bankruptcy.

In your business what is your ***BE***? Who are you as an organization? This is an excellent exercise to explore with your team. Once defined, the ***DO*** becomes much more focused and successful.

Your personal life has another dynamic. For example, another way of viewing this is my unscientific description of addiction: *An external solution for an internal problem.* If our ***BE*** is not okay, we compensate by choosing something outside of ourselves to fill the hole in our ***BE***. Anything to fill the hollow in our being. Anything not to feel this internal discontent. It could be drugs or alcohol. It also could be work, sex, things, religion, or the lives of other people. All of these are successful to fill this hole – temporarily. You are not a bad person if this fits you but consider exploring filling the hole in your ***BE*** with you and your creator.

You are the only one to determine
how you live, your ***DO***
or your ***BE***?

***It always boils down to***
***defective thinking of some kind.***

## The Empty Bucket

Like an empty bucket,
my soul rings hollow when empty
vibrates with desolation … the hollow sound of loneliness.
Every cell in my body does not want to be alone.
My loneliness is frightening …
an all-consuming thought.

If I face this emptiness
acknowledging what is now
rotting inside my soul
then I must face my truth.
My reality.
For in confession of emptiness
I must ask these questions,
why do I have this void,
this dark hole in my soul?
Why is my bucket so empty?

The answer lay heavy upon my wounded heart …
I do not love myself.
If you knew the real me,
behind my mask,
you would not love me too.
It's difficult to be brave …
when so fearful inside.

I have now begun to travel inward
to find and claim the prize of self.
Finding the prize
discovering my worth
claiming it for me.
What valuables I will find
what beauty and abundance to behold?

I will fill my empty bucket

overflowing with spiritual treasures.
The reward of the journey
will be worth the trip,
deep through
the void of my being,
the empty bucket of my soul.

## How You living?

## Connection

The key problem I discovered about myself and often find it when counseling with wounded, depressed, and unhappy people is a lack of connection, a disconnection from themselves. When self-connection is missing, it can be terrifying and the wounded find temporary relief by medicating it with alcohol/drugs, hiding from it in excesses, such as work, sex, religion, etc. or finding temporary relief when connected to another in romantic relationships. Many times, it is a combination of several of these coping skills. These are examples of using external solutions to solve an internal problem.

When another person is the solution, love becomes like the popular song written by Bebo Norma, *Nothing Without You*. If I am "nothing without you," love is a demand for another to solve their disconnect. "I need you to make me okay." With this mindset, a love relationship become toxic, distorted, and can become destructive.

When people experience a disconnection from themselves, they feel it but do not realize the problem. Without this awareness, they develop an obsessive need to connect to someone, somewhere, someway.

With this ardent need, they latch upon something else, another person or group of people - just not to feel disconnected. If this connection is threatened and is the only place, they feel connected, most people will do most anything to keep this connection alive including hanging on to a toxic relationship. Statistically, a battered woman will leave the relationship and return 13 times before she can leave him for good. Many wounded people are so desperate they hang on to hurtful people, bond with gangs, or join cults, anything not to feel disconnected. Think of a teenage boy when offered a joint of marijuana by a friend. He feels so disconnected (remember yourself as an adolescent), his peers become his value system, and so he takes his first hit, often contrary to the basic morals taught in his family.

Consider letting go of the barriers between yourself and others. Let go of the definition our culture has inflicted that it is someone else who gives our life meaning. Learn how to become *okay* deep within. Self-love allows the best part of yourselves to connect with the wondrous parts of others. Letting go and accepting allows you to connect deeper and more profoundly.

*We are here to laugh at the odds and live our lives*
*so well that Death will tremble to take us.*
Charles Bukowski

When the fashion photographer, Rick Guidolti talks about humanity, about what he now sees in his subjects, his face lights up with joy. With this new awareness, he is now free to express the profound love in his heart. The same love that is in your heart screaming to be free of restrictions, limitations, conventions, and definitions of who is okay and who is not okay to love. Freeing others from the prison of definition also releases us to be connected. Then we are free. And in this state - *love is enough.*

## Wolves

Janet Repa, my sister, lives in Santa Fe, New Mexico where she is a successful artist. She called me before an operation on her hands. Eyes and hands are very important to an artist, so I asked her, "Janet, aren't you worried?" Her answer gave me the courage to face some of my own great wolves. "No, I wonder what I will learn."

Many children's stories have made a wolf the villain, as the "Big Bad Wolf" in *The Three Little Pigs.* And wolves have been the antagonist in this book. My apologies to wolves in general and especially to our villain. Wolves are a necessary part of the natural balance and so it is with the wolves who bring us trouble. How can you know joy if you never experienced pain? Embrace the pain, difficult people, and life's unfairness - these are our wolves, these are our teachers. Remember, it was your special wolf who invited you to read this book.

Isn't life just a learning lab? If that indeed is true, and if you view your wolves as your teachers, much of the self-imposed stress is mitigated. Hug all your wolves, listen to their message, be with them at this moment, and accept them as your current reality. Be grateful for the learning available from the experience. Now your wolves no longer are in control. When you build your emotional stability with bricks, not straw or sticks, you have tamed these beasts, and the peace and serenity you so long sought is now yours.

Maybe you are not this optimistic, not ready to embrace your wolves. However, you will be better able to handle life's obstacles if you can appreciate what the encounter has taught you. May you continue to learn the ways of the wolves thus being better able to emerge victorious in those encounters.

## Sufferer's Creed

Roy Campanella played for the Brooklyn Dodgers and won the Most Valuable Player award, and eventually became the second black man in the Hall of Fame. He captured the MVP award twice and at the time of his death in June 1993, he was the only black player to own three MVP trophies. The color of his skin delayed his debut until he was 26 years old and at the age 35, he suffered a broken neck in an automobile accident that ended his playing days and left him crippled. Campanella, like Frankl, knew suffering well.

### A Creed for Those Who Have Suffered

Roy Campanella

I asked God for strength, that I might achieve.

I was made weak, that I might learn humbly to obey…
I asked for health, that I might do great things.
I was given infirmity that I might do better things…

I asked for riches, that I might be happy.
I was given poverty, that I might be wise…

I asked for power, that I might have the praise of men.
I was given weakness, that I might feel the need of God…
I asked for all things, that I might enjoy life.
I was given life, that I might enjoy all things…

I got nothing I asked for but everything I had
hoped for.

Almost despite myself, my unspoken prayers were
answered.

I am, among men, most richly blessed!

After that debilitating accident, it is amazing that he became, "most richly blessed." This is a person who became grateful for his wolves and was blessed by that embrace.

## Fear

Change and human nature have a bipolar relationship. On one end of the spectrum, some people change things just to change things. On the other end, some resists change just to resist. On the resistance end, people can be stuck even when knowing change is necessary, but their fear may be overwhelming. Using an alcoholic as an example, explaining the harmful effects of drinking is not new news - with their strong and intact denial system, your wisdom falls on death ears. When pointing out the unmanageability of their lives which again they know intimately, for they are living it – these facts provide little reason to change. If you gave them the *Big Book of Alcoholics Anonymous,* containing tremendous wisdom and insights – few would respond. All your suggestions are valid, yet it is terrifying giving up a known reality for uncertainty.

Change is only possible when the pain of living such an excruciating life overcomes the fear. More on the alcoholic example, what is successful is joining in the community of others, experienced people who understand the problem, and are willing to share known coping skills vastly superior to drinking. Fear of change is often overwhelming but when progress happens their lives begin to change.

Although corporations do not drink (sic), a similar history often precedes the tipping point of change, where the cost of the past threatens to rob the future. Your organization is no longer in the comfort of denial, but now engaged in the great change process. Your company may need other professionals to view your current condition, provide resources, guide your team toward success, and be your best cheerleader. I am just one of the thousands of professionals available to you during this change process.

*You can't be a winner*
*and be afraid to lose.*
Jack Chapman

You are the best cheerleader to encourage, achieve, and acknowledge progress. If you now are reading this page, you already have done more than most. The world is beset with the "I'm gonna" mentality. When making this mantra of what, "I'm gonna do," and then failing to follow through, you are lying to yourself and more tragically, you learn not to trust yourself. Been there, done that, and let me show you my plaque on the wall.

If I had this book during my business crisis I shared at the introduction, would I have read it? In all honestly, I would not. You are different! You choose to set out on a course of discovery arriving at this moment on this page. Because of your dedication, I can truthfully say, "*I believe in you*".

**Now that you outran the wolf, are you now bettered prepared to get back in the race?**

**Celebrate your progress.**

# Resources

## Turnaround Management

The Turnaround Management Association (TMA) is dedicated to corporate renewal and job preservation. This national organization provides change professionals the opportunity to improve existing skills, develop new ones, exchange knowledge, and network with fellow members from across the United States and the world. TMA is the most professionally diverse organization in the corporate restructuring, renewal, and corporate health space.

> I've been having a tough time but at least this week, I didn't have to have bail money or to bury any bodies.

Established in 1988, TMA has almost 10,000 members in 54 chapters worldwide, including 34 chapters in North America. Members include turnaround practitioners, attorneys, accountants, advisors, liquidators, consultants, as well as academic, government employees, a few business coaches, and members of the judiciary - all working to save distressed businesses, assist management to navigate off-plan events, and help healthy companies avoid similar pitfalls, **www.turnaround.org**

# Acknowledgment

Someone once said, "No one reads acknowledgments." Perhaps they should have said, Acknowledgements are only read by those who should be included, by those who hope to be included but are unsure if they are, and those who should be but are overlooked and experienced the crushing feelings of being ignored. For anyone I left out from this list, please accept my apologies, it was not my intention.

It is most difficult to write a book without the strength of encouragement of others and *Outrun the Wolf* is no exception. All authors face the **Dragon of Doubt** for writing is an exposure of the author's soft underbelly to the intimacy of other's truth, perception, and judgment. These comments can tickle, coddle, satisfy, encourage, or frighten tender author's feelings. This author is the *tenderest* of the tender. Well-deserved criticism is valuable but still often painful. For every negative criticism, I need many positive ones to keep me pointed in the right direction. I am thankful for this support of others and…*gulp*…I am grateful for those comments that hurt, but that I need to hear.

Three people deserve special attention for their help in creating *Outrun the Wolf:* Jeff Sands, Mike Manes, and Jack Chapman. All of us are passionate about our ***Thumb-work,*** how we can be better humans in the corporate world and our families.

Attending a Zoom seminar sponsored by Turnaround Management Association, I heard Jeff Sands' view of corporate turnarounds. I was so inspired by his practicality and care for his clients that, I bought his book, *Corporate Turnaround Artistry*. He tells a joke that is humorous for its profound truth: "...turnarounds are 50% operational, 50% financial, and 50% debtor psychology." With his embracing of the importance of the executive's mental state, I had to contact Jeff.

When we talked, he asked me what I could do to assist in a turnaround as a business coach. I went through his book and pointed out his comments about how important the leadership's attitude and emotional states are in affecting the outcome. One of them," The ability to keep the entrepreneur engaged is often critical to the turn-around process." Having personally experienced a company in trouble when I did not have the necessary tools to take care of my-self, I know how valuable *Outrun the Wolf* would have been to me during those difficult days.

Our only area of disagreement is the reason I wrote *Outrun the Wolf*. On the dustcover, Jeff wrote, "...this book covers every-thing CEOs, business owners ... needs to know." What I found lacking is the insights now included in *Outrun the Wolf*. The vital elements of a successful turnaround of a company is the combina-tion of *Corporate Turnaround Artistry* with this book.

After studying the professional makeup of Turnaround Management Association, most members are directly concerned with solutions that are financial, legal, operational, etc., very few are exclusively focused on the coping skills of the business execu-tive, owner, and/or entrepreneur – debtor psychology. Having personally experienced a company in trouble and not having the tools to take care of myself, this information and coping skills would have been valuable to me during those difficult days.

Never trust an electrician with no eyebrows.

When I embarked on this writing journey, Mike Manes owner of Square One Consulting, who is a business coach, corporate trainer, and friend immediately jumped aboard by supplying many of his writings and ponderings. From one of those writings, came the title, *Outrun the Wolf.* Many times, I had a section finished to my satisfaction only to have one of Mike's ideas challenge that concept, requiring a rewrite.

Jack Chapman was a business client of mine when he owned Plain Jane, Inc. On that contract, I responded to his urgent call. "My employees are in revolt." With a little influence by me and great compassion and business acumen, Jack solved the revolt. Later I was on his board of advisors when he created Louisiana Shuttle Express which he later sold to Reliant Transportation Group. Writing this book, Jack became my part-time grammar cop and the full-time (unpaid) copyeditor where his kind but challenging questioning added to the success of this book.

Jack and I often share our funny but painful experiences in our dysfunctional earlier years. Maybe someday Jack will tell you about the sales talk he presented to co-workers at a national sales meeting of a Fortune 500 company *in his boxer shorts!* He has a way of gaining attention that is still remembered by all those who witnessed his hairy legs.

These three men often supplied moral support that kept me going when my spirit faltered. They encouraged me and freely offered their valuable wisdom. *Outrun the Wolf* is a much better book than I could have written without them. As you have read, I liberally quoted them throughout this book.

Several beta-readers provided many additional insights and constructive comments. They are Joyce Brooks, Pat Canning, Max Scot, Jeff Davis, Bob Hambright, and Kevin Winnett. My bride of many years, Penny is my greatest cheerleader and supporter. She is hoping my writing career will finally pay off and we can retire in the lap of luxury instead of in one of our children's garages. Our kids share the same hope.

Over my writing career, many other people have added their wisdom, perspective, and editorial input into the product you now hold. Teri Bondi told me I could "create a novel in one afternoon." Joan McKenna always was excited about what I was writing, believed in me, and contributed to several other publications. Justin Zyla made me think about you, the reader, "...always write from the perspective of who is reading and how they may view it." Laci Talley and I collaborated on several other books, and her contribution included needed insight, wisdom, and writing skills. Sam Sublet was one of my valued writing mentors. Although he died from an overdose, I still feel his gentle hand on my shoulder when I doubt myself. I miss my friend.

Many of the jokes and aphorisms are random, anonymous internet humor, provided by a high school classmate, Dr. Betty Shepherd. Judith Gosse provided most of the artwork and the cover drawing. Emily Starks did the formatting and Sadaqat Ali formatted the cover.

At a job interview:
Interviewer: *Tell me about yourself.*
Me: *I'd rather not.*
*I really want this job.*

## About the Author

David Walton Earle is a Licensed Professional Counselor (LPC) helping clients with anger management, substance abuse, compulsive gambling, anxiety, depression, and relationships. As a business coach, he combines his counselor skills with his twenty-plus years of executive management experience creating a powerful matrix for transferring leadership skills. He is also a teacher, trainer, author, coach, and alternative dispute professional.

Earle earned a Master of Science from Texas A&M and has held executive management positions in various fields including industrial construction, private investment banking, and corporate troubleshooting. He is the president of the Earle Company, an organization dedicated to change.

He has published four self-help books *Love is Not Enough* (Changing Dysfunctional Family Habits), *Simple Communications for Complicated People* (Communication Made Simple), *What To*

*Do While You Count To 10 (*Management of Strong Emotions); *The Joy of Dysfunctional Families* – A Joke book, and a three-book trilogy of recovery poetry: *Professor of Pain* (A Lesson Before Living), *Iron Mask* (Peace Is Your Birthright), and *Red Roses 'n Pinstripes (*Despair to Meaning). T*he Wisdom of the Twelve Steps* is a series of eight workbooks for the recovering community. His latest is an autobiography, *Contents of a Small Boy's Pocket* (Life Stories from the Deep South). He has also co-authored three other books - two on leadership: *Leadership-Helping Others Succeed* and *Extreme Leadership,* and a joke book, *You Might Need a Therapist If…*

Earle has been on the panel as a mediator and/or arbitrator for various organizations such as U.S. Federal Court-Middle District, Equal Employment Opportunity Commission (EEOC), Financial Industry Regulator Authority - (FINRA), Natural Futures Association - US futures & derivatives industry - (NFA), Federal Deposit Insurance Corporation (FDIC), and the Louisiana Supreme Court. He was an adjunct faculty member of the University of Phoenix for over 10 years.

Earle volunteers as an instructor in the Young Marines program, is a member of the Marine Corp League, and enjoys tennis. He resides in Baton Rouge with his wife, Penny, and retired greyhound, Maggie.

You may contact him at: earlecompany@cox.net

***My Life Will Change... When I Change™.***

## Suggested Reading

*7 Habits of Highly Effective People* - Stephen R. Covey
*A Hole in the Sidewalk* – Claudia Black, Ph.D
*Anger* - Thich Nhat Hanh
*Beyond the Relaxation Response* - Hebert Benson, M.D.
*Big Book of Alcoholics Anonymous* - Bill Wilson
*Circumplex Model for Marriage & Families* – Dr. David Oleson
*Codependency No More* - Melody Beattie
*Corporate Turnaround Artistry* – Jeff Sands
*Daily Reflections for Highly Effective People* - Stephen R. Covey
*Getting to Yes* - William L. Ury, Roger Fister, Bruce M. Patton
*I'm Ok – You're Ok* - Thomas A. Harros, M.D.
*Just Listen* - Mark Goulston
*Learning to Love Yourself* - Sharon Wegscheider-Cruse
*Love* - Leo Buscaglia
*Man's Search for Meaning* - Viktor E. Frankl
*People Can't Drive You crazy if You Don't Give Them the Keys* – Mike Bechle
*Relapse Toolkit* – Claudia Black, Ph.D
*The Magic of Conflict* - Thomas F. Crum
*The Power of Now* - Eckhart Tolle
*The Seven Spiritual Laws of Success* - Deepak Chopra
*The Truth Begins with You* – Claudia Black, Ph.D
*The Way of the Wizard* - Deepak Chopra
*Understanding Co-Dependency* - Sharon Wegscheider-Cruse
*Wake UP!* - Tom Owen-Towle
*You Are What You Think* – David Shoop, Ph.D.

## Disclaimer

All the lessons and coping skills presented in ***Outrun the Wolf*** are the best thinking of the author, my husband. These are his realities, his best learning from living many years in chaos, causing himself and others considerable pain and suffering. Here is the wisdom he collected by changing his life. Yes, he does his own ***thumb work***.

What is collected between its covers is true; however, what he writes and what he practices are sometimes at odds. I know him well.

I love him for his attempts at making our lives better. I see him struggle with his chaos habits sometimes coming directly at me affecting my day. I respect his willingness, sometimes begrudgingly, to hear how his behavior affected me.

Using the principles found in this book has made our lives so much better, but you need to know…your business coach, author, self-help guru, my husband is not *perfect*.

Penny Earle

# Epilogue

Every great book always has an epilogue, right? So does *Outrun the Wolf*. Do you recall the subtitle, **self-care in times of trouble**? What is your wolf? What is your trouble?

> **Trouble is**: pandemic, murders, suicide, wars, floods, earthquakes, robberies, insurrection, divorce, death, kidnapping, sabotage, rejection, separation, bankruptcy, tornadoes, snowstorms, hurricanes, typhoons, shots fired, arrested, lawsuit, arbitration, mediation, financial crisis, robbery, fraud, embezzlement, disowned, espionage, rockslides, avalanche, volcanic eruption, shipwreck, sinking, torpedoed, revolt, riot, lightning strike, operation, broken bones, fight, DUI, auto accident, death, disease, or stubbed toe.

Someone once said, "If you ever want to make God laugh, tell him your plans." Writing about trouble is one thing, experiencing one is quite another reality. **So, if you ever want to make God laugh, tell him your plans.**

Penny and I have reached the age where we must consider plans for our "golden years." So, we adopted the mindset that instead of a retirement home we would move into the "resort." A retirement home does not have the same ring as "resort". Even though we had not moved in yet, we had a name for our new cottage, *The Last Resort*. Quite clever we thought.

Our plan (there is that planning again) was to sell our house on Landsbury Avenue and use that money for the entrance fee to St. James Place retirement community. A large amount is required for the prepaid health care necessary for our *golden years*. September 1st was the move-in date. That was our plan. Happily, ever after.

If plans make God laugh, he giggled as 13.9 inches of rain-soaked our plans in 3 feet of water. Floodwaters in ... ***plans out***.

Imagine most of your furniture, flooring, sheetrock, insulation, interior doors, and many personal items stacked in a disconcerting pile on your front lawn. Many friends and relatives volunteered to gut our home. Backbreaking, heart-wrenching, and dirty work. Smelly too. Having your house flood was *our trouble – our Wolf.* This real-life event did not happen to someone else but to us. This traumatic event caused anger, sadness, depression, and anxiety and greatly challenged all the suggestions, lessons, and advice included in this book.

We gutted our house, turning our once proud home inside out, we were all dirty, tired, and struggling not to be overwhelmed. Trying to seek balance amidst this vast upheaval, I used humor to laugh instead of cry (full disclosure - I did cry at times). Since all my neighbors also flooded, my competitive nature kicked in. If I had to have this ugly pile of discarded valuables, I insisted on my pile being the highest. And it was!

It was life's irony creating my troubling event, upfront and personal. My very own personal wolf.

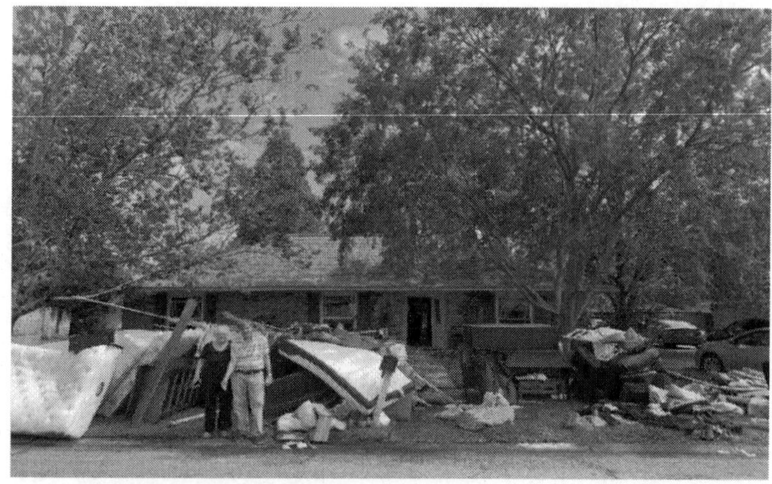

10802 Landsbury Ave, Baton Rouge, LA 70809

I have contracts with many different Employee Assistance Programs (EAP) where I visited many scenes of explosions, murders, robberies, sudden deaths, floods, massive lay off, and business closures. Included in this list of "troubles" was also a case of a missing employee, one pandemic (hopefully never another), a jailbreak, and even sabotage. In this capacity, I help employees with their emotional trauma by empathizing with their experiences, listening to their woes, and providing various coping skills. In these events, I was always the outsider looking in. Just three feet of water in two hours reversed that equation. I was now inside, looking out!

Mother nature's flood confronted all my coping skills to the maximum. As your expert guru in trouble-times, Mr. Know-it-all who throughout this book dispensed wisdom far beyond his years and experienced, three feet of stormwater challenged all these lessons. *Maybe someone wished me a lot of pain*. I am now humbled by the experience. Remember in my naivety when I suggested "Hug all your wolves?" My wolf, disguised as floodwaters, was stinky, wet, and muddy - hard to hug.

Many of Wolf's suggestions worked wonders, some I failed to employ, and some I forgot. Some were reinforced in different but dramatic ways.

My neighbor, Curtis Lee, had his new car flooded. He was so proud, I asked, "Ah, Curtis, your new car?" He nodded his head. "That is such a shame". His gleaming white teeth were bright against his always friendly black face when he smiled, "I'm not going to let this take away my joy!" A few days later when I saw him again, I yelled across our driveways, "Hay Curtis, still got that joy?" Again, that pleasant smile, "I sure do." Just then I was feeling overwhelmed and said, "How about sending some my way?" He reached up and sent a huge chunk of his joy across our yards. That invisible joy comforted me for many days.

Over the years, I have learned to ask. So now in desperation, I had to ask. I asked a lot of people for a lot of things. Since my office flooded, I needed an office to continue seeing clients. I asked. I got one. My car flooded, "Do you know someone who may lend me a car for three months? I got one.

Four wonderful people rescued Penny and me, carrying us out through chest-high water. They earned special hero badges that night. Two kind people offer to share their home and said, "Stay as long as you need." During the 2016 flood, we offered our home as a temporary shelter for two other people who, through no fault of their own, stayed for over 6 months. We knew firsthand how difficult guests can be over an extended stay. We needed a place of our own, a more permanent place to move, preferably free. We didn't have to ask, St. James offered their model apartment, "Three months – no cost." I asked for volunteers, and they came. I asked many times for many things. It was love that responded.

I could not control that pile of discarded belongings standing in my front yard, so I calculated what it would cost if I just walked away and accepted my fate – $350,000 was my estimate. I thought about my thinking and decided that negativity would not be the inspiration source needed. What ***can*** I control? What is my current thinking? What needs to be changed? If this 350k was the bottom of the well, anything I did to decrease this number was something I ***can*** do. Penny bought into this renewed outlook, and we battled mightily to overcome and win back some of our losses. Although many days I felt like I was bailing out the Titanic, crossing out items on the ever-increasing To-Do list reinforced our determination.

During my frantic efforts to regain normalcy, I laughed at my attempt to be grateful … *just grateful*. Many days, I struggled not to gag on my own wisdom. Struggled, but grateful. It is such a peaceful place to be. Just grateful.

***This book has been battled-tested!***

## Heroes:

I started to list who did what for us from the mighty to the insignificant. Since all contributions were valuable, making a hierarchy of deeds proved too restrictive and fraught with discounting someone, so I elected to just list names. Sometimes it was an encouraging call that seem even more important than the sweat being extended on my behalf. These heroes are not listed in order of importance, alphabetically, or chronological order but kind souls who freely gave their labor, finances, and support. It was their love that inspired us to seek that light at the end of the dark and foreboding tunnel.

These wonderful people have our undying appreciation.

Max Scot, Charles Mayeux, Ed Borders, Peter Connelly, Mary Beth Henry, Pat and Hal Canning, Richard Flicker, Juan Cruz, Gayle Hersey, Barbara Walsh, Israel Sublett, Danielle Childers, Victor Hotar, Mitchel Egger, Sherri Wilks, Josh Sublett, Liz Sublett, Aidan Sam, JJ, and Jonathan Yacoub and their mother, Nancy, Earl Davis, Mike Hebert, Jon, Tara, and Evert Johnson, Randy Gomez, Jack Chapman, Patti McGrath, Connie, and Ralph Murphy, Chuck Weirich, Dot Dawson, St James Place, Unitarian Church, Alex and Scarlet Qualls,

Janet, and Joe Repa, Jim Levy, Irene Rampino, a Marine Corp League member – whose name escapes me, Teddy Bryant, Bill Egger, Bob Weirich, Jeanne' and Tony Lewis, Kelly Lastrapes, Joyce Brooks, Jimmy Cason and his mother, Joyce, Robert Baggett, Melissa Craft, Ricky Carroll, Fernando Fernandez, Mike Legett, Maribeth Anderbeck, and Dick Brant.

These are the people who gave me
the strength to hug my wolf.
**I am overwhelmed by their love.**
**And grateful.**

## Second Epilogue

To top off the year 2021 – *a year never to forget*, both Penny and I came down with Covid-19. Thank goodness we were both vaccinated.

For over five months, since the flood, Penny and I worked every day - morning to late at night. We were exhausted. The 10-day quarantined provided the rest that our battered bodies, wore out psychic, and depleted spirits needed.

Made in the USA
Columbia, SC
19 February 2022

56078240R00178